Golden Arches East

Golden Arches East

McDonald's in East Asia

Second Edition

Edited by
James L. Watson

STANFORD UNIVERSITY PRESS
STANFORD, CALIFORNIA 2006

Stanford University Press
Stanford, California
© 1997, 2006, by the Board of Trustees of the
Leland Stanford Junior University
Printed in the United States of America

Library of Congress Cataloging-in-Publication Data

Golden arches east : McDonald's in East Asia / edited by
James L. Watson—2nd ed.
    p. cm.
        Includes bibliographical references and index.
        ISBN 978-0-8047-4988-6 (cloth : alk. paper) —
        ISBN 978-0-8047-4989-3 (pbk. : alk. paper)
        1. McDonald's Corporation. 2. Fast food
restaurants–Social aspects—East Asia. 3. East Asia—
Social life and customs. 4. Globalization—East Asia.
I. Watson, James L.

TX945.5.M33G65 2006
338.7'616647955—dc22   2006001449

Original printing 2006
Last figure below indicates year of this printing:
15   14   13   12   11   10   09   08   07   06

Preface to the First Edition

It seems appropriate to begin with a biography of this project. Why fast food? How did five anthropologists find themselves doing ethnographic studies of McDonald's in East Asia? This is not the sort of study most people think of as the proper subject of anthropology.

I must confess that I was drawn into this project by circumstances not of my own devising. In 1989 Rubie Watson and I made our annual visit to a village in Hong Kong's New Territories, just south of the old Anglo-Chinese border. We have been doing fieldwork in the New Territories since the late 1960s, concentrating on topics that excite anthropologists (if not always the general reader): lineage organization, inheritance patterns, ancestor worship, geomancy, popular religion. Each year we looked forward to treating our host family, including two godsons, to *dim sam* (tea snacks) in Yuen Long, a market town that has evolved into a booming city. Soon after our arrival in early January 1989, our friends proposed: "Let's go to the new place. That's where the kids want to eat."

Later, as we emerged from our taxi-van, I looked up and there, looming in front of me, was a gigantic, three-story, sparkling new McDonald's restaurant. My first reaction can best be described as sensory disorientation: Where was I? I remember muttering to Rubie, "I didn't fly all the way from Boston to eat at McDonald's!" But of course I did, and have continued to do so on every subsequent visit to the New Territories. In the lives of my godsons and their age mates, McDonald's is a central institution. They are transfixed by the place and conspire in ever more creative ways to eat there.

Finally, after numerous visits to the Yuen Long McDonald's, it dawned on me that something had to be done about this phenomenon: it was clearly too important to ignore. I talked four colleagues into joining me in comparative studies of five East Asian settings. Each of us report similar flashes of astonishment when we discovered how deeply fast food chains had affected the lives of people we thought we knew well.

The Golden Arches have become, as readers well know, an icon of international business and popular culture, recognized nearly everywhere on the planet. Ninety-six percent of American children are familiar with Ronald McDonald;[*] the figures are probably equally high in Hong Kong and Tokyo, while Beijing is catching up fast.

Not surprisingly, many people have strong views about McDonald's and assume that all right-thinking individuals share similar attitudes. To some environmentalists and political activists, for instance, McDonald's is an unambiguous symbol of evil. American intellectuals tend to denigrate McDonald's as an expression and instrument of cultural homogenization. Several academics of my acquaintance deny that they have ever crossed the threshold of a McDonald's restaurant; those who do admit to having entered the forbidden territory claim that they were coerced by their children and are always careful to add that

[*] *Welcome to McDonald's*, 1996, McDonald's Corp., McD 5-2940, p. 36.

they hate the food.[†] Other Americans, notably working-class people who survive at or near the minimum wage, treat McDonald's as a godsend—a home away from home where an entire family can eat for under ten dollars. In some countries McDonald's stands for the United States and is treated as a symbol of Yankee imperialism: "About 40 masked men ransacked a McDonald's restaurant in Mexico City today to protest [California proposition 187]. 'Yankee Go Home' [was] among the messages scrawled on the restaurant's window" (*New York Times*, Nov. 9, 1994).

In this book we take the stance that McDonald's is a subject worthy of research in its own right, which means that we do *not* begin with the assumption that everything about the corporation is necessarily bad. In doing so we risk offending the guardians of anthropological correctness. When we presented preliminary reports of our findings at the 1994 Annual Meeting of the American Anthropological Association, a senior scholar queried our motives ("Aren't you just legitimizing corporate hype?"), and another asked pointedly about the source of our research funds. Let me therefore set the record straight: Not one dime, yen, yuan, or won of research support derived from McDonald's Corporation or its East Asian franchise holders. We did not solicit funds from the corporation, nor would we have accepted such money had it been proffered. None of us has served as a paid consultant to McDonald's or any other fast food company. Our funding came from the

---

[†] Ninety-six percent of the U.S. population has visited a McDonald's restaurant at least once; 8 percent of the U.S. population eats at a McDonald's on an average day. Ibid., p. 15.

usual (poverty-stricken) academic sources that support anthropological fieldwork in East Asia. Details can be found in the endnotes to each article.

To dismiss enterprises like McDonald's as somehow unworthy of serious inquiry is not only elitist, it is also suicidal for our discipline. Anthropologists have long prided themselves on tackling the big issues of cultural transformation throughout the world. My graduate students will perhaps forgive me for repeating a mantra they have often heard: "In fieldwork you live where people live, you do what people do, and you go where people go." Increasingly, all over the world, people are going to McDonald's; they are also going to shopping malls, supermarkets, and video stores. If anthropologists do not start going with them, we will soon lose our raison d'être.

In my view, recent theoretical fads have led anthropologists to become increasingly detached from the interests and preoccupations of ordinary people. This book is part of a broader movement to redefine anthropology as the study of everyday life; we focus here on the most basic of human preoccupations—food. But, as we hope to convince our readers, food is only part of the picture. The study of McDonald's, Coca-Cola, Nestle's, Kellogg's, Kentucky Fried Chicken, and Heinz (to name only a few of the most obvious examples) leads the anthropologist into terra incognita, a world of research dominated by business schools, securities firms, and international consultancies. Is it possible for anthropologists to deal with corporate culture in a manner that is consistent with scholarly agendas and yet relevant to the interests of a general readership? Both goals can be accomplished by concentrating on the mundane concerns of ordinary people who are themselves the consumers of Big Macs, Cokes, and cornflakes. Focusing on the mundane is a strategy that allows anthropologists to relate their micro-level investigations—which are grounded in specific communities or groups of people—to the concerns of economists, sociologists, and political scientists who deal with cultural issues at the macro or global level. By its very nature, research on global issues has a seductive quality that encourages analysts to skip across the surface of cultural phenomena, not stopping to dig deeply into the lives of those who are most directly affected by corporations such as McDonald's. This book represents a conscious effort to situate the global in the local. Simply stated, our aim is to determine how McDonald's worldwide *system* has been adapted to suit local circumstances in five distinct societies.

Previous studies of fast food companies have focused on *production*, emphasizing either management or labor. The resulting publications read much like debates between conservatives and liberals: one side celebrates McDonald's as a creator of jobs and opportunity, the other condemns the company for exploiting workers and wasting resources. The authors of this book made a point of interviewing managers as well as workers whenever possible; we also read widely in the business literature devoted to fast foods. But we are primarily concerned with another dimension of the fast food system, namely *consumption*. What do consumers have to say about McDonald's? How is fast food perceived by those who pay to eat it? How do the preferences, biases, and cultural predispositions of customers affect the system of production? This approach may seem rather obvious to readers; it certainly was to us when we first discussed the project. Nevertheless, the consumer's perspective is largely ignored by most scholars who have written about the fast food industry. Literary critics, popular culture specialists, and media analysts tend to concentrate on their own reactions to fast food chains; they prefer to "interrogate" themselves rather than talk to people who actually eat at McDonald's. Other scholars, namely those who focus on business, have explored the managerial and entrepreneurial dimension of McDonald's, paying almost exclusive attention to the concerns of high-level executives. Ordinary customers remain in the background, if indeed they are mentioned at all.

Two of the best books about McDonald's are *Fast Food, Fast Talk* by Robin Leidner and *McDonald's: Behind the Arches* by John Love. Our approach builds on these and other studies, but we differ in one critical respect: we rely, first and foremost, on personal interviews and informal conversations with consumers. As anthropologists we are conditioned to pay close attention to the linguistic forms people use to express themselves, in their own language. We also observe the body language employed by customers and patterns of public etiquette that govern restaurant interactions. Research in other social settings has taught us that actions often speak more directly than words. In designing our joint project we had to reinvent certain features of classic ethnographic methodology. Rather than acting like lone wolves who work in isolation (the usual anthropological scenario), we agreed in advance to address a similar set of questions, and we maintained regular communication via fax and email. Insights from Korea fed our investigations in Hong Kong and Taiwan; the appearance of "Aunt McDonald" in Beijing forced the rest of us to take a closer look at the use of kinship terminology in the corporate context. The five primary contributors all had previous field experience in the society involved (over 25 years in three cases).

As editor of this book, I would like to thank the following

people for help, encouragement, and research assistance: Melissa Caldwell, Bernadine Chee, Sidney Cheung, Kenneth George, Maris Gillette, Jack Glazier, Jing Jun, Liu Tik-sang, Eriberto (Fuji) Lozada, Holly Lynch, Pan Tianshu, Thomas Rawski, Mary Steedly, Anna Watson, Patty Jo Watson, Richard Watson, and Rubie Watson. Pam Summa did a heroic job as text editor and helped at all stages of the research; everyone associated with this book owes her a great debt. Muriel Bell's expert advice and attention to detail were instrumental in making this a better, more readable book. Special thanks go to my godsons, Teng Chin-pang and Teng Chin-hong, without whose inspiration this project would never have gotten off the ground. None of these people, of course, bears any responsibility for the opinions, views, or conclusions presented in this book. That responsibility belongs to the authors.

New Harbor, Maine   J.L.W

Contents

Contributors   xv

Introduction: Transnationalism, Localization, and
Fast Foods in East Asia   1
  James L. Watson

1. McDonald's in Beijing: The Localization of Americana   39
   Yunxiang Yan

2. McDonald's in Hong Kong: Consumerism, Dietary
   Change, and the Rise of a Children's Culture   77
   James L. Watson

3. McDonald's in Taipei: Hamburgers, Betel Nuts, and
   National Identity   110
   David Y. H. Wu

4. McDonald's in Seoul: Food Choices, Identity, and
   Nationalism   136
   Sangmee Bak

5. McDonald's in Japan: Changing Manners and
   Etiquette   161
   Emiko Ohnuki-Tierney

Update:McDonald's as Political Target: Globalization
and Anti-globalization in the Twenty-First Century   183
  James L. Watson

Notes   201
Select Bibliography   239
Index   247

Contributors

SANGMEE BAK is Professor of Cultural Anthropology at Hankuk University of Foreign Studies, Seoul, South Korea. She is the author of *Professional Women's Work, Marriage, and Kinship in Taiwan*, a series of articles on coffee drinking, cell phone use, and high tech culture in Korea.

EMIKO OHNUKI-TIERNEY is Vilas Research Professor, Department of Anthropology, University of Wisconsin at Madison. She is author of many books, including *Rice as Self: Japanese Identities Through Time* and *Kamikaze, Cherry Blossoms, and Nationalisms: The Militarization of Aesthetics in Japanese History*.

JAMES L. WATSON is Fairbank Professor of Chinese Society and Professor of Anthropology at Harvard University. He is author of *Emigration and the Chinese Lineage* and co-editor of *The Cultural Politics of Food and Eating* and *SARS in China: Prelude to Pandemic?*

DAVID Y. H. WU is Honorary Fellow, Institute of Ethnology, Academic Sinica, Taiwan. Formerly Professor and Chair, Department of Anthropology, Chinese University of Hong Kong, he also served as Senior Fellow at the Institute of Culture and Communication, East-West Center, Honolulu. He is author of *The Chinese in Papua New Guinea* and co-author of *Preschool in Three Cultures: Japan, China, and the U.S.A.*

YUNXIANG YAN is Professor of Anthropology and Co-Director, Center for Chinese Studies, University of California at Los Angeles. He is author of *The Flow of Gifts: Reciprocity and Social Networks in a Chinese Village* and *Private Life Under Socialism: Love, Intimacy, and Family Change in a Chinese Village, 1949–1999.*

Golden Arches East

In 1989, immediately after the Berlin Wall fell, two young East Germans crossed the border and happened upon a McDonald's restaurant. Here, in a letter to his cousin, one of them describes the experience: *[Katje] stormed in and I stood outside just opening my eyes as wide as I could. I was shaking so. It was all so modern, white and [made] out of glass, the windows were so amazing, the roof was constructed in a way that's only familiar to us through western newspapers. Katje pulled me inside. I felt like a lost convict who'd just spent 25 years in prison. Katje had some money that we used to buy a Big Mac. I'm sure we behaved in such a way that everyone could see where we came from. Above all, I was in such a state of shock that I was stumbling over everything.*

Daphne Berdahl, Where The World Ended

In October, 1996, McDonald's opened its first restaurant in New Delhi. The event drew protests from Hindu leaders, who criticized the company for serving beef in other parts of the world (though not, of course, in India). A young woman was interviewed while she was waiting for a vegetable burger: *It doesn't matter to me that McDonald's serves beef in its restaurants overseas. I'm here for the experience.*

John Zubrzycki, Christian Science Monitor

Transnationalism, Localization, and Fast Foods in East Asia

James L. Watson

On November 22, 1994, the *Wall Street Journal* announced
that the world's busiest McDonald's restaurant,[1] located in the
heart of Beijing, would have to move to make room for a new
commercial development. Within hours the story was picked
up by wire services and splashed across the pages of newspapers and magazines around the world.[2] McDonald's managers had situated their first Beijing outlet within a stone's throw
of Tiananmen Square, one of China's primary tourist spots
and a public arena for the celebration and contestation of Chinese national identity.[3] News of the move came as a shock to
company officials who were operating on the assumption that
they had a 20-year lease on the premises. The message of the
surprise relocation far outweighed its immediate commercial
impact: If this could happen to McDonald's, potential investors reasoned, no one was safe.

Under ordinary circumstances, news of a restaurant relocation is unlikely to attract much attention. But this, of course,
was no ordinary restaurant: it was McDonald's. The very
name, its "Mc" prefix, and the ubiquitous Golden Arches are

recognized and imitated throughout the world. McDonald's has become a saturated symbol, so laden with contradictory associations and meanings that the company stands for something greater than the sum of its corporate parts.

As the essays in this book demonstrate, McDonald's sells more than food. In Beijing, for instance, a new class of yuppies has embraced the company as a means of connecting to the world outside China. Many of the people Yunxiang Yan interviewed said they did not like the food, but assumed that something more profound was at issue when eating at McDonald's. In Korea, by contrast, hamburgers and similar meat products have long been a feature of the national diet, so the actual taste of McDonald's standard fare is not considered new. But, as Sangmee Bak demonstrates in Chapter 4, many Koreans equate eating a Big Mac with cultural and economic treason. Similarly in Taiwan, eating has become a political act and one's choice of restaurant—mainlander-owned or Taiwanese—may be taken as a reflection of attitudes toward independence or reunification with China. In Chapter 3, David Wu shows how McDonald's and other fast food chains have boomed on this precarious terrain, assisted perhaps by the common perception that "foreign" foods are politically neutral. Meanwhile, in Japan McDonald's has made the transition from exotic to ordinary and, as Emiko Ohnuki-Tierney argues in Chapter 5, the restaurants have blended into the local scene. Much the same can be said of Hong Kong. Since the early 1970s, an entire generation of Japanese and Hong Kong children has grown up with McDonald's; to these people the Big Mac, fries, and Coke do not represent something foreign. McDonald's is, quite simply, "local" cuisine.

McDonald's and the Cultural Imperialism Debate

Today over 30 million customers will be served at approximately 20,000 McDonald's restaurants in over 100 countries (see Table 1). In 1995 the system-wide sales of McDonald's Corporation totaled US$30 billion, $14 billion of which derived from restaurants outside the United States. A new McDonald's opens somewhere in the world every three hours.[4]

TABLE 1
McDonald's Restaurants by Country, 1990–1995

	1990	1995
Systemwide	11,803	18,380
United States	8,576	11,368
Japan	776	1,482
Canada	626	902
Germany	349	649
England	356	577
Australia	269	530
France	150	429
Brazil	63	243
Mexico	21	132
Taiwan	43	111
Sweden	49	106
Hong Kong	51	98
New Zealand	46	98
Philippines	32	83
Singapore	34	78
China	1[a]	62
Malaysia	22	58
South Korea	4	48
Thailand	6	39
Indonesia	0	38

SOURCE: 1995 Annual Report, McDonald's Corp., McD6-3030, p. ii.
[a]Shenzhen Special Economic Zone.

What do these statistics mean? The answer, of course, depends upon one's point of view. Some readers no doubt welcome McDonald's ascendancy as evidence that free market values prevail everywhere, irrespective of geography or cultural differences ("All the World's a McStage").[5] This viewpoint is reflected in the news media that track McDonald's and report on its every triumph ("Big Mac Goes to Mecca").[6] In preparing for this project I read thousands of newspaper, magazine, and trade journal articles about the worldwide fast food industry (see endnotes beginning on p. 203 for a sampling). There can be little doubt that McDonald's enjoys a special, perhaps even privileged, relationship with U.S. media—a tribute to the company's virtuosity in public relations. Positive articles far outweigh negative or even neutral ones. The reverse appears to be true in Britain, owing largely to McDonald's disastrous decision to sue local environmentalists ("Big Mac Makes a Meal of It As Libel Trial Drags On").[7] With the possible exception of Korea, media reports in East Asia tend to be positive. The Chinese media could barely restrain their enthusiasm for McDonald's during the restaurants' first three years of operation in the People's Republic; the company was celebrated as a model of modernization, sanitation, and responsible management.

More recently, however, Chinese political leaders have expressed alarm at the growing influence of McDonald's, Kentucky Fried Chicken (KFC), Pizza Hut, and other foreign food firms. As Chinese state policy has begun to encourage an indigenous fast food industry, local media coverage has shifted accordingly.[8] Chinese leaders appear to be aligning themselves with European and American intellectuals who have long equated McDonald's and its rivals in the fast food industry as agents of *cultural imperialism*—a new form of exploitation that results from the export of popular culture from the United States, Japan, and Europe to other parts of the world.[9] "Culture" in this context is defined as popular music, television, film, video, pulp fiction, comics, advertising, fashion, home design, and mass-produced food. Corporations that are capable of manipulating personal "tastes" will thrive as state authorities lose control over the distribution and consumption of goods and services. Popular culture, in this view, generates a vision, a fantasy, of the good life, and if the Big Mac, Coke, and Disney cartoons are perceived as an integral part of that life, American companies cannot lose.[10]

Theorists who write about cultural imperialism argue that it is the domination of popular culture—rather than outright military or political control—that matters most in the postmodern, postsocialist, postindustrial world.[11] One of the clearest expressions of this view appeared recently on the Op-Ed page of the *New York Times*. The voice is Ronald Steel's: "It was never the Soviet Union, but the United States itself that is the true revolutionary power. . . . We purvey a culture based on mass entertainment and mass gratification. . . . The cultural message we transmit through Hollywood and McDonald's goes out across the world to capture, and also to undermine, other societies. . . . Unlike more traditional conquerors, we are not content merely to subdue others: We insist that they be like us."[12]

McDonald's as a Corrosive Force?

Does the spread of fast food undermine the integrity of indigenous cuisines? Are food chains helping to create a homogenous, global culture better suited to the needs of a capitalist world order?

This book is specifically designed to address such questions. The authors of the following case studies have different perspectives on the cultural imperialism debate, reflecting circumstances in the societies studied. We do not celebrate McDonald's as a paragon of capitalist virtue, nor do we condemn the corporation as an evil empire. Our goal is to produce ethnographic accounts of McDonald's social, political, and economic impact on five local cultures. These are not small-scale cultures under imminent threat of extinction; we are dealing with economically resilient, technologically advanced societies noted for their haute cuisines. If McDonald's can make inroads in these societies, one might be tempted to conclude, it may indeed be an irresistible force for world culinary change. But isn't another scenario possible? Have people in East Asia conspired to change McDonald's, modifying this seemingly monolithic institution to fit local conditions?

The essays in this book demonstrate that the interaction process works both ways. McDonald's *has* effected small but influential changes in East Asian dietary patterns. Until the introduction of McDonald's, for example, Japanese consumers rarely, if ever, ate with their hands; as Emiko Ohnuki-Tierney shows in Chapter 5, this is now an acceptable mode of dining. In Hong Kong, McDonald's has replaced traditional teahouses and street stalls as the most popular breakfast venue. And among Taiwanese youth, french fries have become a dietary staple, owing almost entirely to the influence of McDonald's.

At the same time, however, East Asian consumers have quietly, and in some cases stubbornly, transformed their neighborhood McDonald's into local institutions. In the United

States fast food may indeed imply fast consumption, but this is certainly not the case everywhere. In Beijing, Seoul, and Taipei, for instance, McDonald's restaurants are treated as leisure centers, where people can retreat from the stresses of urban life. In Hong Kong, middle school students often sit in McDonald's for hours—studying, gossiping, and picking over snacks; for them, the restaurants are the equivalent of youth clubs. More will be said about the localization process in the following chapters. Suffice it to note here that McDonald's does not always call the shots.

Globalism and Local Cultures

Those who have followed academic and business trends in recent years are aware that two new "isms" are much in vogue—globalism and transnationalism. Many writers use these terms interchangeably. In my view the two -isms represent different social processes and should not be conflated. Globalism describes an essentially impossible condition that is said to prevail when people the world over share a homogenous, mutually intelligible culture. Proponents of globalism assume that electronic communications and mass media (especially television) will create a "global village."[13] This global system is sustained, the argument proceeds, by technologically sophisticated elites who speak the same language (American English), maintain a common lifestyle, and share similar aspirations. To quote one observer of globalism, Benjamin Barber, the "future [is] a busy portrait of onrushing economic, technological, and economic forces that demand integration and uniformity and that mesmerize peoples everywhere with fast music, fast computers, and fast food—MTV, Macintosh, and McDonald's— pressing nations into one homogeneous global theme park, one

McWorld tied together by communications, information, entertainment, and commerce."[14]

In its most recent guise, globalism has resurfaced as a logical projection of the digital revolution. According to various digirati, notably those associated with *Wired* magazine, Internet enthusiasts have already begun to create a global culture that will negate—or at least undermine—the traditional state.[15] Web visionaries also predict that ideologies based on class, religion, and ethnicity will recede as the global system becomes a reality. This new utopian literature is reminiscent of early Marxist visions of a stateless, classless world devoid of ethnic and religious divisions. Underlying globalist theories is the idea that people the world over will share a common culture, but few of these modern visionaries bother to clarify what they mean by "culture"—it is simply taken for granted.

From the very beginning of anthropology as an academic discipline, debates about the meaning of culture have united and divided anthropologists.[16] Of late, the tone of this debate has become especially strident, separating the good from the bad, the enlightened from the ignorant. In its earlier usage culture was defined by most anthropologists as a shared set of beliefs, customs, and ideas that held people together in coherent groups.[17] In recent decades, however, the notion of coherence has come under attack by ethnosemanticists, who have discovered that people in supposedly close-knit groups (bands of hunters, factory workers, bureaucrats) do not share a single system of knowledge.[18] Culture, therefore, is not something that people inherit as an undifferentiated bloc of knowledge from their ancestors. Culture is a set of ideas, reactions, and expectations that is constantly changing as people and groups themselves change.

In this book the operative term is "local culture," shorthand for the experience of everyday life as lived by ordinary people in specific localities. In using it, we attempt to capture the feelings of appropriateness, comfort, and correctness that govern the construction of personal preferences, or "tastes."[19] Dietary patterns, attitudes toward food, and notions of what constitutes a proper meal (a concept discussed by all contributors) are central to the experience of everyday life and hence are integral to the maintenance of local cultures.

As noted above, there are serious questions attending the use of the term "culture," and the word "local" is similarly problematic. Both notions imply an inherent sameness within a given population, irrespective of class, gender, or status differences. When this style of analysis is carried to its logical extreme the result is essentialism, which leads one to assume that "the Chinese" (for example) share an essential, irreducible core of beliefs and attributes that separates them from other categories of people, such as "the Koreans." It is obvious that all Chinese do not share the same mental framework, nor do they always agree on what constitutes appropriate or correct behavior.

Readers will note that the authors of this book have made efforts to highlight class, gender, and status differences, especially in relation to consumption practices. One surprise was the discovery that many McDonald's restaurants in East Asia have become sanctuaries for women who wish to avoid male-dominated settings. In Beijing and Seoul, new categories of yuppies treat McDonald's as an arena for conspicuous consumption. Anthropologists who work in such settings must pay close attention to rapid changes in consumer preferences. Twenty years ago McDonald's catered to the children of Hong

Kong's wealthy elite; the current generation of Hong Kong hyperconsumers has long since abandoned the Golden Arches and moved upmarket to more expensive watering holes (e.g., Planet Hollywood). Meanwhile, McDonald's has become a mainstay for working-class people, who are attracted by its low cost, convenience, and predictability.

One of our conclusions in this book is that societies in East Asia are changing as fast as cuisines—there is nothing immutable or primordial about cultural systems. In Hong Kong, for instance, it would be impossible to isolate what is specifically "local" about the cuisine, given the propensity of Hong Kong people to adopt new foods. As argued in Chapter 2, Hong Kong's cuisine, and with it Hong Kong's local culture, is a moving target. Hong Kong is the quintessential postmodern environment, where the boundaries of status, style, and taste dissolve almost as fast as they are formed. What is "in" today is "out" tomorrow.

Transnationalism and the Multilocal Corporation

It has become an academic cliché to argue that people are constantly reinventing themselves. Nevertheless, the speed of that reinvention process in places like Hong Kong, Taipei, and Seoul is so rapid that it defies description. In the realm of popular culture, it is no longer possible to distinguish between what is "local" and what is "foreign."[20] Who is to say that Mickey Mouse is not Japanese, or that Ronald McDonald is not Chinese? To millions of children who watch Chinese television, "Uncle McDonald" (alias Ronald) is probably more familiar than the mythical characters of Chinese folklore.

We have entered here the realm of the transnational, a new

field of study that focuses on the "deterritorialization" of popular culture. As Arjun Appadurai notes, the world economy can no longer be understood by assuming that the original producers of a commodity necessarily control its consumption. A good example is the spread of "Asian" martial arts to North and South America, fostered by Hollywood and the Hong Kong film industry.[21] Transnationalism describes a condition by which people, commodities, and ideas literally cross—transgress—national boundaries and are not identified with a single place of origin. One of the leading theorists of this new field argues that transnational phenomena are best perceived as the building blocks of "third cultures," which are "oriented beyond national boundaries."[22]

Transnational corporations are popularly regarded as the clearest expressions of this new adaptation, given that business operations, manufacturing, and marketing are often spread around the globe, to dozens of societies.[23] The Nike Corporation, a U.S.-based firm that began operation in Japan, is an excellent case in point. One of the company's most popular products is the Air Max Penny, inspired by an American basketball player whose nickname is Penny. The shoe contains 52 separate components produced in five countries (Japan, South Korea, Taiwan, Indonesia, and the United States). By the time it is finished, the Penny has passed through at least 120 pairs of hands. The final product is assembled by Chinese workers in a Taiwanese-owned factory just north of Hong Kong; design work is done by American technicians at a research center in Tennessee. Nike itself does not own any factories. Instead, the company relies on an international team of specialists who negotiate with manufacturers, monitor production, and arrange shipment.[24]

The classic model of the transnational corporation assumes a non-national, or even antinational, mode of production controlled from a headquarters complex located somewhere in the First World.[25] Dispersed production and centralized control would certainly appear to be the norm in the transnational food and beverage industry: Coca-Cola's far-flung empire is based in Atlanta; KFC in Louisville; Heinz in Pittsburgh; Kellogg's in Battle Creek, Michigan; Carr's, the biscuit maker, in Carlisle, England. The list could easily fill this page and the next.

At first glance, McDonald's would appear to be the quintessential transnational: It operates in more than 100 countries and maintains a sprawling headquarters complex in Oak Brook, Illinois—the home of Hamburger University. On closer inspection, however, the company does not conform to expectations; it resembles a federation of semiautonomous enterprises.[26] James Cantalupo, President of McDonald's International, claims that the goal of McDonald's is to "become as much a part of the local culture as possible." He objects when "[p]eople call us a multinational. I like to call us *multilocal*," meaning that McDonald's goes to great lengths to find local suppliers and local partners whenever new branches are opened. To support his claims, Cantalupo notes that, in 1991, there were fewer than 20 American expatriate managers working in overseas operations.[27] Yunxiang Yan discovered that only one American—a Chinese-speaker—worked in the Beijing headquarters of McDonald's; all of the managers encountered by Sangmee Bak in Seoul were Korean nationals; and in Japan, decisions have been in local hands since the company's opening in 1971. In fact, it was McDonald's early experience in Japan that set the tone for future overseas operations. As John Love notes, the Japanese case "proved that the key to success in the international market was the same as it was [in the United States]: local control by local owner-operators."[28]

Research in this book reveals that McDonald's International retains at least a 50 percent stake in its East Asian enterprises; the other half is owned by local operators. Soon after McDonald's opened in Korea, a major political debate erupted over the disposition of local profits. Was the goal of the company to enrich American stockholders or to help build the Korean economy? Korean managers confronted their critics by arguing that local franchisees owned half the business and that a high percentage of profits was plowed back into its Korea-based operations. Sangmee Bak notes that local managers insisted that the Korean business environment was so complicated that foreigners could not hope to survive on their own. They took great pride in their accomplishments and told Bak that theirs was a *Korean* business. In Korea—as in China, Taiwan, and Japan—McDonald's goes out of its way to find local suppliers for its operations.[29] Hong Kong, as noted in Chapter 2, is the lone exception; owing to its special geographic circumstances, raw materials are no longer produced there, and nearly everything McDonald's uses has to be imported. (Since its repatriation on July 1, 1997, however, one could argue that Hong Kong no longer relies on "imports," given that most of its supplies come from mainland China.)

McDonald's localization strategy has been so successful that two of its East Asian managers have become international celebrities: Den Fujita, Managing Director, Japan, and Daniel Ng, Managing Director, Hong Kong. These men are credited with turning what appeared to be impossible tasks ("Selling hamburgers in Tokyo or Hong Kong? You must be joking!")

into dramatic success stories.[30] Fujita and Ng are media stars in their respective countries; like Ray Kroc, founder of McDonald's in the United States, they have become entrepreneurial legends who extol the virtues of hard work, personal discipline, and the free market.[31] (Another such living legend is, of course, George Cohon, President of McDonald's Canada and the impresario of McDonald's Moscow; in 1991 *Pravda* proved it had a sense of humor by designating Cohon a "Hero of Capitalist Labor.")[32]

Behind each of these success stories lies the ability to discern, and respond to, consumer needs. Daniel Ng, for instance, established his own research unit and ran focus groups to monitor the changing attitudes of ordinary customers; he is also a keen observer of the popular culture scene in Hong Kong. The independent natures of these local managers (not to mention their sheer chutzpah) underline the obvious: McDonald's transnational success is due in large part to its multilocal mode of operation. There is, however, another critical factor in the equation—good timing.

The Family Revolution in East Asia: Children as Consumers

It is certainly no coincidence that the startup dates for McDonald's (see Table 2) correspond to the emergence of new classes of affluent consumers in the various East Asian countries.[33] Rising incomes have produced dramatic changes in lifestyles, especially among young people who live and work in metropolitan areas. Decisions regarding employment and consumption no longer require consultations with an extended network of parents, grandparents, adult siblings, and other kin. Married women are working outside the home in increasing numbers, which in turn has affected gender relations, child-

TABLE 2
Startup Dates for McDonald's in Various Countries

1955	Franchising begins in U.S.A.	1984	Taiwan
		1985	Thailand
1967	Canada	1985	Mexico
1971	Japan	1986	Turkey
1971	Australia	1988	South Korea
1971	Germany	1990	China (Shenzhen Special
1972	France		Economic Zone)
1973	Sweden	1990	Russia
1974	England	1991	Indonesia
1975	Hong Kong	1992	China (Beijing)
1976	New Zealand	1992	Poland
1979	Brazil	1993	Israel
1979	Singapore	1994	Saudia Arabia
1981	Philippines	1995	South Africa
1982	Malaysia	1996	Croatia

SOURCES: *1994 Student Information Packet*, McDonald's Corporation, McD1-1274, p. 38; *New York Times*, Nov. 12, 1995, and Feb. 5, 1996.

rearing practices, and residence patterns.[34] A majority of newlyweds are opting for neolocality (forming a new household separate from those of their parents) or creating new arrangements that defy convention. In Taiwan, for instance, professional women often insist on living near their own parents, rather than follow the more "traditional" pattern of patrilocality (living with or near the husband's parents). The crucial factor here is the household labor—childminding, cooking, shopping—provided by the working woman's mother, whose assistance makes her daughter's professional life possible.[35]

In response to these changes a new family structure has emerged, one that focuses on the needs and aspirations of the conjugal unit, the married *couple*. Conjugality brings with it an entire set of attitudes and practices that undermine older assumptions regarding the meaning of life.[36] Should married couples strive, regardless of personal cost, to promote the welfare of the larger kin group and support aging parents? Or should they concentrate on building a more comfortable life for themselves and their immediate offspring? Increasingly, the balance is shifting toward conjugality and away from the family norms that guided earlier generations.

The shift also coincides with a dramatic decline in the birthrate and a rise in the amount of money and attention lavished on children. China's single-child-family policy has helped produce a generation of Little Emperors and Empresses, each commanding the affection and economic support of two parents and in many cases four grandparents.[37] In Chapter 1, Yunxiang Yan shows how McDonald's has capitalized on the Little Emperor/ress phenomenon, treating children as independent decision makers who command substantial resources. Similar patterns of indulgence are common in Taiwan (see Chapter 3) and in Japan, where children command impressive amounts of spending money.[38] In 1995, Hong Kong parents gave junior high school students an average of US$107 per month to spend on snacks and entertainment.[39]

McDonald's restaurants first appeared in East Asian cities during the early phases of this family revolution. When one looks closely at the historical sequence summarized below, it is obvious that entrepreneurial flair alone cannot explain the corporation's phenomenal success rate.

Tokyo, 1971

An affluent middle class has matured by the early 1970s,[40] and a new generation of consumers can afford to eat out on a regular basis. McDonald's takeoff corresponds to the emergence of the "teens," a hitherto unrecognized stage in the Japanese life course. For the first time in Japanese history, all young people are expected to stay in school until age 18.[41] These leisured youths become avid consumers of American-style fast foods and popular culture.[42]

Hong Kong, 1975

McDonald's opening date marks the beginning of a long economic boom in Hong Kong as the British colony becomes an international services center and a transshipment port for the China trade. A white-collar middle class rapidly replaces Hong Kong's postwar working class.[43] By the mid-1970s the majority of residents are living in neolocal, conjugal units and are preoccupied with their own offspring rather than a wider network of kin.[44] Children and young adults emerge as full-fledged consumers in the late 1970s and early 1980s. McDonald's becomes the "in" place to eat.

Taipei, 1984

McDonald's is the first foreign food company allowed to operate in Taiwan's previously closed market. The start-up corresponds to the beginning of a new political era, one in which local interests challenge the authoritarian rule of the Nationalist Party. The Golden Arches arrive just as Taiwan reaches takeoff as a major player in the global electronics and computer markets. Taiwan's emerging middle class begins to have time and money to spend on leisure activities. Family patterns change rapidly to accommodate urban life and the regular employment of married women.[45] Older forms of childhood socialization, emphasizing filiality and obedience, are gradually de-emphasized to accommodate practices that encourage consumerism.[46] Taipei's youth embrace McDonald's as a symbol of their new lifestyle.

Seoul, 1988

McDonald's is the first foreign food chain permitted to operate in Korea. An indigenous middle class has emerged after decades of personal sacrifice and deferred gratification by the previous generation of workers. Salaried employees (mostly male) have little spare time for family activities, but their dependents begin to enjoy a lifestyle defined by consumerism.[47] Korean children rapidly become knowledgeable consumers, eager to eat hamburgers, pizza, and American-style chicken. The persuasive power of this new generation is impressive: Many parents who object to foreign imports find themselves arranging birthday parties for their children at McDonald's.[48]

Beijing, 1992

Family patterns in urban China have been changing rapidly since the introduction of economic reforms in the late 1970s and early 1980s. McDonald's enters the Chinese scene during a critical period of class formation; for the first time since the communist victory of 1949, independent entrepreneurs and business people are allowed to operate openly. Affluent families begin to distinguish themselves by engaging in conspicuous consumption and, as outlined in Chapter 1, McDonald's becomes a powerful symbol of the new lifestyle. By the mid-1990s a booming market in children's entertainment (theme parks, video parlors, computer games) has emerged. McDonald's is expanding rapidly in China to capitalize on these cultural developments; plans call for up to 600 outlets by the year 2003.[49]

One conclusion is obvious: McDonald's could not have succeeded in East Asia without appealing to younger generations
of consumers, children and teenagers. The corporation makes a
point of cultivating this market and invests heavily in television advertising aimed specifically at children. Birthday parties
have become a key element in this strategy: Prior to McDonald's entry into the local scene, festivities to mark the specific
birthdates of youngsters were unknown in most parts of East
Asia. In Hong Kong, for instance, calendrical dates of birth
were recorded for use later in life (in matching the horoscopes
of prospective marriage partners, for instance), but until the
late 1970s most people paid little attention to the annual
event—if indeed they remembered it at all.

McDonald's and its rivals in the fast food industry have
promoted the birthday party—complete with cake and candles—in their advertising and, as the case studies in this book
make clear, the celebrations have become the rage among upwardly mobile youngsters throughout East Asia. McDonald's
also introduced other, localized innovations that appeal directly to their youngest customers. In Beijing, the company's
ubiquitous male mascot, Ronald, has been paired with a female
companion known as Aunt McDonald, whose job it is to en-
tertain children and attend parties. In Taipei and Hong Kong,
McDonald's offers parents a special party package that includes
gifts and toys for each participant, plus the services of a hostess
who leads the children in songs and games. Parties of this type
have become an integral feature of the local culture.

More than any other factor, therefore, McDonald's success
is attributable to the revolution in family values that has transformed East Asia. Furthermore, as demonstrated repeatedly in
this book, the localization process depends heavily upon chil-

dren: In Japan and Hong Kong, McDonald's did not make the transition from foreign import to "local" institution until the first generation of childhood consumers began to have children of their own. Generational succession is not yet complete in Taiwan, although as David Wu illustrates in Chapter 3, children are driving the localization process. It is too early to call the outcome in Korea and China, but the research by Bak and Yan (Chapters 4 and 1) demonstrates that children everywhere are powerful agents of social change.

Standardization and Taste: The McDonald's System

One characteristic of this book distinguishing it from previous studies of the fast food industry is our focus on *consumption*: we place primary emphasis on the role of consumers. As noted in the Preface, we have chosen not to concentrate exclusively on *production*. Before we proceed, however, something needs to be said about McDonald's efforts to standardize its product, given that consistency and predictability are important keys to the company's worldwide appeal. What follows is a brief summary of the fast food industry, its history and productive processes. Readers who are interested in specific aspects of production (including management, labor relations, food sourcing, and mechanization) might wish to pursue the references cited in the endnotes.

McDonald's, of course, did not invent fast food, although the corporation is largely responsible for the standardization and automation we now take for granted in the industry. Nearly every country has a candidate for the original "fast" cuisine: fish and chips in Britain, noodles in China, station box lunches (*ekibentō*) in Japan, street kebabs in Turkey, sausage and bread in Germany (which later metamorphosed into the ubiquitous American hot dog).[50] One key to McDonald's success is the constant push to speed up production without sacrificing consistency. Corporate goals announced in late 1995 include the filling of walk-in orders within 90 seconds and a guarantee that customers will never have to wait more than three-and-a-half minutes at drive-through windows. Company representatives monitor performance by making surprise visits to McDonald's outlets every quarter.[51]

McDonald's has created a *system* that depends upon standardized procedures in everything from sandwich assembly to advanced management training at Hamburger University.[52] An excellent summary of McDonald's operating procedures can be found in *Fast Food, Fast Talk*, a study of the standardization of work in the United States; the author, Robin Leidner, characterizes McDonald's as "an exemplar of extreme standardization."[53] A 600-page *Operations and Training Manual* guides production. Nothing is left to chance; photo layouts show where the sauces should be placed on the bun, and the exact thickness of sliced pickles is specified. All equipment at McDonald's restaurants must be purchased from approved suppliers, and the architectural design of both interior and exterior is carefully controlled.[54] McDonald's does not condone "absentee" owners, nor will it work with partnerships (i.e., multiple owners); franchise holders must be involved in the day-to-day management of the restaurant.[55] In 1991 over 20,000 people contacted the company to inquire about new franchises; only 2,000 reached the interview stage and fewer than 200 were accepted.[56]

As Robert Kwan, Managing Director of McDonald's in Singapore, puts it: "McDonald's sells . . . a system, not products."[57] The aim is to create a standardized set of items that taste the same in Singapore, Spain, and South Africa. Many travelers have told me (with a tone of triumph in their voices) that they can indeed perceive slight differences in the taste of Big Macs they have sampled in Beijing or Paris. Such claims are, however, difficult to verify. Thomas Friedman of the *New York Times* reports that he has eaten Big Macs at McDonald's in 14 countries (all, no doubt, in the line of journalistic duty) and maintains that "they all *really do* taste the same."[58] Based on personal visits to McDonald's in the five sites surveyed in this book—plus England, Germany, the Netherlands, and the United States—I side with Mr. Friedman on the question of taste.[59]

McDonald's may not be able to control the taste responses of individual consumers, but it *can* make the experience of eating relatively predictable. The corporation pays close attention to restaurant design, down to the exact measurements of service counters, placement of overhead backlit menus (an innovation that is now widely imitated throughout the world), arrangement of seats and booths, color of walls and style of decorations, and the location of (standardized) disposal bins. Who has not had the uncanny sensation of déjà vu when entering a McDonald's restaurant in a foreign country? "It's just like home."

The familiarity factor is central to McDonald's success, especially in societies like the United States, where job mobility is a regular feature of family life. To many disoriented, lonely children, the Golden Arches symbolize more than just food; McDonald's stands for home, familiarity, and friendship. One finding of this book is that American children are not alone in this response. A surprisingly high percentage of young people in Tokyo, Taipei, and Hong Kong have grown up with Mc-

Donald's as their favorite venue for entertaining family and friends.[60] It was not the power of corporate sponsorship alone that made McDonald's the "official food service partner" during the 1996 Olympic Games in Atlanta. Athletes from around the world were familiar enough with McDonald's fare to accept it without question, thereby avoiding potentially disastrous encounters with strange foods.[61] Americans abroad report similar reactions. On his way home from China after an exhausting business trip, the CEO of Microsoft, Bill Gates, found himself in Hong Kong with a colleague, looking for a place to eat after midnight: "We were really happy to discover that they have 24-hour McDonald's in Hong Kong," said Gates, as he "wolfed down hamburgers."[62]

Modified Menus and Local Sensitivities: McDonald's Adapts

The key to McDonald's worldwide success is that people everywhere know what to expect when they pass through the Golden Arches. This does not mean, however, that the corporation has resisted change or refused to adapt when local customs require flexibility. In Israel, after initial protests, Big Macs are now served without cheese in several outlets, thereby permitting the separation of meat and dairy products required of kosher restaurants.[63] McDonald's restaurants in India serve Vegetable McNuggets and a mutton-based Maharaja Mac, innovations that are necessary in a country where Hindus do not eat beef, Muslims do not eat pork, and Jains (among others) do not eat meat of any type.[64] In Malaysia and Singapore, McDonald's underwent rigorous inspections by Muslim clerics to ensure ritual cleanliness; the chain was rewarded with a *halal* ("clean," "acceptable") certificate, indicating the total absence of pork products.[65]

Variations on McDonald's original, American-style menu exist in many parts of the world: Chilled yogurt drinks (*ayran*) in Turkey, espresso and cold pasta in Italy, teriyaki burgers in Japan (also in Taiwan and Hong Kong), vegetarian burgers in the Netherlands, McSpagetti in the Philippines, McLaks (grilled salmon sandwich) in Norway, frankfurters and beer in Germany, McHuevo (poached egg hamburger) in Uruguay.[66]

Not all McDonald's menu innovations have been embraced by consumers: Witness the famous McLean Deluxe fiasco in the United States and a less publicized disaster called McPloughman's in Britain (a cheese-and-pickle sandwich).[67] The corporation has responded to constant criticism from nutritionists and natural food activists by introducing prepackaged salads, fresh celery and carrot sticks, fat-free bran muffins, and low-fat milk shakes.[68] These efforts may satisfy critics but they are unlikely to change McDonald's public image among consumers, few of whom stop at the Golden Arches for health food.

Irrespective of local variations (espresso, McLaks) and recent additions (carrot sticks), the structure of the McDonald's menu remains essentially uniform the world over: main course burger/sandwich, fries, and a drink—overwhelmingly Coca-Cola. The keystone of this winning combination is *not*, as most observers might assume, the Big Mac or even the generic hamburger. It is the fries. The main course may vary widely (fish sandwiches in Hong Kong, vegetable burgers in Amsterdam), but the signature innovation of McDonald's—thin, elongated fries cut from russet potatoes—is ever-present and consumed with great gusto by Muslims, Jews, Christians, Buddhists, Hindus, vegetarians (now that vegetable oil is used), communists, Tories, marathoners, and armchair athletes. It is understandable, therefore, why McDonald's has made such a fetish of its deep-fried potatoes and continues to work on improving the delivery of this industry winner. The Chairman of Burger King acknowledges that his company's fries are second-best in comparison to those of its archrival: "Our fries just don't hold up." A research program, code-named "stealth fries," is specifically designed to upgrade Burger King's offerings.[69]

Fast Gets Faster: Automation and the Industrialization of Food

A central feature of the McDonald's system is the devolution of work into a series of tasks that can be performed by an average worker with a minimum of training. There are no chefs in a McDonald's restaurant; hamburgers and fries are produced in assembly-line fashion, following the industrial model popularized by Henry Ford.[70] As one observer of the restaurant business notes, the end products of work at McDonald's are neat boxes stored in chutes, hamburgers ready for immediate sale.[71]

McDonald's was certainly not the first enterprise to follow Fordist methods of food production. Starting in the late nineteenth century (and probably much earlier), public dining halls in China divided the cooking process into elementary procedures—cleaning, peeling, chopping, boiling, frying, serving—each performed by a separate team of workers. The results can hardly be called haute cuisine (ask any Chinese student who has had to endure canteen food), but the system does feed hundreds of people in a relatively short time. Assembly-line methods were also followed by various American enterprises that predated McDonald's, including railway dining cars and the Howard Johnson restaurant chain. The first Howard Johnson franchise opened in 1935, and by 1941 the company had grown to 150 outlets serving an emerging market of middle-class motorists.[72] McDonald's expansion can be traced to the post–World War Two boom in automobile traffic and the American infatuation with brand-name products that promised consistency, predictability, and safety.[73] Franchising began in 1955, and by 1963 McDonald's was selling one million hamburgers a day; the first drive-through operation started in 1975, an innovation that today accounts for approximately half of McDonald's sales in the United States.[74]

Advances in automation have revolutionized the worldwide food industry. Even sushi is now becoming a fast food. For $86,000 the Suzumo Machinery Company will provide a sushi robot that turns out 1,200 pieces per hour, four to six times the rate of the most accomplished sushi chef.[75] McDonald's was the first fast food company to use computers that automatically adjust cooking time and temperatures. French fries offer a case in point. In conjunction with researchers at the Argonne National Laboratory near Chicago, McDonald's devised a rapid frying system for frozen potatoes that reduced delivery time by 30 to 40 seconds.[76] Assuming that a high percentage of McDonald's 30 million daily customers order fries, the multiplier effect of 30 seconds more than covers the costs of automation.

Fast food operators in the United States report that their biggest problems are rising labor costs and shortages of reliable workers. The turnover rate for nonmanagerial employees now approaches 300 percent per year in many American cities.[77] Although comparable figures are not readily available for East Asia, management interviews conducted by the five anthropologists who worked on this project reveal a much lower turnover rate in the cities they studied. The cost of labor, however, continues to rise in East Asia, and local operators are quick to embrace new technology that promises to speed up production. The next step in automation is touch-screen computerized ordering systems that release workers from counter duty. A system pioneered by Arby's reduced ordering time from 100 seconds to 45, increasing sales per working hour from $23 to $32 for the average employee.[78]

Consumer Discipline, Education, and Resistance

Does the increasing speed of production necessarily encourage an equally fast rate of consumption? Do customers always conform to management expectations? The fast food business is based on the assumption that customers will hold up their end of an implicit contract: The company promises to provide fast, reliable, inexpensive service if the consumer agrees to pay in advance, eat quickly, and leave without delay, thereby making room for others. The contract also assumes that fast food patrons know what is expected of them, that they have been educated, or disciplined, to behave like "proper" consumers in a modern economy. Scholars who support the cultural imperialism hypothesis would argue that the goal is to turn Russians, Chinese, and Saudis into Americans. As we shall see, however, corporate campaigns to modify consumer behavior do not always go according to plan.

Children in Hong Kong, Tokyo, and Boston learn at a very early age how to place orders, find a table, and eat without embarrassing their friends. Such skills cannot, however, be taken for granted. During McDonald's first weeks of operation in Moscow, employees distributed information sheets to people standing in queues, telling them how to order and what to do after paying. During particularly busy periods, a young woman stood outside the restaurant and spoke through a bull-horn: "The employees inside will smile at you. This does not mean that they are laughing at you. We smile because we are happy to serve you." The tray liners featured illustrations of Big Macs, fries, and shakes, with their component raw materials (cheese, pickles, potatoes, strawberries) in the background.[79] Many Muscovites needed such guidance because their previous experience of service personnel had left them unprepared to be smiled at and because they had no idea what was inside a hamburger, let alone how to eat one.[80] I observed a similar process of consumer education in 1994, outside McDonald's in Beijing. Chinese families frequently gathered around a large, pictorial menu and held lengthy discussions before venturing inside to place an order. In Hong Kong, by contrast, the restaurants have become such a routine feature of the urban landscape that pictorial menus are no longer necessary, although scaled-down versions are still provided for tourists (mostly from the Chinese countryside) who may not be familiar with the fare.

There can be little doubt that McDonald's excels at educating its customers. Convincing them to behave like orderly, disciplined consumers is another matter altogether. An essential feature of any industrialized food system is the queue, a remarkable social institution that is too often taken for granted. Standing in line is not a "natural" human reaction to bottlenecks resulting when one person serves many. In Hong Kong, for instance, queuing for services (at banks, ticket offices, restaurants) was largely unknown until the mid-1970s, when a new generation of locally born people began to transform the social environment. McDonald's is often credited with introducing the queue to Hong Kong consumers, although other innovations (restraining barriers at ferries and taxi ranks) started the trend at least a decade before the company opened for business in 1975. The orderly queues that one sees in Hong Kong today are reflections of a dramatic shift from the immigrant-based culture of the 1950s–1970s ("Hong Kong is a borrowed place and we are living on borrowed time") to the self-confident, affluent culture of the 1980s and 1990s ("Hong Kong is our home and we are proud of it"). When free-for-alls do break out, often instigated by recent arrivals from China, Hong Kong residents stand back and glare their disapproval—a highly effective means of socializing, and thereby disciplining, newcomers.

One must not assume, however, that the queue is a universally accepted feature of modern consumerism. In Leiden, for instance, McDonald's customers regularly refuse to line up during busy periods and form tightly packed clumps in front of order takers. Under normal circumstances Dutch clumps are not disorderly because the local rules of behavior encourage people to negotiate politely among themselves and order in sequence of arrival. Peter Stephenson observed the clumps forming at Leiden's McDonald's and concluded that the local rules of courtesy do not apply in this setting. Dutch teenagers experience "a kind of instant emigration" and behave in a manner they perceive to be American: "Me! Me!" they shout as they struggle for attention at the counter.[81] Rick Fantasia found a similar, although less boisterous, neglect of queuing in French McDonald's, and Melissa Caldwell notes that queues in Moscow tend to dissolve into scrums during busy periods unless corralled by an employee.[82]

On the whole, however, the vast majority of McDonald's customers around the world soon learn to accept the queue, and in some places (such as Hong Kong) they enforce their own form of discipline on miscreants. The physical setting of fast food restaurants encourages this discipline. As Allen Sheldon notes, both customer and employee are standing, thereby establishing an egalitarian relationship, which in turn makes it seem reasonable for consumers to perform tasks that would otherwise be delegated to paid staff: drawing one's own drinks, distributing napkins and flatware, clearing the table. In Sheldon's view McDonald's is a "theater of equality,"[83] especially in contrast to conventional restaurants, where the customer sits and the employee stands, "waiting" for orders.

The egalitarian model does not apply to all McDonald's restaurants, however. Exceptions are made where local dining customs demand more formality. In Rio de Janeiro, for instance, waiters serve Big Macs with champagne in candle-lit restaurants; in Caracas hostesses seat customers, take orders, and deliver meals.[84] Expectations are exactly the opposite in Taipei, Hong Kong, and Beijing: Interviews revealed that consumers preferred the egalitarian model of fast food service. They were attracted to McDonald's precisely because of its lack of pomp and its unrelenting predictability. As Yan notes in Chapter 1, the alternatives to McDonald's are not only expensive, they can lead to embarrassing incidents: What does one do when the big spender at an adjoining table orders shark's fin soup and braised quail? Compete or lose face? At McDonald's the menu is comfortably limited and there is little opportunity for competition. Bak reports that the egalitarian model is also followed in Korea, but with one modification introduced by management: employees sometimes seat diners at tables occupied by others, a practice that maximizes the use of space and incidentally increases the speed of eating. Rather than seeing this practice as an imposition, however, Korean consumers generally appreciate the intervention because it is considered impolite to seat oneself at an occupied table.

Service with a Smile?

To outsiders one of the most peculiar characteristics of American society is the indiscriminate display of goodwill toward perfect strangers, a quality referred to as "friendliness." In the United States customers expect a smile from the clerk, not just an acknowledgment of thanks. Many Americans judge businesses and bureaucracies by the "sincerity" of these smiles. Cities and regions are ranked on a scale of friendliness: Houston is high, Boston is most assuredly low.

Since its inception McDonald's has made friendliness a hallmark of its corporate image. It could be argued that American fast food chains, following McDonald's lead, have transformed a cultural expectation—smiling service—into a commodity. Prior to this intervention, friendly service may have been expected but, as all Americans know, was not always delivered. McDonald's and its imitators promote the cordiality associated with the smile as an integral part of their product: convenience, cleanliness, predictability, and friendliness.[85] Counter staff are trained to project the requisite standard of amiability and to vary their "Thank you" phrases so that customers receive what appear to be personalized messages.[86]

It therefore comes as a shock to many Americans when they travel abroad for the first time and discover that public friendliness is not the universal norm. In fact, the human smile—a complex alignment of facial muscles—is not always interpreted as a symbol of congeniality, openness, or honesty; quite the opposite is often true. In Russia, a visible smile can be tantamount to a challenge.[87] Eye contact is another aspect of the

McDonald's service model that is taken for granted in the United States but has to be taught to new employees in many postsocialist societies. No more than a decade ago, service workers in Russia and China were ranked at the very bottom of the communist status hierarchy. Not surprisingly, they treated the general public with utter contempt. Getting the attention of a waiter or a clerk during the heyday of state socialism took considerable patience and skill.*

McDonald's campaign to make "smiling service" a mainstay of its business image in East Asia may be swimming against the tide of cultural expectations. In Hong Kong, for instance, consumers are automatically suspicious of clerks, hawkers, or service personnel who smile on the job. As outlined in Chapter 2, Hong Kong residents place a high value on public expressions of "seriousness"; workers are expected to assume a facial expression that reflects attention to detail and determination—the result may look more like a frown than a smile, but it projects the right message. Similar reactions are reported by contributors who worked in Taiwan and Korea. In fact, the longer McDonald's operates in an East Asian city, the less evident are the forced smiles.[88] Customers are far more concerned with efficiency, reliability, and hygiene.

*I must confess that I still miss this challenge when traveling in China today; rudeness among hotel and restaurant staff had become a high art form in the 1970s. Following Deng Xiaoping's economic reforms of the 1980s, standards of service began to improve, along with salaries and working conditions.

Cleanliness, Hygiene, and the Public Toilet

Phil Donahue, the original television talk show host, once asked Ray Kroc if he really had cleaned toilets when McDonald's was still a start-up company: "You're damn right I did," Kroc shot back, "and I'd clean one today if it needed it."[89] Cleanliness, in contrast to smiling service, is one feature of the McDonald's corporate system that needs no explanation: clean toilets are universally appreciated. McDonald's is widely credited with starting a revolution of rising expectations among East Asian consumers who had never experienced high standards of public hygiene in the catering trade. In Taipei, Beijing, Seoul, and Hong Kong, local restaurateurs had to match this new standard or watch their customers go elsewhere. Young people, in particular, began to draw an equation between the condition of a restaurant's toilet and the state of its kitchen. Earlier generations of diners had little choice but to ignore unsanitary conditions; there were no alternatives, unless one was prepared to eat at expensive restaurants in major hotels.

One consequence of rising affluence in East Asian cities has been a rejection of traditional street cuisine and a preoccupation with food hygiene. Parents now worry about what their children consume outside the home. There is considerable fear of food poisoning, adulteration, and unsanitary packaging—witness the mass hysteria that erupted over the 1996 outbreak of *e. coli* food poisoning in Japan.[90] In 1994 and 1995 rumors swept through Beijing that dozens of people had died after eating contaminated *youtiar* (deep-fried dough sticks) at roadside stalls. The local press ignored the rumors, but given the high level of cynicism regarding the enforcement of sanitation regulations, this only served to confirm suspicions.[91]

McDonald's appeals to the busy, upwardly mobile middle

classes in East Asian cities precisely because it promises—and delivers—predictability and cleanliness. The Golden Arches brook no surprises. Competing chains, many of which are small operations, try to capitalize on McDonald's reputation with varying degrees of success: In Beijing, Shanghai, and Xi'an a large number of imitators have emerged, with names like McDuck's, Mcdonald's, and Modornal; in Seoul, restaurants called McKiver's (written in Korean) and McDonny's (in English) are common.[92] (Other notable clones are Macdonalds in Durban, South Africa; MacFastFood in Bangalore; McAllan in Copenhagen; and McDharma's in Santa Cruz, California.)[93] Nor are the Golden Arches safe: Winner's Burger, a South Korean chain, featured two upside-down arches as their logo; in Shanghai, a local restaurant called Nancy's Express used a sign with one leg of the double arches missing, thus forming an N; and in Beijing a chain of noodle shops called Honggaoliang ("Red Sorghum") advertises itself with a large H which bears an uncanny resemblance to the Golden Arches.[94]

The equation between McDonald's and reliability is especially strong in China, where competitors not only dress their staff in McDonald's-style uniforms but also engage in what are perhaps best described as public exhibitions of cleanliness. In Beijing, local fast food chains regularly employ one or more workers to mop floors and polish windows—all day long, every day. The cleaners usually restrict their efforts to the entryway, where their performance can best be observed by prospective customers. Beijing residents often watch for such signs before they choose a place to eat.[95] McDonald's is one of the few chains that carries this preoccupation with cleanliness into the kitchens, which are also on display. Yan notes that company officials were happy to conduct tours of their restaurants for the edification of customers, government officials, and even potential rivals.

Conclusion: McDonaldization versus Localization

McDonald's has become such a powerful symbol of the standardization and routinization of modern life that it has inspired a new vocabulary: McThink, McMyth, McJobs, McSpirituality, and, of course, McDonaldization.[96] George Ritzer, author of a popular book entitled *The McDonaldization of Society*, uses the term to describe "the process by which the principles of the fast food restaurant are coming to dominate more and more sectors of . . . society."[97] Ritzer treats McDonald's as the "paradigm case" of social regimentation and argues that "McDonaldization has shown every sign of being an inexorable process as it sweeps through seemingly impervious institutions and parts of the world."[98]

Is McDonald's in fact the revolutionary, disruptive institution that theorists of cultural imperialism deem it to be? Evidence from this book could be marshaled in support of such a view, but only at the risk of ignoring historical process. There is indeed an initial, "intrusive" encounter when McDonald's enters a new market—especially in an environment where American-style fast food is largely unknown to the ordinary consumer. In all five cases surveyed in this book, McDonald's was treated as an exotic import—a taste of Americana—during its first few years of operation. Indeed, the company drew on this association to establish itself in foreign markets. But this initial euphoria cannot sustain a mature business.

Unlike Coca-Cola and Spam, for instance, McDonald's standard fare (the burger-and-fries combo) could not be absorbed into the preexisting cuisines of East Asia. As Bak notes in Chapter 4, Spam quickly became an integral feature of Korean cooking in the aftermath of the Korean War; it was a recognizable form of meat that required no special preparation. Coca-Cola, too, was a relatively neutral import when first introduced to Chinese consumers. During the 1960s, villagers in rural Hong Kong treated Coke as a special beverage, reserved primarily for medicinal use. It was served most frequently as *bo ho la*, Cantonese for "boiled Cola," a tangy blend of fresh ginger and herbs served in piping hot Coke—an excellent remedy for colds. Only later was the beverage consumed by itself, first at banquets (mixed with brandy) and later for special events such as a visit by relatives. There was nothing particularly revolutionary about Coca-Cola or Spam; both products were quickly adapted to suit local needs and did not require any radical adjustments on the part of consumers.

McDonald's is something altogether different. Eating at the Golden Arches is a total experience, one that takes people out of their ordinary routines. One "goes to" McDonald's; it does not come to the consumer, nor is it taken home (in most parts of the world, that is). Unlike packaged products, McDonald's items are sold hot and ready-to-eat, thereby separating the buyer from the acts of cooking and preparation. One consumes a completed set of products, not the component parts of a home-cooked meal.

From this vantage point it would appear that McDonald's may indeed have been an intrusive force, undermining the integrity of East Asian cuisines. On closer inspection, however, it is clear that consumers are not the automatons many analysts would have us believe. The initial encounter soon begins to fade as McDonald's loses its exotic appeal and gradually gains acceptance (or rejection) as ordinary food for busy consumers.

The hamburger-fries combo becomes simply another alternative among many types of ready-made food.

The process of localization is a two-way street: It implies changes in the local culture as well as modifications in the company's standard operating procedures. Key elements of McDonald's industrialized system—queuing, self-provisioning, self-seating—have been accepted by consumers throughout East Asia. Other aspects of the industrial model have been rejected, notably those relating to time and space. In many parts of East Asia, consumers have turned their local McDonald's into leisure centers and after-school clubs. The meaning of "fast" has been subverted in these settings: It refers to the *delivery* of food, not to its consumption. Resident managers have had little choice but to embrace these consumer trends and make virtues of them: "Students create a good atmosphere which is good for our business," one Hong Kong manager told me as he surveyed a sea of young people chatting, studying, and snacking in his restaurant.

The process of localization correlates closely with the maturation of a generation of local people who grew up eating at the Golden Arches. By the time the children of these original consumers enter the scene, McDonald's is no longer perceived as a foreign enterprise. Parents see it as a haven of cleanliness and predictability. For children McDonald's represents fun, familiarity, and a place where they can choose their own food—something that may not be permitted at home.

The case studies in this book also make it clear that localization is not a unilinear process that ends the same everywhere. McDonald's has become a routine, unremarkable feature of the urban landscape in Japan and Hong Kong. It is so "local" that many younger consumers do not know of the company's foreign origins. The process of localization has hardly begun in China, where McDonald's outlets are still treated as exotic outposts, selling a cultural experience rather than food. At this writing it is unclear what will happen to expansion efforts in Korea; the political environment there is such that many citizens will continue to treat the Golden Arches as a symbol of American imperialism. In Taiwan the confused, and exhilarating, pace of identity politics may well rebound on American corporations, in ways as yet unseen. Irrespective of these imponderables, McDonald's is no longer dependent on the United States market for its future development. In 1994 McDonald's operating revenues from non-U.S. sales passed the 50 percent mark; market analysts predict that by the end of the 1990s this figure will rise to 60 percent.[99]

As McDonald's enters the twenty-first century, its multilocal strategy, like its famous double-arches logo, is being pirated by a vast array of corporations eager to emulate its success. In the end, however, McDonald's is likely to prove difficult to clone. The reason, of course, is that the Golden Arches have always represented something other than food. McDonald's symbolizes different things to different people at different times in their lives: Predictability, safety, convenience, fun, familiarity, sanctuary, cleanliness, modernity, culinary tourism, and "connectedness" to the world beyond. Few commodities can match this list of often contradictory attributes. One is tempted to conclude that, in McDonald's case, the primary product is the experience itself.

CHAPTER 1

McDonald's in Beijing: The Localization of Americana

Yunxiang Yan

On April 23, 1992, the largest McDonald's restaurant in the world opened in Beijing. With 700 seats and 29 cash registers, the Beijing McDonald's served 40,000 customers on its first day of business.[1] Built on the southern end of Wangfujing Street near Tiananmen Square—the center of all public politics in the People's Republic of China—this restaurant had become an important landmark in Beijing by the summer of 1994, and the image of the Golden Arches appeared frequently on national television programs. It also became an attraction for domestic tourists, as a place where ordinary people could literally taste a bit of American culture. New McDonald's restaurants appeared in Beijing one after another: two were opened in 1993, four in 1994, and ten more in 1995; by the end of 1996, there were 29 outlets in Beijing.[2] According to Tim Lai, the company's General Manager, the Beijing market is big enough to support 100 McDonald's restaurants, and McDonald's plans to open 600 outlets in China by century's end.[3]

The astonishing growth of the Beijing McDonald's has to be understood in the context of recent changes in Chinese society.

There is a new tendency to absorb foreign cultural influences and transform them into local institutions, a trend that the Chinese political system resisted during the Maoist era (1949–78). In the case reviewed here, both the McDonald's management and staff on the one hand and the Beijing customers on the other have been active participants in the localization process. To analyze this process, I first examine the image of McDonald's in the minds of ordinary Chinese people. Then I look at McDonald's efforts to fit into the Chinese market, as well as the ways in which Beijing consumers have appropriated McDonald's for their own use.

The Big Mac as a Symbol of Americana

In October 1, 1993, National Day in China, a couple in their early seventies had dinner at the McDonald's restaurant on Wangfujing Street. They had been invited to celebrate the holiday at McDonald's by their daughter and son-in-law, who spent almost 200 yuan for the dinner, an unimaginably large sum in the view of the elderly couple. The experience of eating in a foreign restaurant struck them as so significant they had their picture taken in front of the Golden Arches and sent it to their hometown newspaper, along with another photo they had had taken on October 1, 1949, in Tiananmen Square—celebrating the first National Day of the People's Republic of China. Their story was later published by the newspaper, with the two contrasting photographs. In the 1949 photo, the two young people appear in identical white shirts, standing slightly apart, their thin faces betraying undernourishment in hard times. In the 1993 photo, a portly woman proudly holds her husband's left arm, and the two are healthy looking and fashionably dressed. They took a taxi to McDonald's and, while crossing Tiananmen Square, they remembered how poor they had been in 1949 and realized how much China has changed in the interim.[4]

At first glance, this news story reads like the typical propaganda skit that one still finds in official Chinese media, with its constant play on "recalling the bitterness of old China and thinking of the sweetness of the new society" (*yiku sitian*). However, in this case it is McDonald's—a capitalist, transnational enterprise—that symbolizes the "sweetness" of current life. What is even more interesting, the headline of the story reads: "Forty-Four years: From *Tu* to *Yang*." The terms *tu* and *yang* have been paired concepts in the everyday discourse of Chinese political culture since the nineteenth century. In common usage, *tu* means rustic, uncouth, and backward, whereas *yang* refers to anything foreign (particularly Western), fashionable, and quite often, progressive. The juxtaposition of these common terms demonstrates how McDonald's and its foreign (*yang*) food have become synonymous with progressive changes that make life more enjoyable in contemporary China.

In the eyes of Beijing residents, McDonald's represents Americana and the promise of modernization.[5] McDonald's highly efficient service and management, its spotless dining environment, and its fresh ingredients have been featured repeatedly by the Chinese media as exemplars of modernity.[6] McDonald's strict quality control, especially regarding potatoes, became a hot topic of discussion in many major newspapers, again with the emphasis on McDonald's scientific management as reflected in the company's unwavering standards.[7] According to one commentator who published a series of articles on McDonald's, the company's global success can be traced to its highly standardized procedures of food production, its scientific recipes, and its modern management techniques. As the title of his article ("Seeing the World from McDonald's") suggests, each restaurant represents a microcosm of the transnational,[8] so much so that, according to another article by the same author, many American youths prefer to work at McDonald's before they leave home to seek work elsewhere. The experience of working at McDonald's, he continues, prepares American youth for any kind of job in a modern society.[9]

Other news items associate the success of transnational food chains with their atmosphere of equality and democracy. No matter who you are, according to one of these reports, you will be treated with warmth and friendliness in the fast food restaurants; hence many people patronize McDonald's to experience a moment of equality.[10] This argument may sound a bit odd to Western readers, but it makes sense in the context of Chinese culinary culture. When I asked my Beijing informants about the equality factor, they all pointed out that banquets in Chinese restaurants are highly competitive: people try to outdo one another by offering the most expensive dishes and alcoholic beverages. It is typical for the host at a banquet to worry that customers at neighboring tables might be enjoying better dishes, thus causing him or her to lose face. To avoid such embarrassment, many people prefer to pay the extra fees necessary to rent a private room within a restaurant. Such competition does not exist at McDonald's, where the menu is limited, the food is standardized, and every customer receives a set of items that are more or less equal in quality. There is no need to worry that one's food might be lower in status than a neighbor's. For people without a lot of money but who need to host a meal, McDonald's has become the best alternative.

During the autumn of 1994 I conducted an ethnographic

survey of consumer behavior in Beijing. I discovered that the stories commonly told about McDonald's have taken on a surreal, even mythic tone. For instance, it is believed among a number of Beijing residents that the potato used by McDonald's is a cube-shaped variety. A 20-year old woman working at McDonald's told me in all seriousness about McDonald's secret, cube-shaped potatoes, the key to the corporation's worldwide success. She was also fascinated by the foreign terms she had learned in the short time she had worked there, terms such as *weisi* (waste), *jishi* (cheese), and *delaisu* (drive-through). The first two are straight transliterations of the English terms, but the third is both a transliteration and a free translation: it means "to get it quickly." These half-Chinese, half-English terms are used by employees and customers alike, making their experiences at McDonald's restaurants exotic, American, and to a certain extent, modern.

In this connection the ways Beijing McDonald's presents itself in public are also worth noting. By the autumn of 1994, McDonald's had not yet placed any advertisements on Beijing television. According to the General Manager, it was pointless to advertise McDonald's on television because Chinese commercials, unlike their counterparts in the West, appear only during the interval between programs. After watching one program, audiences tend to switch to another channel, which means that advertisements have little chance of being seen. Newspapers and popular magazines were regarded as a better way to present McDonald's public image. In the Beijing region, McDonald's relied on Berson-Marsteller, a transnational public relations company, to deal with the Chinese news media. The main source of information about McDonald's in China is a short booklet that sketches the history of the American-based corporation and its famous business philosophy, QSC & V, or quality, service, cleanliness, and value. The absence of what might be called hard news has led Chinese reporters to repeat McDonald's corporate philosophy of QSC & V—which, incidentally, reinforces the Chinese government's promotion of upgrading and modernizing the local business environment.

McDonald's local management has also made efforts to promote the corporation's image as an exemplar of modernity. For instance, a five-minute tour of the kitchen is provided upon request at each of the Beijing restaurants. I went on three such tours at different locations, and all were identical. My guides—McDonald's employees responsible for public relations—showed me all the machines, stoves, and other special equipment and explained how they work. I was then shown the place where employees wash their hands (following strict procedures) and the wastebins that contained food that was no longer fresh enough to meet the McDonald's standards. Throughout the five-minute tour, one message was emphasized repeatedly: McDonald's foods are cooked in accordance with strict scientific methods and are guaranteed fresh and pure.

In addition to the freshness and purity of its food, McDonald's management also emphasizes its nutritional value. In a published interview, a high-level manager maintains that the recipes for McDonald's foods are designed to meet modern scientific specifications and thus differ from the recipes for Chinese foods, which are based on cultural expectations. A central feature of this "scientifically designed" food is that it includes the main nutritional elements a human being needs daily: water, starch, protein, sugar, vitamins, and fat. Thus when one spends 10 to 15 yuan to have a standardized meal at McDonald's, one is guaranteed enough nutrition for half a day.[11] The idea that McDonald's provides healthy food based on nutritional ingredients and scientific cooking methods has been widely accepted by both the Chinese media and the general public. In Japan, too, until the mid-1980s, McDonald's food was believed to be nutritious and healthy; it is only in recent years that the Japanese public has begun to worry about the negative effects of fast food.[12]

Given the general eagerness for modernization, shared by both the government and ordinary people, and, in the realm of consumption, the growing appetite for all things foreign, or Western (*yang*), McDonald's has benefited greatly from the cultural symbolism it carries. Bolstering the "genuineness" of its food, the Beijing restaurant keeps its menu identical to that of its American counterpart. By 1994 the sale of Big Mac hamburgers accounted for 20 percent of local McDonald's sales, a figure higher than the comparable one for Taiwan.[13] This figure has been interpreted by McDonald's management as an indicator that Beijing customers have no problem accepting American-style cuisine.

But what is it that the Beijing customers have accepted—the hamburgers or the ambience? My ethnographic inquiry reveals that whereas children are great fans of the Big Mac and french fries, most adult customers appear to be attracted to McDonald's by its American "style" rather than its food. Many people commented to me that the food was not really delicious and that the flavor of cheese was too strange to taste good. The most common complaint from adult customers was *chi bu bao*, meaning that McDonald's hamburgers and fries did not make one feel full; they are more like snacks than meals. I conducted a survey among students at a major university in Beijing and collected 97 completed questionnaires.[14] Table 1 shows the in-

TABLE 1
Evaluation of McDonald's Food

Sensation after eating	Male (N=29)		Female (N=68)		Total
	"Filling"	"Unfilling"	"Filling"	"Unfilling"	
Perceived as for-mal meal	3	2	17	1	23
Perceived as snacks	3	21	20	30	74
Total	6	23	37	31	97

SOURCE: Survey carried out by the author at Beijing University on Oct. 11 and 14, 1994.

formants response to two questions: (1) Is McDonald's food a formal meal or a snack? (2) Does McDonald's food make you feel full?

Only one-fourth of my informants regarded McDonald's food as a formal meal, and most of these respondents were women students (18 out of 23). Accordingly, 24 of the 29 men students (83 percent) perceived McDonald's food as snacks (*xiaochi*). Regarding the sensation of fullness, 54 informants (56 percent) did not feel they had had a "satisfying" meal at McDonald's, and, not surprisingly, this sentiment appeared most commonly among young men—23 of the 29 male students (79 percent)—while fewer than half the women respondents found McDonald's food unsatisfying. Those who treated McDonald's food as a formal meal were more likely to feel full: only 3 of 23 such informants complained of *chi bu bao* (not feeling full). One implication of the findings is that the perception of McDonald's as a provider of meals or of snacks is largely determined by the capacity of the food to make one feel full. It seems that women are more likely to feel full, and hence a larger proportion of women are ready to accept McDonald's food as a formal meal.

The Chinese food system is based on a basic division of *fan* (grains and other starches) and *cai* (vegetable and/or meat dishes). "To prepare a balanced meal, it must have an appropriate amount of both *fan* and *ts'ai* [*cai*], and ingredients are readied along both tracks."[15] According to these principles, the McDonald's hamburger—a patty of meat between layers of bread—is not a properly prepared meal. As a Beijing worker commented, at best a hamburger is the equivalent of *xianbing*, a type of Chinese pancake with meat inside, which no one would treat as a daily meal. In Chinese terms, foods like *xianbing* are classified as "small eats" (*xiaochi*), a term close to "snack." The logic is very clear: a McDonald's hamburger is reinterpreted as a foreign (*yang*) form of *xianbing* and thus as foreign "small eats" (*yang xiaochi*). No doubt this is why 75 percent of my informants classified McDonald's foods as snacks, and 55 percent of them did not feel full after eating at McDonald's restaurants.

It seems ironic that although people have reservations about the food at McDonald's, they are still keen on going there. Why? Most informants said that they liked the atmosphere of the restaurant, the style of eating, and the experience of being there. In other words, the attraction of McDonald's is that it offers, not filling food, but a fulfilling experience. Or, as a local writer says, it is the culture of fast food that draws Beijing consumers to these restaurants.[16]

In fact, before McDonald's entered the Beijing market, Kentucky Fried Chicken (KFC), followed by Pizza Hut, had aroused considerable consumer interest in imported fast foods. According to an early report on KFC, people did not go to

KFC to eat the chicken; instead they enjoyed "eating" (consuming) the culture associated with KFC. Most customers spent hours talking to each other and gazing out the huge glass window that overlooks a busy commercial street—thereby demonstrating their sophistication to the people who passed by.[17] Some local observers have argued that the appeal of Chinese cuisine is the taste of the food itself, and that, by contrast, Western food relies on its presentation. The popularity of imported fast food is thus taken as a demonstration that consumers are interested in the spectacle, the show, that this new form of eating permits.[18] Prior to McDonald's opening in Beijing, the company's name was already popular among trendy consumers and it was only natural that, when the first restaurant was opened in Beijing in April 1992, thousands lined up for hours in order to partake of the experience, along with the new cuisine offered by this famous restaurant.

By the end of 1994, although more foreign restaurants such as the Hard Rock Cafe and Pizza Hut had opened, McDonald's remained a fashionable, popular restaurant. Eating at McDonald's had become a meaningful social event for Beijing residents, though to be sure, different people came to the restaurant for different reasons. Many people, especially those constrained by their moderate income, visited McDonald's restaurants only once or twice, primarily to satisfy their curiosity about American food and culinary culture. A considerable proportion of customers were tourists from outlying provinces who had only heard about McDonald's or seen its Golden Arches in the movies. Tasting American food has recently become an important aspect of Chinese tourism in Beijing, and those who achieve this goal boast about it to their relatives and friends back home. There are also local customers, however, who frequent McDonald's regularly. A "Trade Area Survey" conducted by the management of Beijing McDonald's in one of its outlets shows that 10.2 percent of their customers frequented the restaurant at least four times a month in 1992, a figure that jumped to 38.3 percent in 1993.[19] Based on my observations and interviews, frequent customers fall into three groups: yuppies, young couples, and children (accompanied by their parents). Despite differences in social background, all except for the children mentioned McDonald's eating environment and good service as the primary reason they came, and most, if not all, of my informants emphasized that eating at McDonald's was a significant culinary and cultural experience.

For younger Beijing residents who have higher incomes and wish to be "connected" more closely to the outside world, eating at McDonald's, Kentucky Fried Chicken, or Pizza Hut has become an integral part of their new lifestyle, a way for them to participate in the transnational cultural system. As one informant commented: "The Big Mac doesn't taste great; but the experience of eating in this place makes me feel good. Sometimes I even imagine that I am sitting in a restaurant in New York City or Paris." One late morning I talked with a young man, age 22, a graduate of the Beijing Institute of Foreign Languages, while we sat in a McDonald's restaurant. He ordered two Big Macs, one chicken sandwich, one Filet-o-Fish, one large Coke, and an ice cream sundae—all for himself. During our conversation, he told me that he was working for a Japanese company, earning a monthly salary of 3,500 yuan (more than $400), which in 1994 was ten times the average wage of an ordinary worker. When I asked how much he spent on fast food, he said he didn't know and didn't care: "I think I am better off than my friends who went to study abroad. Staying in my hometown, I can enjoy all such foreign goods as long as I make money. You see, today I have to attend a formal banquet for a business lunch and I will only drink when I get there. Unlike those *tu* [rustic] guys, I prefer eating at McDonald's to a noisy Chinese restaurant."

Throughout my fieldwork I talked with more than a dozen yuppies like this young man, all of whom were proud of their newly attained habit of eating foreign fast food. Although some emphasized that they just wanted to save time, none finished their meals within 20 minutes. Like other customers, these young professionals arrive in small groups or come with girl- or boyfriends and enjoy themselves in the restaurant for an hour or more. Eating foreign food, and consuming other foreign goods, has become an important way for these Chinese yuppies to define themselves as middle-class professionals.

Young couples from all social strata are also frequenters of McDonald's because the eating environment is considered romantic and comfortable. The restaurants are brightly lit and clean and feature light Western music; except during busy periods they are relatively quiet. In addition to the exotica of hamburgers, the restaurant offers milk shakes, apple pie, and ice cream, all of which makes McDonald's one of the best places in Beijing to conduct courtship. As mentioned above, the variety of foods offered is, by Chinese standards, limited, and the expenditure is predictable, meaning that no one need fear being drawn into a competition of conspicuous consumption at McDonald's. This is particularly important for young men who need to take their girlfriends or wives out for a treat but have limited budgets: they know they will not lose face in this foreign cultural context. By 1994, McDonald's seven Beijing restaurants had all made efforts to create a relatively remote, private service area with tables for two only. In some of these restaurants, the area was nicknamed the "the lovers' corner."

There is another special enclosure in every Beijing McDonald's called "children's paradise." Unlike the quiet, romantic "lovers' corner," this area is always noisy, full of children who are running around and playing while they eat. As in other parts of East Asia (notably, as Chapters 2 and 3 show, Hong Kong and Taipei), Beijing children are loyal McDonald's fans. One employee told me that parents often asked her why their children liked McDonald's food so much. Some even suspected, she said, that the Big Mac contained a special, hidden ingredient; otherwise their children would not be so attracted to this exotic food. During my interviews with students in a primary school, one nine-year-old boy told me that his dream is to buy a huge box of hamburgers and eat them every day. Several youngsters expressed the desire to open a McDonald's restaurant of their own when they grow up. I will have more to say about how McDonald's appeals to children in the next section. Here I want to emphasize that children do not come alone: they are usually brought to McDonald's by their parents or grandparents.

I once interviewed a middle-aged woman whose daughter had just won an essay contest at McDonald's. She told me that she did not like the taste of hamburgers, and her husband simply hated them. But their daughter loved hamburgers and milk shakes so much that their family had to visit McDonald's nearly every week. Children's fondness for McDonald's, however, may present difficulties for parents with limited economic resources. As one man, a worker, noted, although his salary did not allow him to eat out, when his son asked him to go to

McDonald's, he never said "No." He would cut back his expenses in some other area so he could afford the meal.

It should be noted that eating at McDonald's is still a big treat for low-income people, and that as of 1994, a dinner at McDonald's for a family of three normally cost one-sixth of a worker's monthly salary. The price is definitely not considered a bargain and is not the reason why Beijing consumers come to McDonald's. As a young woman worker commented: "It's rather expensive to eat here at McDonald's. I have to work for two days in order to have a Big Mac set meal. But for a high-fashion restaurant the price is okay." Thus, working-class families have to save their money to eat at McDonald's. As noted in my opening vignette, many feel they should arrive by taxi, making the trip more luxurious and memorable. For such people, the McDonald's experience has less to do with food than it does with a chance to explore American culture or to give their children a special treat.

The representation of McDonald's as a symbol of American culture not only has drawn Beijing customers to new forms of dining but also has led them to accept new patterns of behavior. For instance, in 1992 and 1993 customers in Beijing (as in Hong Kong and Taiwan) usually left their rubbish on the table, letting the restaurant employees do the clean-up work. The main reason for this kind of behavior was that people regarded McDonald's as a formal restaurant where they had paid for full service. However, during the summer of 1994 I observed that about a fifth of the customers, many of them fashionably dressed youth, carried their own trays to the wastebins. From subsequent interviews I discovered that most of these people were regular customers, and they had learned to clean up their tables by observing what foreigners did. Interestingly enough, several informants told me that when they threw out their own rubbish, they felt they were more "civilized" (*wenming*) than other customers because they knew the proper behavior. It was also obvious that McDonald's customers spoke in lower tones than customers in other, Chinese-style eateries. They were also more careful not to throw rubbish on the ground or to spit near McDonald's outlets. Similarly, a comparison of customer behavior in McDonald's and that in comparably priced or more expensive Chinese restaurants shows that people in McDonald's were, on the whole, more self-restrained and polite toward one another. One possible explanation for this difference is that the symbolic meanings of the new food, along with customers' willingness to accept the exotic culture associated with fast food, has affected people's table manners in particular and social behavior in general.[20]

Fast Food Slowing Down: Appropriation and Localization

A further question arises: Is the Beijing McDonald's genuinely American? In the United States it is commonplace to equate McDonald's food with low cost and fast service. Americans worry about the nutritional value and the fat content of McDonald's hamburgers, but the restaurants remain popular because of the savings they offer in money and time. Few Americans (of my acquaintance, at least) think of McDonald's as an elegant place to relax and "be seen." From a cultural point of view, McDonald's, like many other products of industrialization and modernization, is treated by most Americans as simply a necessity of modern life.[21] In Beijing, by contrast, the Big Mac was rapidly transformed into a form of haute cuisine, and McDonald's became a place where people could gain status simply by eating there. A scrutiny of social interactions in Beijing's McDonald's reveals that what appears to be the same institution represents radically different things in the two societies. These differences are so profound that the presumed "American style" of the Beijing restaurants has itself been transformed; McDonald's has become a caricature of its intended symbolic association. It represents a localized, Chinese version of Americana, as reflected in the following five aspects.

First, Beijing McDonald's consciously presents itself as a Chinese company, on the grounds that the Chinese partner owns 50 percent of the business. The company also emphasizes that 95 percent of the food used by Beijing McDonald's, including potatoes and beef, is locally produced, and, of 1,400 staff members in 1994, only three held foreign passports, and all of them were ethnic Chinese.[22] Here the intriguing point is that localization was precisely the goal of McDonald's management in Beijing. A spokesman stated in 1993: "McDonald's wants to be here long term. The hedging strategy is localization and expansion."[23] During a 1994 interview, Tim Lai, General Manager of Beijing McDonald's, told me, "Ours is a company that provides millions of people with good service and high-quality fast food. In Beijing, McDonald's should be local rather than American or exotic. It should become China's McDonald's." He also emphasized that his goal was to make McDonald's food part of the everyday diet of ordinary Beijing residents. While McDonald's remains essentially American in terms of menu, services, and management, the company has made serious efforts to adapt to the Chinese cultural setting.

To present itself as a local company, all the McDonald's restaurants in Beijing actively participated in community affairs and established special relations with local schools and neighborhood committees. For instance, every year at the beginning of the new school term, McDonald's presents small gifts, such as caps and stationery, to the first graders in the nearby schools, and offers Ronald McDonald Scholarships to those who excelled as students the previous year.[24] On Teachers' Day 1994, the staff members visited local schools and presented gifts to teachers.[25] McDonald's also delegated employees to help police officers direct traffic during rush hours and clean the street in front of its restaurants. More interestingly, the company hoists the Chinese national flag every morning in front of its major restaurant near Tiananmen Square, and a special flag-raising ceremony was organized on September 26, 1994, in anticipation of the Chinese National Day (October 1). People's Liberation Army soldiers who guard the national flag in Tiananmen Square were invited to participate in this ceremony, turning the event into an important news story.[26]

The second feature of the localization process is that McDonald's, with its climate-controlled environment and soft music, has become a place to "hang out"—a function that contradicts its original, American purpose. During off-peak hours it is common for people to walk into McDonald's just for a drink or a snack. Sitting with a milk shake or a packet of fries, customers often spend 30 minutes to an hour, and sometimes longer, chatting with one another, reading newspapers, or holding business meetings. I once observed two people seated in a McDonald's restaurant for over two hours, discussing handbag sales. As indicated earlier, young couples and teenagers are particularly fond of frequenting McDonald's because they consider the environment romantic. Women in all age groups tend to spend the longest time in McDonald's, irrespective of whether they are alone or with friends. By contrast, unaccompanied men rarely linger after finishing their meal. The main reason for this gender difference, according to my informants, is the absence of alcoholic beverages at McDonald's.

My research confirmed the impression that most customers in Beijing claim their tables for longer periods of time than do their American counterparts. The average dining time in Beijing (autumn 1994) was 25 minutes during busy times and 51 minutes during slack periods. American-style fast food has obviously slowed down in Beijing. An interesting footnote to this phenomenon is that 32 percent of my informants in a survey of 97 college students regarded McDonald's as a symbol of leisure and emphasized that they go there to relax.

Similar views appear to be common among older people. In August 1994, I had an intensive interview with two retired women in their late fifties after I had seen them for the third time in less than two weeks at the same McDonald's restaurant. They were sisters who lived in different parts of the city, one in the south and the other in the north. When the elder sister read the news of McDonald's opening in April 1992, they decided to meet at the restaurant on Wangfujing Street, which is midway between their residences. It has become a routine for them to order a hamburger and a drink and then chat for one or two hours—sometimes even longer. They told me that they liked the setting; it is clean, bright, and air-conditioned, better than their memories of Beijing's old-style teahouses. They were quite knowledgeable about McDonald's; they knew about grand openings for restaurants in Beijing, Shanghai, and Tianjin, and closely followed news about working conditions and management issues. When I asked if there were other regular older customers like themselves, they said "of course," and, smiling, told me they had made some new friends at McDonald's.

Beijing consumers have appropriated the restaurants not only as leisure centers but also as public arenas for various personal and family rituals. The most popular ritual (and also the one promoted by McDonald's) is, of course, the children's birthday party, about which I have more to say below. Although less formalized (and without the restaurant's active promotion), private ceremonies are also held in the restaurants for adult customers, particularly for young women in peer groups (the absence of alcohol makes the site attractive to them). Of the 97 college students in my survey, 33 (including nine men) have attended personal celebrations at McDonald's: birthday parties, farewell parties, celebrations for receiving a scholarship to an American university, and term-end parties. One academic couple in their early fifties told me that they have held family celebrations at McDonald's restaurants to mark three occasions: their youngest son's return after graduating from a university in another city, their thirtieth anniversary, and the wife's recent salary increase. They chose McDonald's as the site of these ceremonies for two reasons: (1) it is new and more stylish than what they perceive as the vulgar traditional Chinese restaurants; and (2) it is relatively inexpensive for a decent family banquet (they pointed out that it was difficult to spend more than 30 yuan at McDonald's, whereas a good Chinese banquet may cost 100 yuan a head).

Until its recent relocation,[27] McDonald's flagship restaurant near Tiananmen Square remained the most popular site for personal rituals and group activities. In May 1993, a group of young contemporary artists organized an exhibit to be held in this McDonald's restaurant, displaying trendy art and fashionable clothes. Some items were politically charged, including a cowboy jacket with the former USSR national flag upside down on the back. This exhibit was sponsored by two research institutes in Beijing and, through personal connections, the organizers were able to mobilize some high-ranking officials and famous scholars to attend the show. At the last minute, Beijing public security closed the exhibit, on the grounds that it would cause a traffic jam. The real reason for police interference, according to several people involved, was the exhibit's timing (close to the June 4th anniversary of the 1989 democracy demonstration) and the location (three blocks from Tiananmen Square). To date this is the only event with political implications involving a McDonald's restaurant, but it does illustrate the ritual function that the fast food chain has assumed in the public perception of Beijing consumers.

The multifunctional use of McDonald's is due in part to the lack of cafes, teahouses, or ice cream shops in Beijing; it is also a consequence of the management's effort to attract as many customers as possible by creating an inviting environment. It is clear that the local management has accepted their customers' perceptions of McDonald's as a special place which does not fit preexisting categories of public eateries. They have not tried to educate Beijing consumers to accept the American view that "fast food" means that one must eat fast and leave quickly. How does the management solve problems of space during busy hours? I was told that the problem was often self-resolved, because a huge crowd of customers naturally creates pressure on those who have finished their meal and, more important, during busy hours the environment is no longer relaxing.

The emphasis on creating a Chinese-style family atmosphere constitutes the third feature of the localization process. The interior walls of local restaurants are covered by posters and slogans emphasizing family values. To enhance the family atmosphere, McDonald's has deliberately hired employees from different age groups and assigned some older employees to work in the dining area as receptionists (more on this below). It has become increasingly common for people of multiple generations in a family to have their Sunday lunch or dinner at McDonald's. Given that many parents do not live with their married children in Beijing and that eating out is an important family event, such a meal embodies the harmony and solidarity of an extended family—the ideal of private life in Chinese culture. Understandably, Beijing McDonald's has made its leading slogan, "Get together at McDonald's; enjoy the happiness of family life" (*huanju meidanglao; gong xiang jiating le*). During holidays, such as Chinese New Year and Mid-Autumn Festival, the restaurants extend their hours, offer small gifts, and host various activities, such as performances by volunteers. The idea behind these activities, according to the General Manager, is to make McDonald's seem like a real home for those customers who are unwilling or unable to go home for holidays. This family atmosphere has been repeatedly featured in local newspapers, which has in turn brought more customers into the restaurants.[28] As a result, people coming alone to McDonald's to save money and time, common in the United States, are rare in Beijing's restaurants.

It is well known that McDonald's in the United States also presents itself as a family restaurant, and this image has been widely accepted by American consumers. According to Conrad Kottak, McDonald's popularity partly rests on the fact that the restaurant offers a sanctuary, a home away from home, to Americans who are traveling or at home. "In this familiar setting, we do not have to consider the experience. We know what we will see, say, eat, and pay."[29] In other words, what makes McDonald's a family restaurant in American society is its ordinariness, its predictability, and, of course, its low prices. Americans therefore frequent McDonald's for a casual lunch rather than a formal dinner. For the same reason, Americans usually do not go to McDonald's to celebrate a personal or family event, nor do they visit McDonald's on holidays. In Beijing, by contrast, it is precisely the experience of eating foreign food that draws people to McDonald's; in every respect (including the absence of chopsticks), McDonald's represents the unfamiliar, extraordinary, nonroutine, and unhomelike. Thus, people frequent McDonald's not for a casual lunch but for a formal meal or even a celebration. Consequently, Sundays and holidays are the busiest time for McDonald's restaurants in Beijing. What makes McDonald's a family restaurant is the restaurant's effort to provide a pleasant and fashionable place for people to celebrate their family harmony and solidarity in public.

The fourth feature of the localization of McDonald's in Beijing is that, in contrast to the American practice of substituting technology for human workers,[30] the Beijing McDonald's relies heavily on personal interactions with customers. In everyday operations, one or two public relations staff in each outlet are always available to answer customers' questions. Each restaurant assigns five to ten female receptionists to take care of children and talk with parents. These receptionists are referred to by the kinship title "Aunt McDonald," following the common term for Ronald McDonald, known as "Uncle McDonald" in Taiwan, Hong Kong, and Beijing. One task of these receptionists is to establish long-term friendships with children and other customers who frequent the restaurant, in the attempt to personalize what might otherwise be a purely business transaction.[31] Ms. Chen, a 21-year old "Aunt McDonald," told me that after working in the restaurant for seven months, she had made more than 100 young friends, ranging in age from three to twelve. Children ran into the restaurant every day, she said, and greeted her: "Aunt McDonald, how are you?" (or, "Aunt Chen" if they know her last name). She usually talked with the children and their parents before they went to the counter to order food. Although admitting that making friends was her duty, she added: "This also makes me feel good, as if I am in a big family. I feel particularly happy and proud of myself when I walk down the street and children recognize me." The feeling is obviously mutual: as several parents told me, their children come to McDonald's not only for the food, but also for fun and the special attention they receive from the receptionists. A mother said: "The best part is the feeling that there is some *renqing* [goodwill, concern, sentiment] at McDonald's." In a sense, therefore, McDonald's management has responded to a local expectation of social interactions—namely, the need to build good personal feelings (*renqing*) between staff and customers—to secure a long-term, mutually beneficial relationship.[32]

Interestingly enough, Aunt and Uncle McDonald do not confine their activities to the restaurant. After making friends with the youngest customers, the staff members who play Aunt or Uncle McDonald record the children's names, addresses, and birthdates on a special list called "Book of Little Honorary Guests." Later they visit the children's families and their kindergarten and primary schools. Congratulatory letters are sent to the children prior to their birthdays, with warm greetings from Uncle McDonald.[33]

Finally, McDonald's localization strategies have centered on children as primary customers. Because of the Chinese government's single-child policy,[34] in most families children are the object of attention and affection from up to half a dozen adults: their parents and their paternal and maternal grandparents. The demands of such children are always met by one or all of these relatives, earning them the title "Little Emperors" or "Empresses." When a Little Emperor says, "I want to eat at McDonald's," this means that the entire family must go along. It is no wonder that McDonald's management knows that "Children are our future." The above-mentioned "Book of Little Honorary Guests" is only one of the strategies that Beijing McDonald's has devised to introduce its product into the heart of Chinese families via the fantasy world of children. Birthday parties are a central feature of this strategy. Arriving with five or more guests, a child can expect an elaborate ritual performed, free of charge, in a special enclosure called "Children's Paradise." The ritual begins with an announcement over the restaurant's loudspeakers—in both Chinese and English—giving the child's name and age, together with Uncle McDonald's congratulations. This is followed by the recorded song "Happy Birthday," again in two languages. Aunt McDonald then entertains the children with games and presents each of them with small gifts from Uncle McDonald. During the ceremony all food and drinks are served by Aunt McDonald, making the children feel important.

A feature of the "Little Emperor" phenomenon in contemporary China is that most parents want their one child to become an important personage in the future and thus make various investments in his or her education. It is common, for instance, for working-class parents who know little about music or computers to attend a weekly piano lesson or computer class with their child. During the class they work even harder than their child does, because they want to be able to help with homework. Taking parents' great expectations of their children into consideration, the McDonald's management decided to promote learning in their restaurants. Paper and pens are provided so children can draw pictures; essay contests are held for primary and secondary school students; and children's programs, with parents acting as the audience, are hosted in some restaurants. For instance, in September 1994, eight McDonald's outlets in Beijing and Tianjin sponsored a "My Teacher" essay contest, to celebrate Teachers' Day (September 10); the 160 winners of this contest received gifts and a Certificate of Merit from the restaurants.[35] Every evening in a McDonald's located in east Beijing, two "Aunt McDonald" receptionists lead children in dance for twenty minutes and then give the participants small gifts. The manager of this restaurant told me that, in order to make sure every child can participate in dancing, staff members create new kinds of dance for the children. "We want the parents to know," she explained, "that children are attracted to our restaurant not only by food—there are a lot of things children can learn here."

In August 1994, the first McDonald's "theme restaurant" was opened, inspired by famous theme parks such as Disneyland. The interior of the restaurant was decorated like a large ship, and staff members wore blue-and-white sailor uniforms instead of traditional McDonald's uniforms. The restaurant has developed a program called Uncle McDonald's Adventure, which encourages children to imagine that they are traveling around the world on a big ship guided by Uncle McDonald. The basic idea, according to the manager, is to increase children's knowledge of world geography and encourage them to create an imagined world by and for themselves.

During my interviews with pupils in a primary school, I discovered that Ronald McDonald is a very popular figure among children. Not one of the 68 youngsters (from the third to sixth grade) I spoke with failed to recognize the image of Ronald McDonald; most students appeared very excited when I asked about him. All the children said they liked Ronald because he was funny, gentle, kind, and—several added—he understood children's hearts. About one-third believed that Ronald McDonald came from America; the majority insisted that he came from the McDonald's headquarters in Beijing. When I asked these children to tell me the most interesting experience they had had at McDonald's, a sixth grader said it was the time he went to McDonald's with four friends to celebrate his birthday, unaccompanied by adults. They made a reservation so that Aunt McDonald had prepared a table for them in advance and helped them recite poems, sing songs, and play games. A third-grader said she was very happy when she heard her own name announced over the loudspeakers at McDonald's, accompanied by "Happy birthday to you." When I was about to leave after finishing my group interview, a third grade boy ran up to me and asked: "Are you Uncle McDonald?" "No, I'm not. Why?" "You have his eyes." Assuming a serious demeanor, the boy then showed me a pen with a small hamburger on it—a gift he had received from Ronald McDonald. It became clear to me that for this little boy and many of his friends, Uncle McDonald is real, and, as such, he is also an important influence on these children's lives.

It should be noted that McDonald's special appeal to children is partially and indirectly due to its association with

Americana and modernity—a theme I explored in the preceding section. As mentioned above, a large number of adult customers were brought into McDonald's restaurants by their children or grandchildren, and continue to go there even though in many cases they dislike or cannot afford the foreign food. The question arises, Why is children's demand for McDonald's food such a powerful motivator for parents? It is true that parental affection, particularly in families with only one child, has led many parents and grandparents to surrender to their children's demands. However, my interview with a mother who frequently accompanies her daughter to McDonald's provides a clue to another kind of answer.

This woman told me that after almost a year of "adapting" to the foreign food, she had begun to enjoy it and now takes her daughter to McDonald's at least twice a week. When I asked whether the price was high, she said it was acceptable for a foreign restaurant and added, "I want my daughter to learn more about American culture. She is taking an English typing class now, and I will buy her a computer next year." It is clear that eating a Big Mac and fries, like learning typing and computer skills, is part of the mother's plan to expose her daughter to American culture. In other words, she wants her daughter to learn not only the skills needed in a modern society, but also to eat modern food so she will grow up to be a successful person who knows how to enjoy a modern way of life. If the daughter was fond of some "low food," such as the corn gruel commonly consumed by villagers in North China, would the mother have been so willing to meet her child's demand? It is very unlikely.

This woman's case is by no means unique in contemporary China. Rational considerations play as important a role as affection in most parents' responses to their children. Particularly for those middle-aged parents who missed the opportunity for social mobility during the chaotic Cultural Revolution period (1966–76), their children's achievements give them a vicarious way to realize the lost dreams of their own youth. Thus parents make every effort to encourage their children to learn all kinds of skills (including computer and piano) that are supposedly necessary in the modern world, and will save money to meet their children's demand for food, clothes, and toys that are considered modern. Parental efforts of this type can even follow the child across the Pacific Ocean. Several Chinese students who have recently come to the United States to attend college told me that their parents always remind them from home to eat cheese, because the parents believe it is cheese that makes Americans so physically strong and energetic. Here food is directly related not only to its nutritional value but also to its symbolic power. Children's influence on their parents, then, is directly related to the parents' hope that their children's lives will be better than their own. As Jack Goody notes in his study of dietary changes in an African society, one reason for the shift in food-consumption patterns is the idea that children are their parents' investment in the future, part of "an effort to maintain and advance the standards of attainment."[36]

The Rise of Consumerism and McDonald's Instant Success

In the early 1980s, McDonald's started to negotiate with Chinese authorities, in the hope that the Golden Arches might eventually enter the largest consumer market in the world. Beginning in 1983, apples from China were bought for apple pies sold by McDonald's in Japan, and later, food distribution and processing facilities were developed in China.[37] The actual opening of McDonald's restaurants in Beijing, however, did not occur until 1992. In the interim, there were revolutionary changes in Chinese consumption patterns. After fifteen years of economic reform and improvements in living standards, a large number of people in Beijing began to buy things simply out of the desire to possess things and the joy of shopping, instead of restricting their purchases to basic needs (as during the Maoist era). The reflection of this trend in the food culture is that people are now interested in different cuisines, and dining out has become a popular form of entertainment among those who have a little extra spending money. For these people, cleanliness and nutrition have superseded low prices as the main criteria for selecting a restaurant, because they can now afford to worry about their health. It is in this social context of mass consumption and consumerism that McDonald's appeals to so many Chinese customers.

Consumption has been an important feature of the political agenda underlying the government's promotion of economic reforms. In an effort to revitalize Chinese market forces, reformers encouraged consumer spending during the early 1980s. A famous slogan at that time was *nengzheng huihua*, which means "being able to make money and knowing how to spend it." This slogan was in direct conflict with the official ideology of Maoist socialism, which emphasized "hard work and simple living." Not surprisingly the Chinese mass media were filled with debates about the new consumerism. At the theoretical level, critiques of "premature consumption" (*chaoqian xiaofei*) and "hyperconsumption" (*gao xiaofei*) dominated these discussions. In practice, however, the rise of consumerism appears to be an irreversible trend. According to 1994 statistics released by the Chinese Consumers Society, the average expenditure per capita had increased fourfold in the previous decade. The ratio of "hard consumption" (of food, clothing, and other necessities of daily life) to "soft consumption" (of entertainment, tourism, fashion, and socializing) has changed from 3:1 in 1984 to 1:1.2 in 1994.[38] A new wave of mass consumption began in 1990, concentrating on interior decoration, private telephones and pagers, air conditioners, body building machines, and tourism.[39] Stories of the conspicuous consumption of luxury items among the new rich and increasing demands for imported goods have become a dominant feature of Chinese popular culture.[40] Some Chinese scholars have argued that the growth of a luxury commodity market is the hallmark of a modern way of life and a phenomenon characteristic of post-industrial societies.[41]

A good indicator of the escalating demands for consumption is the changing concept of the "three big items" (*san dajian*), by which is meant the three luxury items that confer the most status on their owner. During the 1960s and 1970s the "three bigs" were wristwatches, bicycles, and sewing machines. Families saved for years to buy these expensive items (an average of 200 yuan each). In the 1980s, color television sets, refrigerators, and washing machines, each costing at least 1,000 yuan, had become the new "three bigs." By the early 1990s, the "three bigs" were a telephone, an air conditioner, and a VCR. For the new entrepreneurial class the stakes have become so high that the three bigs are a flat, a private car, and modern communication devices such as mobile phones and fax machines. According to a 1994 survey, 2 percent of Chinese qualified as members of the new rich and were spending their money to acquire these "three super bigs."[42]

TABLE 2
Monthly Spending Money Claimed by Beijing Youth

Money available (yuan)[a]	Number of informants	Percentage
1 to 499	347	34.7
500 to 999	469	46.9
1,000 to 1,499	94	9.4
1,500 to 1,999	48	4.8
2,000 to 2,499	20	2
2,500 to 2,999	6	0.6
Above 3,000	16	1.6
Total	1,000	100

SOURCE: Survey results quoted in Pian Ming, "Beijing qingnian rexing gaodang shangpin" (Beijing Youth Keen on Luxury Commodities), *China Industrial and Commercial Times*, July 16, 1994.
[a]At the time of this survey, 1 yuan equals about $0.12 in U.S. currency.

The purchasing power of young people in Beijing has increased dramatically over the past decade; they have played a leading role in the trend toward consumerism. In early 1994 a Japanese consulting company conducted a survey among 1,000 Beijing youths between the ages of 16 and 30. The results are astonishing. Table 2 shows the amount of money controlled by these young people.

Two thirds of the informants had 500 yuan or more to spend per month. With so much money available to them, what are the most desirable commodities for these youths? The survey shows that 53 percent hope to buy a flat, and 57 percent would like to have a car.[43] It is no wonder that driving schools have done a booming business in recent years.[44]

For ordinary citizens, shopping has become an increasingly important part of everyday life; as noted earlier, people have begun to purchase goods that they want but do not necessarily need.[45] The most impressive evidence of this change is that children are very knowledgeable about Beijing's modern shopping malls and the commodities available there. A primary school teacher told me that children in her class know much more about brand names than do many of the teachers. Every Monday, these children talk about their experiences in shopping malls over the past weekend. To test children's knowledge of commodities, I asked my two nephews, both aged nine, to identify the cars in a newly published auto magazine. To my surprise, they quickly recognized the names and manufacturers of more than half the cars depicted.

With regard to food, an important feature of this emerging consumerism is a growing interest in eating out. According to a report in a Chinese consumer magazine, nearly 75 percent of Beijing residents who are on fixed work schedules no longer have breakfast at home: they eat at food stalls on the streets or in restaurants that provide breakfast, including foreign eateries such as Vie de France or Uncle Sam's. Frequent restaurant dining has become a popular form of entertainment among virtually all social groups.[46] According to a survey conducted by the Beijing Statistics Bureau in early 1993, nutritional value and convenience are the top concerns for most Beijing residents when choosing a restaurant. The most interesting discovery of this survey is that consumers showed a strong interest in sampling non-Chinese cuisines. Nearly half the informants (49.7 percent) had eaten at Western-style restaurants, including McDonald's or KFC.[47]

In response to increasing consumer demand, thousands of restaurants and eateries have opened in recent years. By early 1993, there were more than 19,000 eating establishments in

Beijing, ranging from five-star hotel restaurants to street stalls. More than 5,000 were state-owned, 55 were joint ventures or foreign-owned, and the remainder, 14,000, were owned by private entrepreneurs or independent vendors (*getihu*). The turnover rate was equally impressive: for every two restaurants that opened in 1993, one went out of business.[48]

In spite of this boom, Beijing residents still complain that it is difficult, and sometimes even hazardous, to eat out. A public panic of sorts swept through Beijing in the early 1990s. Rumors circulated of people dying after eating at street stalls or in unlicensed diners run by recent immigrants from the countryside. According to one set of stories, vendors of *youbing* (fried pancakes), a staple of the traditional Beijing breakfast, were said to have used laundry detergent as a fermentation agent—poisoning an untold number of people.[49] Many of my Beijing informants complained that they had two choices when eating Chinese-style food: to pay a lot for a fancy restaurant where the food is clean and safe, or to risk their life in a place where they have no idea what went on in the kitchen.

It is obvious that there is an urgent need for clean, reliable, medium-priced family restaurants in the Beijing market. Western fast food restaurants meet this need. It is precisely in the domain of hygiene that the local fast food restaurants, imitators of KFC and McDonald's, have failed to meet consumer expectations. As one observer points out, it is easy to build the "hardware" of a fast food industry, namely, the restaurants; but the "software" (service and management) cannot be adopted overnight. One of the most important features of McDonald's software is a high standard of hygiene, including the cleanliness of the eating environment and the freshness of the food.[50] The Beijing media constantly cite McDonald's for its attention to hygiene, in contrast to the dismal standards maintained by its local competitors.[51] As recent investigations show, the increasing demand for good hygiene derives from Beijing residents' awareness of the relationship between food preparation and health,[52] an awareness that parallels improved living standards and the rise of consumerism over the past fifteen years. Given the continued growth of the Chinese economy during the 1990s, the demand for clean and reliable food is likely to make transnational food chains increasingly popular among Beijing consumers.

Conclusion: The Golden Arches in the Local-Global Nexus

McDonald's experience in Beijing is a classic case of the "localization" of transnational systems. Efficiency and economic value—the two most important features of McDonald's in the United States—appear to be far less significant in Beijing's cultural setting. When Chinese workers load their families into a taxi and take them to McDonald's, spending one-sixth of their monthly income in the process, efficiency and economy are the least of their concerns. When customers linger in McDonald's for hours, relaxing, chatting, reading, enjoying the music, or celebrating birthdays, they are taking the "fast" out of fast food. It is clear that McDonald's restaurants in Beijing have been transformed into middle-class family establishments, where people can enjoy their leisure time and experience a Chinese version of American culture.

This Chinese version of American culture, as stated at the beginning of this chapter, is a result of the interactions between the McDonald's management and staff, on the one hand, and Beijing customers on the other hand. As a symbol of Americana and modernity, McDonald's food became popular among the newly emerging middle class and also among ordinary citizens who were curious about American food. A consequence of the powerful appeal of representing Americana is the conversion of McDonald's hamburgers and fries, ordinary daily fare in America, into precious and stylish foreign cuisine in Beijing. Such a transformation, however, is not to the company's long-term advantage. Like other leading transnational corporations, McDonald's development relies on its capability to increase consumer demand and expand the fast food market. McDonald's foods are intended for large numbers of ordinary consumers and thus must be, as Sidney Mintz has noted, "transformed into the ritual of daily necessity and even into images of daily decency."[53] In other words, to build on their initial success, McDonald's restaurants must localize their foods (and some of their cultural associations as well), converting them into something that is routine and ordinary for Beijing residents, while somehow maintaining their image as the symbol of the American way of life. This is why McDonald's management has gone to such extraordinary lengths to fit into the local cultural setting.

The other side of the localization process has two dimensions: (1) Beijing consumers' appropriation of McDonald's food and culture; and (2) the responses of local catering businesses and the rise of Chinese-style fast foods. The first dimension has been examined earlier in this chapter (one of the most obvious results of appropriation is the multifunctional use of McDonald's outlets). The notion of fast food (*kuaican*) itself is not new in Chinese culinary culture, which also has something to do with the way consumers have appropriated McDonald's food. I discovered that many informants regarded McDonald's, together with KFC and Pizza Hut, as but one of many cuisines available in the national capital. The real fast food, they said, is *hefan* (which literally means "boxed rice"), the various foods in styrofoam boxes sold at street stalls. When people sit at a table in a comfortable restaurant like McDonald's, they treat it as a formal event, and consequently spend as much time as possible over their food.

The success of foreign fast food chains posed a challenge to the local catering industry and, starting in 1990, many local restaurants met this challenge by creating their own versions of fast food. They started by imitating KFC, and several kinds of fried chicken soon appeared on the market, with names like Ronghua Chicken and Xiangfei Roast Chicken. The competition between local imitators and foreign fast food chains peaked in 1992 and early 1993. Beijing media termed it the "fast food war."[54] Since then, most local competitors have turned to Chinese-style fast food, such as noodles, rice dishes, and Chinese pancakes. The best known example is the Beijing Fast Food Company, a corporation established in 1993 and comprising nearly a thousand local restaurants and street stalls. The company offered more than 50 varieties of food, including five set meals: roast duck, stir-fried rice, dumplings, noodles, and meat pancakes, all served with soup and an appetizer.[55] Several of the leading figures in this business, former employees of KFC or McDonald's who had learned management techniques on the job, claimed that, by combining modern methods of preparation and hygiene with traditional Chinese cuisine, they could recapture Beijing's fast food market from the control of foreign chains.[56] Interestingly enough, a key feature of this indigenization process is that McDonald's has been taken as a model of management and food hygiene by local imitators as well as by government officials. I was told by a public relations officer that every month McDonald's conducts several dozen tours of its restaurants for the benefit of local government officials or catering companies.[57] The most famous restaurant in Beijing—Quanjude Roast Duck Restaurant—sent its management staff to McDonald's in 1993, and then introduced its own "roast duck fast food" in early 1994.[58]

This study demonstrates that analysts would be well advised to pay more attention to the responses of local people before drawing grand conclusions about the impact of transnational corporations. The emerging global culture is marked by diversity rather than uniformity, because local cultures, as Richard Adams notes, "continue to yield new emergent social entities, new adaptive forms brought into being in order to pursue survival and reproduction both through and in spite of the specific work of capitalism."[59] Daniel Miller's analysis of an American soap opera in Trinidad reveals, for instance, that Trinidadian audiences have positively appropriated this foreign product into their social life. The geographic origin of imported culture has become increasingly less relevant; what really matters is its local consequence.[60]

In my view, the most significant contribution made by transnational institutions like McDonald's is that people can use them as bridges to other cultures. In the present case, it is American culture that makes the Beijing McDonald's ultimately attractive to Chinese consumers. The customers want a "taste" of America, and the outcome of their pursuit is the creation of a Chinese version of American fast food culture. McDonald's success in Beijing can therefore be understood only in the context of this localization process. Given the centuries-long development of Chinese cuisine, it is only natural that foreign foods have undergone the transformative process of localization. It is also tempting to predict that, twenty years from now, the "American" associations that McDonald's carries today will become but dim memories for older residents. A new generation of Beijing consumers may treat the Big Mac, fries, and shakes simply as local products.

CHAPTER 2

McDonald's in Hong Kong: Consumerism, Dietary Change, and the Rise of a Children's Culture

James L. Watson

On a cold winter afternoon in 1969 my neighbor, Man Tso-chuen, was happy to talk about something other than the weather. Over tea, Mr. Man continued the saga of his lineage ancestors who had settled in San Tin village, Hong Kong New Territories, over six centuries earlier. Local history was our regular topic of conversation that winter and the story had already filled several notebooks. Suddenly he stopped, leaned back in his chair, and began to describe a meal he had eaten. He recounted—in exacting detail—the flavor and texture of each dish, the sequence of spices, and the order of presentation:

Blue crab and bean curd soup, laced with ginger and served in porcelain steam pots; red snapper braised in soy sauce with green onions; crackling roast piglet; pop-eyed delta shrimp, scalded for 15 seconds in boiling water; *dim sam* (steamed dumplings) shaped and colored like goldfish; stuffed whole chicken plastered with star anise and baked for a full day in clay; newly harvested, first-crop Panyu county rice served with fresh *bak choi* (vegetable), stir-fried in chicken fat.

Food for the gods. Mr. Man's account was so vivid I assumed he was referring to a wedding banquet he had attended a few days earlier in the nearby town of Yuen Long. Only later did I learn from his wife that fifty years had elapsed since he had enjoyed that meal—as a 16-year-old—in the city of Guangzhou (Canton); his father had taken him along on a business trip, and they had been invited to a banquet in one of South China's premier restaurants.

My neighbor's preoccupation with food was by no means unusual. Meals like the one described above are signal experiences in the lives of nearly everyone I have encountered during my 28 years of fieldwork in Hong Kong and the adjoining province of Guangdong. Whatever their station in life, hawker or billionaire property developer, the people of this region are intensely proud of their cuisine, indisputably one of China's finest.[1] "We are Cantonese," Mr. Man would proclaim whenever we sat down to eat together, "We have the best food in the world."

Given such strongly held views, how does one explain the phenomenal success of American-style fast food in Hong Kong and, increasingly, in Guangzhou—the two epicenters of Cantonese culture and cuisine? Seven of the world's ten busiest McDonald's restaurants are located in Hong Kong.[2] When McDonald's first opened in 1975, few thought it would survive more than a few months. By January 1, 1997, Hong Kong had 125 outlets, which means that there was one McDonald's for every 51,200 residents, compared to one for every 30,000 people in the United States.[3] Walking into these restaurants and looking at the layout, one could well be in Cleveland or Boston. The only obvious differences are the clientele, the majority of whom are Cantonese-speakers, and the menu, which is in Chinese as well as English.

Transnationalism and the Fast Food Industry

Does the roaring success of McDonald's and its rivals in the fast food industry mean that Hong Kong's local culture is under siege? Are food chains helping to create a homogenous, "global" culture better suited to the demands of a capitalist world order? Hong Kong would seem to be an excellent place to test the globalization hypothesis, given the central role that cuisine plays in the production and maintenance of a distinctive local identity. Man Tso-chuen's great-grandchildren are today avid consumers of Big Macs, pizza, and Coca-Cola; does this somehow make them less "Chinese" than their grandfather?

It is my contention that the cultural arena in places like Hong Kong is changing with such breathtaking speed that the fundamental assumptions underlining such questions are themselves questionable. Economic and social realities make it necessary to construct an entirely new approach to global issues, one that takes the consumers' own views into account. Analyses based on neomarxian and dependency (center/periphery) models that were popular in the 1960s and 1970s do not begin to capture the complexity of emerging transnational systems.[4]

This chapter represents a conscious attempt to bring the discussion of globalism down to earth, focusing on one local culture. The people of Hong Kong have embraced American-style fast foods, and by so doing they might appear to be in the vanguard of a worldwide culinary revolution. But they have not been stripped of their cultural traditions, nor have they become "Americanized" in any but the most superficial of ways. Hong Kong in the late 1990s constitutes one of the world's most heterogeneous cultural environments. Younger people, in particular, are fully conversant in transnational idioms, which include language, music, sports, clothing, satellite television, cybercommunications, global travel, and—of course—cuisine. It is no longer possible to distinguish what is local and what is not. In Hong Kong, as I hope to show in this chapter, the transnational *is* the local.

Eating Out: A Social History of Consumption

By the time McDonald's opened its first Hong Kong restaurant in 1975, the idea of fast food was already well established among local consumers. Office workers, shop assistants, teachers, and transport workers had enjoyed various forms of takeout cuisine for well over a century; an entire industry had emerged to deliver mid-day meals direct to workplaces. In the 1960s and 1970s thousands of street vendors produced snacks and simple meals on demand, day or night. Time has always been money in Hong Kong; hence, the dual keys to success in the catering trade were speed and convenience. Another essential characteristic was that the food, based primarily on rice or noodles, had to be hot. Even the most cosmopolitan of local consumers did not (and many still do not) consider cold foods, such as sandwiches and salads, to be acceptable meals. Older people in South China associate cold food with offerings to the dead and are understandably hesitant to eat it.

The fast food industry in Hong Kong had to deliver hot items that could compete with traditional purveyors of convenience foods (noodle shops, dumpling stalls, soup carts, portable grills). The first modern chain to enter the fray was

Café de Coral, a local corporation that began operation in 1969 and is still a dominant player in the Hong Kong fast food market (with 109 outlets and a 25 percent market share, compared to McDonald's 20 percent market share in 1994).[5] Café de Coral's strategy was simple: It moved Hong Kong's street foods indoors, to a clean, well-lighted cafeteria that offered instant service and moderate prices; popular Cantonese items were then combined with (sinicized) "Western" foods that had been popular in Hong Kong for decades. Café de Coral's menu reads like the *locus classicus* of Pacific Rim cuisine: deep-fried chicken wings, curry on rice, hot dogs, roast pork in soup noodles, spaghetti with meat balls, barbecued ribs, red bean sundaes, Ovaltine, Chinese tea, and Coca-Cola (with lemon, hot or cold). The formula was so successful it spawned dozens of imitators, including three full-scale chains.

American-style fast foods were, of course, familiar to many Hong Kong travelers, but it was not until McDonald's opened its first restaurant on January 8, 1975, that ordinary consumers had a chance to sample this cuisine. The three elements of McDonald's basic "set" (hamburger, fries, Coke) had all been available in Hong Kong since at least the mid-1950s. Hamburgers were offered, primarily as children's food, at Hong Kong's ubiquitous Russian restaurants (with names such as Cherikoff's and Chanteclair), run by immigrants who had fled Russia and then Shanghai in the wake of communist takeovers. It was in these establishments, and in the coffee shops of major hotels, that the Hong Kong middle classes learned to eat Western food. People who had a basis for comparison always avoided locally produced hamburgers. British-style "chips" (thick-cut, deep-fried potatoes) were similarly available in Hong Kong but never appealed to Chinese consumers. Coca-Cola, by contrast, had since its introduction in the late 1940s become one of the colony's most popular beverages.[6]

McDonald's mid-1970s entry also corresponded to an economic boom associated with Hong Kong's conversion from a low-wage, light-industrial outpost to a regional center for financial services and high-technology industries. McDonald's takeoff thus paralleled the rise of a new class of highly educated, affluent consumers who thrive in Hong Kong's ever-changing urban environment—one of the most stressful in the world.[7] These new consumers eat out more often than their parents and have created a huge demand for fast, convenient foods of all types.[8] In order to compete in this market, McDonald's had to offer something different. That critical difference, at least during the company's first decade of operation, was American culture packaged as all-American, middle-class food.

To understand how an American chain became a leading player in Hong Kong's culinary scene, one has to consider the role of management. Daniel Ng, Managing Director and charter franchise owner of McDonald's Hong Kong, turned what rivals had dismissed as a losing proposition ("Hamburgers in Hong Kong?") into one of the colony's most celebrated success stories.[9] Mr. Ng, an American-educated engineer, made the fateful decision *not* to compete with local, Chinese-style cuisine. As he put it to me: "If I had hired the best chef in Hong Kong to make Chinese dumplings for us, no one would come because no one would believe an American restaurant can produce good dumplings. I wouldn't have come myself."[10]

What would attract local consumers, he decided, was straightforward, uncompromising American food. During the first few years the chain's name, McDonald's, was not translated but was displayed—deliberately—in English, to emphasize its foreign character. Only after the company had established itself, and its identification as a producer of quality products was secure, did Mr. Ng decide to transliterate the name into Chinese characters.

The transliteration process was a delicate one, given the long history of disasters attending the rendition of foreign names in Chinese. Mr. Ng decided to capture the sound of "McDonald's," in three homophonic characters, rather than create a name that would convey meaning—thus making the company appear to be a Chinese enterprise. Many local people reacted badly when Kentucky Fried Chicken first entered the Hong Kong market and chose a Chinese name that meant, literally, "Hometown Chicken." "Kentucky is certainly not my hometown," one longtime resident exclaimed.[11] (KFC later dropped this name and began using a transliterated title based on sound rather than literal meaning.)

Hong Kong McDonald's hoped to avoid confusion by adopting a version of the three-character phrase used to represent a well-known local street, MacDonnell Road. In the company's first attempt the last character was written as the common term for female slave (*nu*) and, after much discussion, it was dropped in favor of *lao*—the dictionary meaning of which is labor or work. The resulting name is pronounced *mak dong lou* in Cantonese, or *mai dang lao* in Mandarin. Taken together these characters convey no obvious meaning, but any speaker of Chinese will instantly recognize the construction as the transliteration of a foreign name. It thus captures the message that Mr. Ng and his staff hoped to impart to the Hong Kong consumer: This place offers something different.

Mental Categories: Snack Versus Meal

As in other parts of East Asia, McDonald's faced a serious problem when it began operation in Hong Kong: Hamburgers, fries, and sandwiches were perceived as snacks (Cantonese *siu sihk*, literally "small eats"); in the local view these items did not constitute the elements of a proper meal. This perception is still prevalent among older, more conservative consumers who believe that hamburgers, hot dogs, and pizza can never be "filling." Many students stop at fast food outlets on their way home from school; they may share hamburgers and fries with their classmates and then eat a full meal with their families at home. This is not considered a problem by parents, who themselves are likely to have stopped for tea and snacks after work. Snacking with friends and colleagues provides a major opportunity for socializing (and transacting business) among southern Chinese. Teahouses, coffee shops, bakeries, and ice cream parlors are popular precisely because they provide a structured yet informal setting for social encounters. Furthermore, unlike Chinese restaurants and banquet halls, snack centers do not command a great deal of time or money from customers.

Contrary to corporate goals, therefore, McDonald's entered the Hong Kong market as a purveyor of snacks. Only since the late 1980s has its fare been treated as the foundation of "meals" by a generation of younger consumers who regularly eat non-Chinese food. Thanks largely to McDonald's, hamburgers and fries are now a recognized feature of Hong Kong's lunch scene. The evening hours remain, however, the weak link in McDonald's marketing plan; the real surprise was breakfast, which became a peak traffic period (more on this below).

The mental universe of Hong Kong consumers is partially revealed in the everyday use of language. Hamburgers are referred to, in colloquial Cantonese, as *han bou bao*—*han* being a homophone for "ham" and *bao* the common term for stuffed buns or bread rolls. *Bao* are quintessential snacks, and however excellent or nutritious they might be, they do not constitute the basis of a satisfying (i.e., filling) meal. In South China that honor is reserved for culinary arrangements that rest, literally, on a bed of rice (*fan*). Foods that accompany rice are referred to as *sung*, probably best translated as "toppings" (including meat, fish, and vegetables).[12] It is significant that hamburgers are rarely categorized as meat (*yuk*); Hong Kong consumers tend to perceive anything that is served between slices of bread (Big Macs, fish sandwiches, hot dogs) as *bao*. In American culture the hamburger is categorized first and foremost as a meat item (with all the attendant worries about fat and cholesterol content), whereas in Hong Kong the same item is thought of primarily as bread.[13]

From Exotic to Ordinary: McDonald's Becomes Local

Following precedents in other international markets,[14] the Hong Kong franchise promoted McDonald's basic menu and did not introduce items that would be more recognizable to Chinese consumers (such as rice dishes, tropical fruit, soup noodles). Until recently the food has been indistinguishable from that served in Mobile, Alabama, or Moline, Illinois.[15] There are, however, local preferences: the best-selling items in many outlets are fish sandwiches and plain hamburgers; Big Macs tend to be the favorites of children and teenagers. Hot tea and hot chocolate outsell coffee, but Coca-Cola remains the most popular drink.

McDonald's conservative approach also applied to the breakfast menu. When morning service was introduced in the 1980s,

American-style items such as eggs, muffins, pancakes, and hash brown potatoes were not featured. Instead, the local outlets served the standard fare of hamburgers and fries for breakfast. McDonald's initial venture into the early morning food market was so successful that Mr. Ng hesitated to introduce American-style breakfast items, fearing that an abrupt shift in menu might alienate consumers who were beginning to accept hamburgers and fries as a regular feature of their diet.[16] The transition to eggs, muffins, and hash browns was a gradual one, and today most Hong Kong customers order breakfasts that are similar to those offered in American outlets. But once established, dietary preferences change slowly: McDonald's continues to feature plain hamburgers (but not the Big Mac) on its breakfast menu in most Hong Kong outlets.

Management decisions of the type outlined above helped establish McDonald's as an icon of popular culture in Hong Kong. From 1975 to approximately 1985, McDonald's became the "in" place for young people wishing to associate themselves with the laid-back, nonhierarchical dynamism they perceived American society to embody. The first generation of consumers patronized McDonald's precisely because it was *not* Chinese and was *not* associated with Hong Kong's past as a backward-looking colonial outpost where (in their view) nothing of consequence ever happened. Hong Kong was changing and, as noted earlier, a new consumer culture was beginning to take shape. McDonald's caught the wave of this cultural movement and has been riding it ever since.

Anthropological conventions and methodologies do not allow one to deal very well with factors such as entrepreneurial flair or managerial creativity. Ethnographers are used to thinking in terms of group behavior, emphasizing coalitions and communities rather than personalities. In studies of corporate culture, however, the decisive role of management—or, more precisely, individual managers—must be dealt with in a direct way. This takes us into the realm of charisma, leadership, and personality.[17]

Thanks largely to unrelenting efforts by Mr. Ng and his staff, McDonald's made the transition from an exotic, trendy establishment patronized by self-conscious status seekers to a competitively priced chain offering "value meals" to busy, preoccupied consumers. Today, McDonald's restaurants in Hong Kong are packed—wall-to-wall—with people of all ages, few of whom are seeking an American cultural experience. Twenty years after Mr. Ng opened his first restaurant, eating at McDonald's has become an ordinary, everyday experience for hundreds of thousands of Hong Kong residents. The chain has become a local institution in the sense that it has blended into the urban landscape; McDonald's outlets now serve as rendezvous points for young and old alike.

A comparative survey of prices, carried out in June 1994, demonstrates that McDonald's fare is equal in price to that of its competitors in the fast food sector or cheaper.[18] Furthermore, when other categories of food purveyors are considered (Chinese restaurants, noodle shops, teahouses, dumpling stalls), the appeal of McDonald's is even more understandable: an average "value meal" is less than half the price of a simple lunch in one of Hong Kong's middle-ranking teahouses or noodle shops. Translated into U.S. dollar terms (see Table 1), McDonald's prices in Hong Kong were, until 1997, the cheapest in the world.[19]

The transformation from exotic to ordinary may be repeating itself just across the Hong Kong border in the Shenzhen

TABLE 1

Comparative Prices, June 1994

(US$1 = HK$7.8)

Item	Cambridge, Mass. (6/5/94)a US$	Hong Kong, Central Distr. (6/16/94)b US$	HK$
Big Mac	2.09	1.19	9.20
Regular Hamburger	0.59	0.54	4.20
Medium Fries	1.09	0.71	5.50
Medium Coca-Cola	0.99	0.62	4.80
Apple Pie	0.85	0.51	4.00
Chicken Sandwich	2.29	1.06	8.20
Fish Sandwich	1.85	1.05	8.10
Coffee, regular	0.80	0.62	4.80
Egg McMuffin	1.57	0.93	7.20
Chicken McNuggets	1.89	1.15	8.90
Cheeseburger	0.69	0.61	4.70
Hash Browns	0.69	0.39	3.00

[a]Collected by Bernadine Chee.
[b]Collected by J. L. Watson.

Special Economic Zone, where Mr. Ng was the pioneer franchise holder for several McDonald's restaurants. Shenzhen was one of the first regions in the People's Republic to benefit from Deng Xiaoping's economic reforms (starting in the early 1980s) and has subsequently become a boom town characterized by a curious combination of socialist bureaucracy and bare-knuckled, frontier capitalism. The consumer scene in Shenzhen is similar, in some respects, to Beijing's as described by Yan in Chapter 1. In both cities McDonald's is perceived as an upmarket restaurant, offering American food (and culture) to a new class of entrepreneurs and professionals who can afford the experience. The first Shenzhen outlet opened on October 8, 1990, and had 12,590 transactions that day—breaking the world record for McDonald's restaurants, set eight months earlier in Moscow.[20] By February 1997, there were 27 McDonald's in Shenzhen, serving nearly two million people, a small number of whom, including children of high-level communist cadres, are beginning to treat the Big Mac and fries as common features of their diet.

Sanitation and the Invention of Cleanliness

Besides offering value for money, another key to McDonald's success was the provision of extra services, hitherto unavailable to Hong Kong consumers. Until the mid-1980s, a visit to any Hong Kong restaurant's toilet (save for those in fancy hotels) could best be described as an adventure. Today, restaurant toilets all over the territory are in good working order and, much to the surprise of visitors who remember the past, they are (relatively) clean. Based on conversations with people representing the full range of social strata in Hong Kong, McDonald's is widely perceived as the catalyst of this dramatic change. The corporation maintained clean facilities and did not waver as new outlets opened in neighborhoods where public sanitation had never been a high priority. Daniel Ng recalled how, during the early years of his business, he had to re-educate employees before they could even begin to comprehend what corporate standards of cleanliness entailed.[21] Many workers, when asked to scrub out a toilet, would protest that it was already cleaner than the one in their own home, only to be told that it was not clean enough. McDonald's set what was perceived at the time to be an impossible standard and, in the process, raised consumers' expectations.[22] Rivals had to meet these standards in order to compete. Hong Kong consumers began to draw a mental equation between the state of a restaurant's toilets and its kitchen. In pre-1980s public eateries (and in many private homes), the toilet was located inside the kitchen. One was not expected to see any contradiction in this arrangement; the operative factor was that both facilities had to be near the water supply. Younger people, in particular, have begun to grow wary of these arrangements and are refusing to eat at places they perceive to be "dirty."

Without exception my informants cited the availability of clean and accessible toilets as an important reason for patronizing McDonald's.[23] Women, in particular, appreciated this service; they noted that, without McDonald's, it would be difficult to find public facilities when they are away from home or office. A survey of one Hong Kong outlet in June 1994 revealed that 58 percent of the consumers present were women,[24] a sex ratio similar to the Korean figures cited by Sangmee Bak (see Chapter 4). For many Hong Kong residents, therefore, McDonald's is more than just a restaurant; it is an oasis, a familiar rest station, in what is perceived to be an inhospitable urban environment.

What's in a Smile? Friendliness and Public Service

American consumers expect to be served "with a smile" when they order fast food, but as noted in the Introduction, this is not true in all societies. In Hong Kong people are suspicious of anyone who displays what is perceived to be an excess of congeniality, solicitude, or familiarity. The human smile is not, therefore, a universal symbol of openness and honesty. "If you buy an apple from a hawker and he smiles at you," my

Cantonese tutor once told me, "you know you're being cheated."

Given these cultural expectations, it was difficult for Hong Kong management to import a key element of the McDonald's formula—service with a smile—and make it work. Crew members were trained to treat customers in a manner that approximates the American notion of "friendliness." Prior to the 1970s, there was not even an indigenous Cantonese term to describe this form of behavior. The traditional notion of friendship is based on loyalty to close associates, which by definition cannot be extended to strangers. Today the concept of *public* friendliness is recognized—and verbalized—by younger people in Hong Kong, but the term many of them use to express this quality is "friendly," borrowed directly from English. McDonald's, through its television advertising, may be partly responsible for this innovation, but to date it has had little effect on workers in the catering industry.

During my interviews it became clear that the majority of Hong Kong consumers were uninterested in public displays of congeniality from service personnel. When shopping for fast food most people cited convenience, cleanliness, and table space as primary considerations; few even mentioned service except to note that the food should be delivered promptly.[25] Counter staff in Hong Kong's fast food outlets (including McDonald's) rarely make great efforts to smile or to behave in a manner Americans would interpret as friendly. Instead, they project qualities that are admired in the local culture: competence, directness, and unflappability. In a North American setting the facial expression that Hong Kong employees use to convey these qualities would likely be interpreted as a deliberate attempt to be rude or indifferent. Workers who smile on the job are assumed to be enjoying themselves at the consumer's (and management's) expense: In the words of one diner I overheard while standing in a queue, "They must be playing around back there. What are they laughing about?"

Consumer Discipline?

As noted in the Introduction, a hallmark of the American fast food business is the displacement of labor costs from the corporation to the consumers. For the system to work, consumers must be educated—or "disciplined"—so that they voluntarily fulfill their side of an implicit bargain: We (the corporation) will provide cheap, fast service, if you (the customer) carry your own tray, seat yourself, and help clean up afterward. Time and space are also critical factors in the equation: Fast service is offered in exchange for speedy consumption and a prompt departure, thereby making room for others. This system has revolutionized the American food industry and has helped to shape consumer expectations in other sectors of the economy. How has it fared in Hong Kong? Are Chinese customers conforming to disciplinary models devised in Oak Brook, Illinois?

The answer is both yes and no. In general Hong Kong consumers have accepted the basic elements of the fast food formula, but with "localizing" adaptations. For instance, customers generally do not bus their own trays, nor do they depart immediately upon finishing. Clearing one's own table has never been an accepted part of local culinary culture, owing in part to the low esteem attaching to this type of labor. During McDonald's first decade in Hong Kong, the cost of hiring extra cleaners was offset by low wages. A pattern was thus established, and customers grew accustomed to leaving without attending to their own rubbish. Later, as wages escalated in the late 1980s and early 1990s, McDonald's tried to introduce self-busing by posting announcements in restaurants and featuring the practice in its television advertisements. As of February 1997, however, little had changed. Hong Kong consumers, unlike the Beijing yuppies Yan describes in Chapter 1, have ignored this aspect of consumer discipline.

What about the critical issues of time and space? Local managers with whom I spoke estimated that the average eating time for most Hong Kong customers was between 20 and 25 minutes, compared to 11 minutes in the United States fast food industry.[26] This estimate confirms my own observations of McDonald's consumers in Hong Kong's central business districts (Victoria and Tsimshatsui). A survey conducted in the New Territories city of Yuen Long—an old market town that has grown into a modern urban center—revealed that local McDonald's consumers took just under 26 minutes to eat.[27]

Perhaps the most striking feature of the American-inspired model of consumer discipline is the queue. Researchers in many parts of the world have reported that customers refuse, despite "education" campaigns by the chains involved, to form neat lines in front of cashiers (see Introduction, pp. 27–30). Instead, customers pack themselves into disorderly scrums and jostle for a chance to place their orders. Scrums of this nature were common in Hong Kong when McDonald's opened in 1975. Local managers discouraged this practice by stationing queue monitors near the registers during busy hours and, by the 1980s, orderly lines were the norm at McDonald's. The disappearance of the scrum corresponds to a general change in Hong Kong's public culture as a new generation of residents, the children of refugees, began to treat the territory as their home. Courtesy toward strangers was largely unknown in the 1960s: Boarding a bus during rush hour could be a nightmare and transacting business at a bank teller's window required brute strength. Many people credit McDonald's with being the first public institution in Hong Kong to enforce queuing, and thereby helping to create a more "civilized" social order. McDonald's did not, in fact, introduce the queue to Hong Kong, but this belief is firmly lodged in the public imagination.[28]

Hovering and the Napkin Wars

Purchasing one's food is no longer a physical challenge in Hong Kong's McDonald's but finding a place to sit is quite another matter. The traditional practice of "hovering" is one solution: Choose a group of diners who appear to be on the verge of leaving and stake a claim to their table by hovering nearby, sometimes only inches away. Seated customers routinely ignore the intrusion; it would, in fact, entail a loss of face to notice. Hovering was the norm in Hong Kong's lower- to middle-range restaurants during the 1960s and 1970s, but the practice has disappeared in recent years. Restaurants now take names or hand out tickets at the entrance; warning signs, in Chinese and English, are posted: "Please wait to be seated." Customers are no longer allowed into the dining area until a table is ready.

Fast food outlets are the only dining establishments in Hong Kong where hovering is still tolerated, largely because it would be nearly impossible to regulate. Customer traffic in McDonald's is so heavy that the standard restaurant design has failed to reproduce American-style dining routines: Rather than ordering first and finding a place to sit afterward, Hong Kong consumers usually arrive in groups and delegate one or two people to claim a table while someone else joins the counter queues.[29] Children make ideal hoverers and learn to scoot through packed restaurants, zeroing in on diners who are about to finish. It is one of the wonders of comparative ethnography to witness the speed with which Hong Kong children perform this reconnaissance duty. Foreign visitors are sometimes unnerved by hovering, but residents accept it as part of everyday life in one of the world's most densely populated cities. It is not surprising, therefore, that Hong Kong's fast food chains have made few efforts to curtail the practice.[30]

Management is less tolerant of behavior that affects profit margins. In the United States fast food companies save money by allowing (or requiring) customers to collect their own napkins, straws, plastic flatware, and condiments. Self-provisioning is an essential feature of consumer discipline, but it only works if the system is not abused. In Hong Kong napkins are dispensed, one at a time, by McDonald's crew members who work behind the counter; customers who do not ask for napkins do not receive any.[31] This is a deviation from the corporation's standard operating procedure and adds a few seconds to each transaction, which in turn slows down the queues. Why alter a well-tested routine? The reason is simple: napkins placed in public dispensers disappear faster than they can be replaced.

When the majority of Hong Kong consumers were growing up in the 1960s and 1970s self-provisioning was largely unknown and caterers rarely allowed customers to serve themselves. Expectations only began to change in the late 1970s, with the introduction of Western-style buffets in some of Hong Kong's larger hotels. The innovation was a smashing success and launched a culinary revolution: Buffets allowed the newly affluent middle classes to sample a wide range of Euro-

pean, Thai, Indian, Mexican, and Japanese foods without reference to indecipherable menus and strange forms of etiquette
that might embarrass novice diners. Owing largely to buffets,
local diners (especially young adults) tend to be far more adventurous than their counterparts in Taipei and Beijing.

Buffets, like fast food outlets, depend upon consumers to
perform much of their own labor in return for reduced prices.
Abuse of the system—wasting food or taking it home—is taken
for granted and is factored into the price of buffet meals. Fast
food chains, by contrast, operate at lower price thresholds
where consumer abuse can seriously affect profits.

Many university students of my acquaintance reported that
they had frequently observed older people pocketing wads of
paper napkins, three to four inches thick, in restaurants that
permit self-provisioning. Management efforts to stop this behavior are referred to, in the Cantonese-English slang of Hong
Kong youth, as the "Napkin Wars." Younger people were ap-
palled by what they saw as the waste of natural resources by a
handful of customers. As they talked about the issue, however,
it became obvious that the Napkin Wars represented more—in
their eyes—than a campaign to conserve paper. The sight of
diners abusing public facilities reminded these young people of
the bad old days of their parents and grandparents, when Hong
Kong's social life was dominated by refugees who had little
stake in the local community. During the 1960s and 1970s,
economic insecurities were heightened by the very real prospect that Red Guards might take over the colony at any moment.[32] The game plan was simple during those decades: Make
money as quickly as possible and move on. In the 1980s a new
generation of local-born youth began treating Hong Kong as
home and proceeded to build a public culture better suited to

their vision of life in a cosmopolitan city. In this new Hong Kong, consumers are expected to be sophisticated and financially secure, which means that it would be beneath their dignity to abuse public facilities. Still, McDonald's retains control of its napkins.

Resistance, Environmental Protests, and Charity

Some readers might be tempted to interpret the Napkin Wars, together with other departures from McDonald's standard model of operation (prolonged dining and hovering), as evidence that local people are actively resisting efforts by the corporation to turn them into disciplined, compliant consumers. An argument to support such claims could be constructed, but it would not, in my opinion, be an accurate reflection of social life in Hong Kong. Throughout my research I gave respondents ample scope to make critical comments about McDonald's or to express hostility toward transnational corporations. In Chapter 4, Sangmee Bak demonstrates convincingly that South Korean consumers are hyperconscious of the political implications of eating at McDonald's. Concern about the activities of transnational corporations and their efforts to establish beachheads in the local economy is never far from the surface in Korean public discourse; the rhetoric of resistance is evident in the speech of ordinary citizens, and is not restricted to elite groups of intellectuals and students.

In Hong Kong, by contrast, denunciations of transnational corporations do not figure prominently in public or private conversations. The reason, no doubt, is that Hong Kong is by its very nature a creation of the world capitalist economy; it could not have survived as a quasi-independent entity since World War Two without the active involvement of international banks, foreign corporations, and outside investors. In this setting McDonald's does not stand out as an obvious target of politically inspired debate. It is but one of literally hundreds of transnational corporations that operate in Hong Kong's complex economy.

McDonald's imports nearly everything it uses in Hong Kong: beef, eggs, potatoes, lettuce, cooking oil, apple pies, paper containers. The corporation has made efforts to buy more materials in China, but many items were still being imported from the United States as late as 1993—including Idaho potatoes.[33] In other parts of East Asia, an imbalance of this magnitude would be seized upon by the local media as evidence of American economic imperialism. McDonald's makes special efforts to use local suppliers for its operations in China and Korea, just as it does in England, Brazil, and Russia.[34] Hong Kong is perhaps a unique case: The local economy no longer produces any of the basic ingredients that constitute McDonald's fare. It would be pointless to single out this corporation, among the hundreds that operate in Hong Kong, for not relying on local products.

This is not to suggest that McDonald's has escaped criticism. On October 15, 1992, and again on the same date in 1993, university students organized public demonstrations outside one of Hong Kong's busiest McDonald's (at the Star Ferry concourse, Tsimshatsui). The date was chosen to correspond to similar protests held in other parts of the world, aimed at drawing public attention to McDonald's alleged abuse of the environment. Student protesters distributed a broadsheet accusing the corporation of purchasing beef that had been raised in rain forest zones.[35] McDonald's has made it a firm international policy to avoid buying beef from such sources,[36] but, like urban legends in the United States, the rumor continues to circulate. The broadsheet also denounced McDonald's for transplanting an American-style "junk culture" (*laji wenhua*), paraphrasing materials first published by activists in England. One might assume that accusations like this would draw considerable attention in Hong Kong where the media are quick to capitalize on public demonstrations. Footage of the protest was broadcast on that evening's television news, but it did not lead to further activities and most students with whom I spoke considered the affair to have been a nonstarter. Ripples of protest continue to surface in Hong Kong, but McDonald's has not been the target of regular demonstrations or hypercritical media coverage, as it has in Mexico, England, and France.[37]

Quite the opposite, in fact, is true. The corporation has made great efforts to present itself as a champion of environmental awareness and public welfare in Hong Kong. McDonald's sponsors a series of ecology camps for Hong Kong school children and Green Power workshops at local universities.[38] The company is also responsible for Asia's first Ronald McDonald House for Sick Children, a charitable institution paralleling American models.[39] Advertisements promote McDonald's as a *local* institution, with a clear stake in the overall health of the community: "We live here too," declares a leaflet (published in Chinese and English) distributed to customers in 1994.[40] Compared to its rivals in the Hong Kong fast food industry, McDonald's stands out as a company that has made efforts to involve itself in community activities; detractors have had a difficult time portraying it as a corporate villain.[41]

Children as Consumers

During the summer of 1994, while attending a business lunch in one of Hong Kong's fanciest hotels, I watched a waiter lean down to consult with a customer at an adjoining table. The object of his attention was a six-year-old child who studied the menu with practiced skill. His parents beamed as their prodigy performed; meanwhile, sitting across the table, a pair of grandparents sat bolt upright, scowling in obvious disapproval. Twenty years ago the sight of a child commanding such attention would have shocked the entire restaurant into silence. No one, save the immediate party (and this observer), even noticed in 1994.

Hong Kong children rarely ate outside their home until the late 1970s, and when they did, they were expected to eat what was put in front of them. The idea that children might actually order their own food or speak to a waiter would have outraged most adults; only foreign youngsters (notably the offspring of British and American expatriates) were permitted to make their preferences known in public. Today, Hong Kong children as young as two or three participate in the local economy as full-fledged consumers, with their own tastes and brand loyalties. Children now have money in their pockets and they spend it on personal consumption, which usually means snacks.[42] In response, new industries and a specialized service sector has emerged to "feed" these discerning consumers. McDonald's was one of the first corporations to recognize the potential of the children's market; in effect, the company started a revolution by making it possible for even the youngest consumers to *choose* their own food.

McDonald's has become so popular in Hong Kong that parents often use visits to their neighborhood outlet as a reward for good behavior or academic achievement. Conversely, children who misbehave might lose their after-school snacking privileges or be left at home while their siblings are taken out for a McDonald's brunch on Sunday. During interviews parents reported that sanctions of this type worked better than anything they could think of to straighten out a wayward child: "It is my nuclear deterrent," one father told me, in English.

Many Hong Kong children of my acquaintance are so fond of McDonald's that they refuse to eat with their parents or grandparents in Chinese-style restaurants or *dim sam* teahouses. This has caused intergenerational distress in some of Hong Kong's more conservative communities.[43] In 1994, a nine-year-old boy, the descendant of illustrious ancestors who settled in the New Territories eight centuries ago, talked about his concerns as we consumed Big Macs, fries, and shakes at McDonald's: "A-bak [uncle], I like it here better than any place in the world. I want to come here every day." His father takes him to McDonald's at least twice a week, but his grandfather, who accompanied them a few times in the late 1980s, will no longer do so. "I prefer to eat *dim sam*," the older man told me later; "that place [McDonald's] is for kids." Many grandparents have resigned themselves to the new consumer trends and take their preschool grandchildren to McDonald's for mid-morning snacks—precisely the time of day that local teahouses were once packed with retired people. Cantonese grandparents have always played a prominent role in child minding, but until recently the children had to accommodate to the proclivities of their elders. By the 1990s grandchildren were more assertive and the mid-morning *dim sam* snack was giving way to hamburgers and Cokes.

The emergence of children as full-scale consumers has had other consequences for the balance of domestic power in Hong Kong homes. Grade school children often possess detailed knowledge of fast foods and foreign (non-Chinese) cuisines. Unlike members of the older generation, children know what, and how, to eat in a wide variety of restaurants. Specialized information is shared with classmates: Which chain has the best pizza? What is ravioli? How do you eat a croissant? Food, especially fast food, is one of the leading topics of conversation among Hong Kong school children. Grandchildren frequently assume the role of tutors, showing their elders the proper way to eat fast food. Without guidance, older people are likely to disassemble the Big Mac, layer by layer, and eat only those parts that appeal to them.[44] Hong Kong adults also find it uncomfortable to eat with their hands and devise makeshift finger guards with wrappers. Children, by contrast, are usually expert in the finer points of fast food etiquette and pay close attention to television ads that feature young people eating a variety of foods. It is embarrassing, I was told by an 11-year-old acquaintance, to be seen at McDonald's with a grandfather who does not know how to eat "properly."

Many Hong Kong kindergartens and primary schools teach culinary skills, utilizing the lunch period for lessons in flatware etiquette, menu reading, and food awareness (taste-testing various cuisines, including Thai, European, and Indian).[45] Partly as a consequence, Hong Kong's youth are among the world's most knowledgeable and adventurous eaters. One can find a wide range of cuisines in today's Hong Kong, rivaling New York City for variety. South Asian, Mexican, and Spanish restaurants are crowded with groups of young people, ages 16 to 25, sharing dishes as they graze their way through the menu.

Culinary adventures of this nature are avoided by older residents (people over 50), who, in general, have a more restricted range of food tolerance.

Ronald McDonald and the Invention of Birthday Parties

Until recently most people in Hong Kong did not even know, let alone celebrate, their birthdates in the Western calendrical sense; dates of birth according to the lunar calendar were recorded for divinatory purposes but were not noted in annual rites. By the late 1980s, however, birthday parties, complete with cakes and candles, were the rage in Hong Kong. Any child who was anyone had to have a party, and the most popular venue was a fast food restaurant, with McDonald's ranked above all competitors. The majority of Hong Kong people live in overcrowded flats, which means that parties are rarely held in private homes.

Except for the outlets in central business districts, McDonald's restaurants are packed every Saturday and Sunday with birthday parties, cycled through at the rate of one every hour. A party hostess, provided by the restaurant, leads the children in games while the parents sit on the sidelines, talking quietly among themselves. For a small fee celebrants receive printed invitation cards, photographs, a gift box containing toys and a discount coupon for future trips to McDonald's. Parties are held in a special enclosure, called the Ronald Room, which is equipped with low tables and tiny stools—suitable only for children. Television commercials portray Ronald McDonald leading birthday celebrants on exciting safaris and expeditions.[46] The clown's Cantonese name, Mak Dong Lou Suk-Suk ("Uncle McDonald"), plays on the intimacy of kinship and has helped transform him into one of Hong Kong's most familiar cartoon figures.[47]

During the course of this project I found myself being drawn ever more deeply into the world of children, paying close attention to the ways they judge themselves and their peers. Around the age of four, Hong Kong children begin to develop a fine-tuned sense of social distinction that is reflected in consumption patterns.[48] I soon discovered that the birthday cake is an infallible status marker among younger consumers; specifically, the type and quality of fruit used to decorate the cake is what matters most. Here, in capsule form, is the ranking system as seen by one nine-year-old in June 1994:

Top Rank: American blueberries and fresh raspberries.
Second Rank: Fresh strawberries and kiwi fruit.
Third Rank: Fresh peaches and melon.
Bottom Rank: Canned, mixed fruit ("fruit cocktail").

The cake-rating system is constantly changing as new types of fruit are introduced to the Hong Kong market. Not surprisingly, children usually learn about these consumer innovations long before their parents. McDonald's has formed an alliance with a local bakery chain to provide party cakes that reflect current fashions, notably in ranks two and three as outlined above. The top category is seen only at celebrations in Hong Kong's fanciest hotels, which compete among themselves to create new versions of expensively adorned cakes for wealthy clients. Such parties are, of course, private, but word soon filters out and within days children all over Hong Kong become aware (to cite a 1994 example) that raspberries are "in" and strawberries are "out"—even though most of my young informants had never actually seen a raspberry.

McDonald's as a Youth Center

Weekends may be devoted to family dining and birthday parties for younger children, but on weekday afternoons, from 3:00 to 6:00 P.M., McDonald's restaurants are packed with teenagers stopping for a snack on their way home from school. In many outlets 80 percent of the late afternoon clientele appear in school uniforms, turning the restaurants into a sea of white frocks, light blue shirts, and dark trousers. The students, aged between 10 and 17, stake out tables and buy snacks that are shared in groups. The noise level at this time of day is deafening; students shout to friends and dart from table to table. Few adults, other than restaurant staff, are in evidence. It is obvious that McDonald's is treated as an informal youth center, a recreational extension of school where students can unwind after long hours of study.

Hong Kong schools place heavy demands on their students and enforce strict discipline on the premises. The interlude at McDonald's, by contrast, is not monitored by teachers or parents. McDonald's staff keep a sharp watch for possible fights or disruptions, but trouble of this nature rarely breaks out in fast food restaurants. Managers know by sight most of the gang members in their neighborhood and sometimes delegate a (large) male employee to shadow potential troublemakers—standing uncomfortably close to them, watching every move. Partly as a consequence McDonald's is commonly regarded as a safe haven where hard-working students can unwind without fear of crossing the Triads. The image of safety is reinforced by a ban on smoking (since 1991) and the absence of alcohol. Youths more inclined toward drinking, smoking, and gambling frequent traditional-style eateries (teahouses, noodle shops) and rarely appear at McDonald's in groups, although they might steal in by themselves to eat quickly or purchase a take-out meal. It is the students, with their book bags and computers, who have claimed McDonald's as their own.

In contrast to their counterparts in the United States, where fast food chains have devised ways to discourage lingering, McDonald's in Hong Kong does not set a limit on table time. When I asked the managers of several Hong Kong outlets how they coped with so many young people chatting at tables that might otherwise be occupied by paying customers, they all replied that the students were "welcome." The obvious strategy is to turn a potential liability into an asset: "Students create a good atmosphere which is good for our business," said one manager as he watched an army of teenagers—dressed in identical school uniforms—surge into his restaurant. Large numbers of students also use McDonald's as a place to do homework and prepare for exams, often in groups. Study space of any kind, public or private, is hard to find in overcrowded Hong Kong. During the 1970s and 1980s, the situation was so desperate that dozens of students would sometimes occupy the departure hall of Hong Kong's international airport, ignoring the loudspeakers and the general chaos for a few hours of study.

For Hong Kong's hard-pressed youth, McDonald's represents something more than a simple snack center: it is commercial space temporarily transformed into private space. Home is likely to be a tiny apartment in a thirty-story public housing block, with shared bedrooms and minimal privacy. Interviews with teenagers revealed that McDonald's is perceived as a place that offers more space, in the literal sense of distance between tables, than any other public eatery in Hong Kong (save for the more expensive restaurants). Competing chains are indeed more crowded, with barely enough room to squeeze between tables. When young people enter their local McDonald's after school, many feel that they have come "home." This is carried to an extreme by a small number of teenagers, mostly girls, who try to avoid conflict with parents or siblings by staying in the restaurants until closing time (usually 10:00 P.M.). Treating McDonald's as a substitute home is common enough in Hong Kong for social workers to treat it as a recognizable syndrome, signaling trouble in the family.[49]

Conclusions: Whose Culture Is It?

In concluding this chapter, I would like to return to the questions raised in my opening remarks: In what sense, if any, is McDonald's involved in these cultural transformations (the creation of a child-centered consumer culture, for instance)? Has the company helped to create these trends, or merely followed the market? Is this an example of American-inspired, transnational culture crowding out indigenous cultures? For the children who flock to weekend birthday parties, McDonald's restaurants are associated with fun, familiarity, and friendship. McDonald's is not perceived as an exotic or alien institution: the children of Hong Kong have made it their own. And this, of course, is precisely the point that many critics would seize upon triumphantly, arguing that the Hong Kong case illustrates the power, the hegemony, of cultural imperialism—convincing consumers that the transnational *is* the local.

Personally, I do not believe that these issues are so easily resolved. The deeper I dig into the lives of consumers themselves, in Hong Kong and elsewhere, the more complex the picture becomes. Having watched the processes of culture change unfold for nearly thirty years, it is apparent to me that the ordinary people of Hong Kong have most assuredly *not* been stripped of their cultural heritage, nor have they become the uncomprehending dupes of transnational corporations. Younger people—including many of the grandchildren of my former neighbors in the New Territories—are avid consumers of transnational culture in all of its most obvious manifestations: music, fashion, television, and cuisine. At the same time, however, Hong Kong has itself become a major center for the *production* of transnational culture, not just a sinkhole for its *consumption*. Witness, for example, the expansion of Hong Kong popular culture into China, Southeast Asia, and beyond: "Cantopop" music is heard on radio stations in North China, Vietnam, and Japan; the Hong Kong fashion industry influences clothing styles in Los Angeles, Bangkok, and Kuala Lumpur; and, perhaps most significant of all, Hong Kong is emerging as a center for the production and dissemination of satellite television programs throughout East, Southeast, and South Asia.[50]

A lifestyle is emerging in Hong Kong that can best be described as postmodern, postnationalist, and flamboyantly transnational. The wholesale acceptance and appropriation of Big Macs, Ronald McDonald, and birthday parties are small, but significant aspects of this redefinition of Chinese cultural identity. In closing, therefore, it seems appropriate to pose an entirely new set of questions: Where does the transnational end and the local begin? Whose culture is it, anyway? In places like Hong Kong the postcolonial periphery is fast becoming the metropolitan center, where local people are consuming and simultaneously producing new cultural systems.

Meanwhile, Hong Kong has become a Special Administrative Region under the sovereignty of the People's Republic of China. In the years leading up to the 1997 transition, Hong

Kong government officials had to deal with an increasing number of immigrants from China, many of whom had little experience of life in an ultramodern city. In 1995 the Department of Education started an "induction" program to acquaint mainland children with Hong Kong's public amenities before they entered local schools. The program included visits to a sports center, a library, a shopping mall, a subway station, and—the last stop—a McDonald's restaurant, where the new immigrants enjoyed Big Macs, fries, and Cokes at government expense.[51]

McDonald's has become such a routine feature of Hong Kong's urban environment that most young people cannot imagine life without it. In 1995 local newspapers followed the plight of a seven-year-old who had grown up in Hong Kong but, because of immigration irregularities, had been deported to live with relatives in China. Months later, when he was allowed back across the border to rejoin parents and siblings in Hong Kong, reporters asked him what he most wanted to do. Without hesitation he replied: "Take me to McDonald's."[52]

CHAPTER 3

McDonald's in Taipei: Hamburgers, Betel Nuts, and National Identity

David Y. H. Wu

McDonald's reception in Taiwan tells us a great deal about the Taiwanese people and their attempts to forge new cultural identities in a world characterized by globalism and postindustrial realignments. In Taiwan today, as in contemporary South Korea, eating is a political act. Let us begin with one person's journey—my own—through the political terrain of food.[1]

A Brief Culinary and Cultural History

I was raised in Taiwan as a native speaker of Taiwanese (Min-nan or southern Fujian dialect) and, like most of my generation, was educated in Mandarin, the "national language" (*guoyu*) of China. I left the island for graduate studies in the United States in 1966 and did not return to Taiwan for ten years. On my first visit home, in the mid-1970s, Taipei appeared little changed. At this point I began making annual visits, and I noticed gradual changes. Then suddenly, in the mid-1980s, the rate of change accelerated, becoming more dramatic and, for me, more alienating. These changes were reflected most visibly in food and foodways. Perhaps as a returning "native son" who had made a life for himself in the diaspora, I considered food more important than other aspects of Taiwanese culture. For me food has always been equated with "home."

One of the most obvious changes was the radical transformation of Taipei's always thriving restaurant trade. During the 1960s and 1970s, the city was renowned as the repository of the great cuisines of mainland China; I still recall, with a pleasure difficult to describe, the culinary wonders of the Peking, Shandong, Zhejiang, Jiangsu, Hunan, Sichuan, and Yunnan restaurants (to mention only the most obvious), with one or more of them, it seemed, on nearly every street corner. Established by refugees from the Chinese mainland in the 1950s, these restaurants were known for their "authentic" regional Chinese cuisines. Their chefs made every effort to maintain the taste and special characteristics of the foods of their native provinces.

By the mid-1980s most of these mainland-style restaurants had either disappeared or were hidden away in obscure neighborhoods. Compared to the newer "Taiwanese-style" and Western establishments, the mainlander restaurants seemed small, dirty, run-down, and old-fashioned in both décor and presentation. Fans of "authentic" Chinese cuisines also began to complain that the food did not taste as good as it did in the 1960s.

What happened? To understand the virtual disappearance of mainlander cuisine, one needs to know more about recent Taiwanese history and its close involvement with the Cold War.

Although the majority of Taiwanese are descendants of early Chinese migrants from Fujian (and some are Hakka people from both Fujian and Guangdong provinces), they had undergone considerable acculturation in Japanese ways during the period of Japanese colonial rule (1895–1945). The newcomers from China who arrived after World War Two were mostly civil servants, merchants, and military personnel. Using local (Min-nan) terms, the Taiwanese called them *ah-soã*, people from the distant mountains in China, or later, *goa-seng-ah*, "outcomers" from other provinces. Both these terms were later considered derogatory. More polite terms are *waishengren*, a Mandarin term meaning "people from outside the province," as distinct from *benshengren*, "people of the province of Taiwan." Mainlanders are also referred to (in Mandarin) as *daluren*, "people from the mainland."

It is therefore not surprising to hear new terms that have emerged in recent years to distinguish local cuisine, such as *taigoan-liauli* ("Taiwan cuisine"). *Liauli*, for "cooking," or "cuisine," is of Japanese derivation, whereas mainlander cuisine is referred to as *goa-seng-cai* (*cai* is the Mandarin term for cooked dishes or cuisine). By the 1970s two types of food had become popular metaphors in Min-nan for these two ethnic groups: *han-chu*, or sweet potato, refers to Taiwanese, and *o-ah*, or taro, represents mainlanders. The origins of these ethnic classifiers lie in the army, where the cheap and nutritious sweet potato represented Taiwanese recruits, while the expensive, tasteless, and (in folk belief) less nutritious taro stood for the drill sergeants—nearly all of whom were mainlanders.

Discontent with the corrupt Kuomintang (KMT or Nationalist party) officials who ruled Taiwan led to island-wide protests and demands for local autonomy on February 28, 1947. A few weeks later, with the aid of reinforcements from the mainland, Nationalist military forces massacred thousands of Taiwanese leaders and intellectuals. In 1949 the Nationalists were defeated on the Chinese mainland by Communist armies; thousands more Nationalist soldiers and their supporters followed their leader, Chiang Kai-shek, to Taiwan—determined to use it as a base from which to recover the mainland. A new "temporary" capital of the Republic of China was set up in Taipei, in opposition to Mao Zedong's Communist capital in Beijing. From 1949 to the late 1980s, the Nationalist government on Taiwan imprisoned anyone suspected of Communist sympathies (broadly defined as anti-KMT) or promoting Taiwan's independence from mainlander rule. Well into the 1980s, no public mention or media coverage of ethnic conflict on Taiwan was allowed. Cultural differences—in language, customs, and lifestyles—deepened the ethnic division between the mainlanders and the Taiwanese.

The Korean War and Cold War politics reinforced authoritarian KMT rule on Taiwan, which was implicitly supported by the United States. American military bases proliferated on Taiwan, and in the 1950s American popular culture, including music, food, and fashion, began to exert a strong influence on Taiwan's youth. The ruling KMT government maintained the myth that the mainlanders' regime in Taipei was the true government, as well as the cultural representative, of all China until 1979, when the United States extended full diplomatic recognition to the People's Republic of China. Dozens of other nations quickly followed suit, thereby diplomatically isolating the island nation. Following these events, even the most outspoken supporters of the KMT—notably mainlanders—began to rethink the meaning of being "Chinese" in Taiwan. Economic growth in the 1970s created an affluent middle class of local-born Taiwanese who would no longer tolerate repressive

KMT policies and preferential treatment for mainlanders in public affairs. By the mid-1980s, many Taiwanese took to the streets in protest and demanded wider participation in government, as well as the autonomy of Taiwan as a nation. With the March 1996 election of native Taiwanese Lee Teng-hui as President of the Republic of China, a new era of local politics and relations with the mainland has emerged. The expression of Taiwanese identity in the 1990s has affected every aspect of popular culture, including food and cuisine. Noteworthy, too, is the continuing influence of Japanese commerce in Taiwan, reviving a popular penchant for things Japanese, including food and fashion. For elderly Taiwanese (President Lee included), Japanese culture has become enmeshed in the newly emerging representation of Taiwanese cultural identity.[2] Native Taiwanese are becoming increasingly reluctant to identify themselves as "Chinese," especially in the wake of the Communists' missile tests and belligerent feints during the 1996 election.

These events set the stage for contemporary developments in popular culture on Taiwan. As in many cosmopolitan centers around the world, Taipei's streets are now clogged with people and traffic, while high-rise buildings and huge department stores have transformed the physical landscape. International clothing styles have become popular, and so have international foods and eateries. One of these, of course, is McDonald's.

McDonald's and the Revival of Taiwanese Localism

In 1984 the first McDonald's restaurant opened in east Taipei, on a street that sported hundreds of nouvelle shops, including supermarkets, clothing boutiques, and restaurant chains serving Korean barbecue, Hong Kong–style seafood, Italian pasta, and Japanese-style coffee. These commercial outlets constituted the leading edge of a global, cosmopolitan culture that entered Taipei in the wake of the economic boom of the 1970s.

The foreign food invasion was an obvious feature of Taipei's dramatic physical transformation, yet it did not signal the elimination or even the decline of native Taiwanese cuisine. In fact, a countercurrent was evident: the revival of the island's indigenous food traditions. On one of our trips home in the mid-1980s, my wife and I were presented with a visual metaphor for the two cultural traditions that coexist in contemporary Taiwan. On our way from the Chiang Kai-shek International Airport to Taipei (a journey that usually takes more than an hour), the driver made a detour to avoid the traffic jams on the motorway. We drove down a dusty road lined with used-car lots, junkyards, and cargo-storage hangars. Passing a truck depot near the motorway on-ramp, we saw dozens of colorful kiosks sporting neon signs that advertised betel nuts for sale. At the time I was struck by the seeming incongruity of this image: betel nuts, a traditional stimulant, for sale along a modern superhighway? It was not until later that I made a connection between these betel-nut stalls and the appearance of McDonald's. In my mind, they represent the two poles of ethnic consciousness and cultural identity in Taiwan today.

Whereas McDonald's is a reflection of the globalization process that has transformed Taiwan into a modern industrial power and a center of world business, betel-nut chewing is associated with the symbolic revival of a "Taiwanese" rural lifestyle among people who are searching for ways to construct a new national identity. Eating hamburgers is perceived as cosmopolitan, a way to connect with the world beyond Taiwan, while the people (mostly men) who chew betel nuts wish to connect with their Taiwanese roots and think of themselves as down-to-earth Taiwanese natives. The politics of Chinese nationalism (mainlander versus Taiwanese) is also reflected in this culinary confrontation.

Betel Nuts

The origin of betel-nut chewing in Taiwan has been little studied. We know that it was a popular habit among the indigenous peoples of Southeast Asia. Archaeologists have found evidence of betel-nut chewing in Taiwan as early as 4,000–4,500 years ago, when they uncovered neolithic sites on the southern tip of Taiwan with human remains showing tooth damage caused by chewing the nuts.[3] Betel nuts were also popular among Taiwan's aboriginal peoples, as evidenced by records of early contact with Han immigrants and European explorers. The Chinese in Fujian and Guangdong also have a long history of betel-nut chewing, and even in Hong Kong as late as the 1940s, betel nuts were served along with cigarettes at banquets. Similarly in Taiwan prior to the influx of mainland refugees in the late 1940s, chewing betel nuts was as popular as smoking tobacco. As a child I often saw my parents bring a small gift pack of betel nuts for their elders when calling on friends or relatives in the countryside.

Betel-nut trees are a kind of palm, looking much like the coconut palm but not as tall. The nuts are sold by the dozen or half dozen in their natural state (like fresh individual olives) or prepared ready for consumption at nut stalls. In northern Taiwan, the sellers cut an incision in the nut, insert some red-tinted limestone paste, and squeeze in a small piece of the stem from the flower of the *lou hiu*, an ivy plant. In southern Taiwan the nuts are prepared without the incision; a whole fresh nut is wrapped in a *lou hiu* leaf, like a wonton. Limestone paste is spread on the leaf before wrapping the nut. The leaf and flower stem add a strong minty and peppery flavor; the limestone increases the pungency of the nuts. This combination, as I discovered for myself, causes a burning sensation in the mouth, similar to what happens when eating hot chili peppers, and an immediate sense of dizziness. With regular usage, the sensation changes (I am told) to one of mild intoxication and relaxation.

Chewing nuts produces a mouthful of red-stained saliva, requiring the chewer to frequently spit blood-colored juice on the floor, on streets, or on walls. Educated city people, especially urban mainlanders, find this habit offensive in the extreme. During the first decades of contact between the elite mainlanders and local Taiwanese, betel-nut chewers were perceived as country bumpkins. By the 1960s only farmers, the elderly, and the southern aboriginal peoples pursued the habit, and in Taipei the sale of nuts was confined to small sections in the southwest and northwest parts of the city, where ethnic Taiwanese residents were concentrated. By the 1970s, few urbanites were seen chewing betel nuts in public.

A revival of the habit and a sudden surge of stalls selling betel nuts in Taiwan's major cities corresponds, significantly, to a period of political liberalization that began in the late 1980s. At that time the Taiwanese and grass-roots-based Democratic Progressive Party was legalized and began to win elections for county mayors and council members. The KMT relaxed its monopoly on media production and publication, and the search for historical facts about the oppression and massacre of

Taiwanese in 1947 flourished. The emergence of a local identity coincided with growing interest in things Taiwanese: an inward search, especially among the young, for the history, artifacts, language, and food habits of Taiwan.

In contemporary Taiwan betel-nut chewing has become a new status symbol, a sign of heightened ethnic awareness. The price of chewing has risen along with its prestige. In the summer of 1994, one vendor quoted NT$100 (about US$4) for 15 nuts, four to five times the average cost a decade earlier. The larger nuts were more expensive, double the price just quoted. One informant admitted that chewing nuts can be a very expensive habit, much more costly than smoking foreign cigarettes. During the months of March and April, when the nuts are in short supply because the trees are in flower, a single nut could be sold for NT$20–$25 (US$.80 or more).

One university-educated businessman who ran a wholesale business in Taipei explained to me how he picked up the habit of betel-nut chewing: "When factory workers from southern Taiwan came to deliver goods to me, I had to buy nuts and share with them, in the same way we offer cigarettes to visitors. In Taipei, nut vendors or nut shops are found on every street corner, and adolescents are frequently caught chewing betel nuts in Taipei schools." Indeed, a government publication reported in 1994 that the per capita rate of consumption was 800 nuts per year.[4] In the village where I did my first fieldwork nearly thirty years ago, housing and consumption patterns show clear evidence of the unprecedented wealth generated by the recent expansion of local betel-nut plantings. One study noted that the land area devoted to betel nuts on Taiwan now exceeded that of rice paddies.[5] While journalists puzzle over the increased popularity of betel nuts, citing medical evidence for the nuts' ability to raise body heat during winter, few observers related the fad to psychological concerns and the pursuit of newfound ethnic identities. The betel-nut craze also corresponds to a boom in Taiwan's "native" cuisine. By the mid-1980s the most popular (and expensive) restaurants in Taipei promoted themselves as purveyors of "authentic, original, Taiwan farm food" (to quote one ad). Foods described in Taiwanese or Hakka dialect—nearly impossible for a Mandarin-speaker to decipher—began to appear on menus. New dishes were invented to embrace foods associated with Taiwan's pristine (i.e., pre-Chinese) diet, notably the sweet potato. Mainlanders traditionally scorned tuberous foods and embraced rice as the foundation of Chinese haute cuisine. It is no coincidence that Taiwan separatists have adopted the sweet potato as a symbol of their movement. The outline of the sweet potato (drawn to resemble a relief map of Taiwan) appears today on flags, posters, and products of all kinds.

During the past twenty years the politics of identity have affected every aspect of Taiwan's popular culture, including food and foodways. The culinary scene became even more complex in 1984, when McDonald's—the first of what would become a steady stream of transnational food chains—was granted permission to open in Taiwan. To many consumers, McDonald's represented something new and different, a third option beyond the realm of the Chinese-versus-Taiwanese competition.

McDonald's in Taiwan: The First Decade

Many Taipei residents were already familiar with hamburgers when McDonald's opened its first outlet in 1984. I remember vividly my first hamburger, eaten in a Western-style restaurant located in the Taipei theater district. The year was

1964, and the Chinese menu described what I was eating as a "German Hamburg minced beef cake"; I also had an "ice-cream soda" (a scoop of ice cream in a glass of soda water).

During the early 1980s I noticed that hamburgers served as a meal in themselves were available in tourist hotels, and hamburger-style dishes were sold by indigenous fast food outlets. However, hamburgers (*han bao* or *han bao bao*, literally meaning Hamburg or Hamburg meat dumpling) did not become a household term in Taipei until the arrival of McDonald's. The company first called itself Mai-Dang-Lao in Chinese, a phonetic rendering that captured the English name but confused many early consumers. The three Chinese characters literally mean "wheat-must-labor." In Hong Kong and some other places, the name Mai-Dang-Nu, or "wheat-become-slaves," was also found. Later the Chinese name was standardized as Mai-Dang-Lao, now used in Hong Kong, Beijing, and Chinese communities in the United States.

The McDonald's company had targeted the Taiwan market in 1980, when government restrictions still prohibited foreign enterprises from entering the food or food-processing business.[6] According to company representatives, three factors contributed to McDonald's decision to open restaurants in Taiwan. First, there was still a U.S. military base in Taipei and a sizable American community. Second, there was an increasingly large Taiwanese population who had firsthand experience of the United States. Many Taiwanese had worked or studied in the States and had returned with a family. Third, there was an increasing number of upper-middle-class children with cross-cultural exposure and plenty of spending money. This group of youngsters typically had at least one parent who had been educated in the United States. In addition, the McDonald's survey noted the growth of a Taiwanese middle class who had been exposed to international cultures.

As noted above, McDonald's was the first foreign food enterprise allowed in Taiwan. This was a signal achievement, recognized as such by the local business community. The company was chosen for this honor in part because of its record of high standards in hygiene and production. David Sun served as McDonald's local partner during the first decade of operation. In 1994 Bill Rose, an American with international experience, took over as Chairman of McDonald's Taiwan.

There were 131 McDonald's restaurants in Taiwan by June 30, 1996.[7] In an interview, Chairman Rose predicted that by the end of the century, Taiwan would have up to 500 outlets if the business kept pace with demand. A Taiwanese commercial newspaper quoted the Managing Director of McDonald's as stating that the company's turnover was NT$2 billion (approximately US$80 million) during the first half of 1994. By September 1994, turnover had exceeded US$110 million. Rose maintained that, "In terms of real dollars, among worldwide McDonald's organizations, Taiwan had the highest growth in 1994."[8]

Local newspapers also reported that in late 1994, McDonald's was negotiating with the Council for Economic Construction to make Taiwan the company's operating headquarters for the entire Asian-Pacific region (which includes Hong Kong, China, Japan, Korea, the Philippines, Malaysia, Thailand, New Zealand, and Australia).[9] In conjunction with this move, McDonald's proposed to increase its capital investment in Taiwan by NT$780 million (US$31 million), causing a sensation in the local business community. Rose was quoted as saying that 75 percent of this new capital would be used to expand and renovate existing restaurants; commentators speculated that this meant McDonald's might become more deeply involved in Taiwan's real estate market.[10]

McDonald's phenomenal success has attracted a great deal of media attention in Taiwan, not all of it favorable. During the 1970s, radical writers and intellectuals had accused the government of exploiting the cheap labor market in Taiwan and conspiring with foreigners, especially Americans and Japanese, to oppress its own people. In the 1980s McDonald's was often equated with the "invasion" of American culture and values. By the 1990s, the growth of indigenous business giants appears to have overshadowed the new foreign companies and the public outlook has changed accordingly. The anti-American sentiments that affect McDonald's operations in Korea are less apparent in Taiwan of the mid-1990s. Nor is McDonald's an unambiguous symbol of cultural imperialism.

On April 29, 1992, bombs exploded in McDonald's restaurants in Taipei and Kaohsiung, killing a policeman and injuring two employees. All 57 outlets then open in Taiwan were closed for the day. The incidents garnered worldwide attention, arousing conjectures that the McDonald's bombings reflected Third World resentment over American domination of the business world.[11] It later became clear, however, that the bombings were the work of extortionists and local racketeers. Such incidents had occurred before, directed at Taiwanese businesses and wealthy families. McDonald's no doubt became a target after media reports publicized the "amazing story" of how in that year McDonald's in Taiwan had become one of the most profitable centers of McDonald's worldwide business. In a sense, therefore, the bombing shows that McDonald's is now treated like any other business in Taiwan, more a target of opportunity than a symbol of oppression.

McDonald's and Taiwan's Youth Culture

McDonald's restaurants have become the favorite hangout for primary- and junior-high-school students, who gather there every day between three and six in the afternoon. Many do their homework while eating and drinking in groups, sharing tables. McDonald's is perceived as an acceptable recreation center for "good" students from "respectable" schools, unlike their analogues of the 1950s or 1960s—the "tough" students with bad school records who congregated at juice bars or billiards parlors. With its reputation as an acceptable and decent place for customers who like to read and write, McDonald's has no incentive to discourage lingering students, even though they may buy little but spend long hours in the restaurant. McDonald's management maintains an inviting environment that is cool in the summer, warm in the winter, clean, comfortable, and soothing (with quiet music).

The company has also helped change attitudes toward work and employment among Taiwanese young people. Prior to the 1980s, a young Taiwanese with a high-school education would not consider taking a poorly paid, low-prestige job in a restaurant. McDonald's achieved the unimaginable, establishing itself as an acceptable employer of high-school and university students. For young people McDonald's rapidly became synonymous with fun, modernity, and prestige. The Western work environment was an added incentive, imparting the idea that diligence leads to international success. The standard company policy of training inexperienced workers and promoting young people to managerial positions was also attractive to prospective employees during the 1980s. Be the mid-1990s, however, the comparatively low wages paid for what became known as hard work began to dampen the enthusiasm of many young people and reduced McDonald's career appeal. These reactions were not unique to the fast food industry; Taiwan is facing a severe labor shortage and soaring wage rates. Taiwan's population has become much more affluent since McDonald's opened, with a corresponding rise in expectations among potential employees.

Nonetheless, McDonald's and its competitors were largely responsible for changing traditional, wholly negative attitudes toward employment and career opportunities in Taiwan's service industries. McDonald's awarded scholarships to part-time employees who maintained good grades in school. The image of McDonald's as promoting "family, education, and environment" is still a key element in the company's marketing strategy. By mid-1994, more than 200 local managers had attended Hamburger University in the United States, where they were trained in everything from food production to marketing. Many of these managers were young people who had been promoted from within the company, a fact well known to other employees. Their experience in the United States put these managers on a fast track for future promotion. McDonald's further nurtures its image as a prestigious organization by holding hygiene workshops for managers at one of Taipei's most luxurious hotels.

The widespread employment of teenagers in the fast food industry has contributed to the spending power of this sector of the population—a radical change from earlier generations (such as my own), who were totally dependent on their parents for spending money. This income in turn is spent on clothing, entertainment, music, and—of course—food. Fast food restaurants have also helped to socialize a new generation of Taiwanese children and teenagers who have grown accustomed to dining out with friends, much as adults do. Children as young as seven or eight are adept at eating in restaurants, using napkins, and wielding knives and forks in the Western manner. One middle-aged man from a working-class background commented to me: "Fast food suits young people's taste. Nowadays when the entire family decides to go out to eat, we have problems deciding where to go. The older generation [meaning parents in their forties] wants Chinese food."

McDonald's as Sanctuary: Home Away from Home

In a study of McDonald's in the United States, the anthropologist Conrad Kottak describes how family members go through the rituals of ordering and eating food; it is clear from their actions that Americans feel comfortable and safe in McDonald's.[12] We can almost say that the Golden Arches offer the promise of security and safety—a kind of sanctuary, removed from the uncertainties of life outside. I must admit that I was surprised to find a similar set of attitudes prevailing in Taipei, where many consumers treat McDonald's as a home away from home. Furthermore, in many neighborhoods Taiwanese have transformed the essentially "foreign" setting of McDonald's into a place at once familiar and indigenous.

During the summer and autumn of 1994, my wife and I concentrated our field research on one McDonald's restaurant in a Taipei suburb. It has in recent years become a kind of community center for students, teachers, parents, and grandparents. This particular McDonald's is a place for people of all

ages to visit, eat, gossip, and otherwise pass the time. It also became clear to us that the restaurant offered a sanctuary from
family tension, a respite from loneliness, and relief from the
heat. This establishment has become "localized" in that it plays
a key role in the routines of everyday life for many people
who live in the neighborhood. The atmosphere here is very
different from that which prevailed in Taiwan's first McDonald's restaurant, which was located in an elegant district and
frequented primarily by yuppies, foreigners, and thrill-seeking
teenagers.

As the same customers frequent the same McDonald's outlet
day after day, they become acquainted with one another; they
not only exchange greetings, but sometimes tell one another
stories about themselves and their family life. The following
accounts will give readers the flavor of these encounters.

Grandma in Waiting

At a certain McDonald's restaurant in Taipei, a woman in
her seventies arrives every morning at 7:00 A.M., when the
doors open for the day. She travels by bus from Yonghe (an
hour's trip), rain or shine (*feng-yu wu-zu*), according to another
customer. She usually buys only a cup of tea or a cold drink,
yet she stays in the restaurant for the entire day. She does not
eat beef (a dietary restriction fostered by Buddhism) and brings
her own lunch box to the restaurant. She discreetly eats this
lunch during the slack late-morning hours, when the employees are not paying much attention to customers. (The Chinese
expression for this is *tou-tou chi*, eating like a thief.) At lunch
time, her grandson (a fifth-grader from the nearby school)
comes to meet her. The grandmother then buys food and
drinks for her grandson. After eating lunch, the boy returns to

school, but the grandmother remains in McDonald's until school is out at 3:30 P.M., when she walks her grandson to the bus station. (He lives in Neihu, in the opposite direction from her home in Yonghe.) She then proceeds home to Yonghe by herself.

One day in late June 1994, the grandson told her that she did not need to come again until autumn because the school term was ending the next day, and the long summer vacation was about to begin. The boy added: "Tomorrow, Daddy and Mommy will take us to the Philippines for a vacation." The woman asked why she had not been told, and the boy replied, "Mom asked Dad not to tell you." In early November 1994, during our second round of field investigations in this McDonald's restaurant, the same woman was there again, following— unchanged—her daily routine of waiting for her grandson.

Avoiding Mother-in-Law

A teacher at the school that figures in the previous anecdote was on bad terms with her mother-in-law. When classes ended each day, at 3:30 in the afternoon, she chose to sit in the nearby McDonald's rather than going directly home. She was accompanied by her two children, who were students in the same school. They usually stayed in the restaurant until 5:30 P.M., by which time she assumed that her husband would be home. "She would not arrive home one minute earlier than her husband. That shows how much she hates to be alone with her mother-in-law," another customer commented. The teacher controlled her own income and kept a special bank account separate from the joint family funds. The mother-in-law was in charge of household chores, including the cooking. Every school day afternoon the daughter-in-law sat in McDonald's, chatting with other customers while her two children snacked and played by themselves.

McDonald's as Temple Bazaar

When I first walked into the McDonald's restaurant discussed above, I could not believe how crowded it was. It was early afternoon on a weekday during the hot summer of 1994. Every seat was occupied; booths were packed with entire families, representing three generations in many cases. People moved in and out of the restaurant constantly, making the two glass doors resemble a merry-go-round. The lines in front of the counter never cleared. There were people walking in all directions; young children ran around, screaming loudly to show their excitement and pleasure. The noise level rivaled the old-fashioned teahouses I remembered from my younger days when I first visited Hong Kong. (Then, too, I thought the sound deafening.) This Taipei McDonald's had the same basic décor as a McDonald's in the United States, right down to the slogans painted on the wall (in English), but the customers were behaving quite differently.

On the following Saturday afternoon when I walked to this restaurant, I noticed a block away that something unusual was happening. A crowd had gathered, motor bikes were parked on the sidewalks nearby, and smoke was rising from a whole array of food vendors' carts clustered just outside the restaurant. Food hawkers sold sausages, roast squid, fishcakes, and traditional herbal drinks (*qingcaocha*) only inches from McDonald's glass windows. This particular restaurant was located on the ground floor of a five-story building, across the street from a primary school (with 6,500 students) and a city park. In front of McDonald's, along the elevated sidewalks, dozens of people stood chatting, eating, waiting, or just watching. The crowds, the constant flow of people, and the assembled vendors all helped to create, in my mind, the atmosphere of a temple festival or rural market. This festive atmosphere was the closest thing I had seen in modern Taipei to the "heat and noise" (Mandarin *renao*, Taiwanese *lauze*) of an old-fashioned temple bazaar.

Thus, it is not the food alone that draws people to McDonald's; rather it is the "action" unfolding in the surrounding neighborhood. Here people can count on seeing friends, hearing gossip, finding snacks (not just hamburgers), and making business contacts. In the past, Taiwanese temples were often flanked by snack stalls and food hawkers; this is still true in some parts of Taiwan, but in the major cities fast food outlets now play the role of social magnet. McDonald's is particularly important in this respect because local management is always careful to place the restaurants in central locations, fronting a plaza or adjoining a large school. It should not be surprising, therefore, that the Golden Arches has more symbolic meaning for many youngsters than does the local temple.

Space and Time: Life in McDonald's

Consumers in the Taipei McDonald's under investigation tend to spend much more time on the premises than do their counterparts in the United States or Hong Kong. As noted earlier, single individuals often treat McDonald's as a place to read, think, or simply kill time—often for over an hour at a sitting. I observed many older people who ordered a cup of tea and sat, quietly by themselves, for an entire morning. Business people frequently arrived with briefcases and used the restaurant for meetings lasting for over an hour. Young people treated McDonald's as a meeting place and a convenient setting for courtship. In no instance did I observe McDonald's staff trying to eject any of these customers; nor were efforts made to make lingerers feel uncomfortable. It is clear that from the local perspective, McDonald's is public space, much like a park or library. As long as customers do not disrupt business or disturb others, they are allowed to occupy seats and use facilities.

Young mothers with children came in for breakfast or a snack, and might leave their toddlers in the playroom at the back of the restaurant. On holidays and weekends, this space is used for birthday parties, with a woman employee acting as hostess for the group. Around lunchtime on weekdays, the restaurant was jammed with school children wearing their characteristic uniforms, arriving in groups of three or four, sometimes accompanied by a mother or grandmother. These youngsters chatted and ate like adults, with an air of sophistication and command that would not have been thinkable one generation ago.

McDonald's and School Lunch

With an estimated population of some five million, Taipei has room for a great variety of catering and restaurant businesses. During the early period of McDonald's operation, the company had to confront the local cultural notion that proper meals are based on rice. Working-class adults whom we interviewed reported a strong clash in culinary values emerging in their families, with their children favoring fast foods such as hamburgers and pizza while the older generation preferred rice-based meals when they ate out. "We don't feel full without rice, but these youngsters are used to *kuai-can* [fast food] that has no *fan* [rice]. These things are strange to our stomachs," observed one middle-aged worker.[13] Lunch boxes or *biandang* (borrowed from the Japanese *bentō* popular since before World War Two) are still popular and can be purchased from caterers or fast food restaurants in nearly every neighborhood in Taipei for only NT$30–40 (US$1.50). These lunches consist of rice in various forms, with condiments such as fish, vegetables, or bean curd. In Chinese-style fast food restaurants and sidewalk snack stalls, traditional dishes such as *lurofan* or *lobapng* (braised pork on rice) costs less than NT$30. At McDonald's, by contrast, the set meal cost around NT$90 in 1994 prices.[14] In spite of (or perhaps because of?) this price differential, many children opt for McDonald's hamburgers rather than lunch boxes when given the choice.

During the summer of 1994 we interviewed a teacher who works in the primary school mentioned earlier, near the McDonald's restaurant we were observing. Every morning students order lunch at their "credit club" (*fulishe*), which is managed by fellow students. They can choose either a lunch box (*biandang*) or a hamburger (*hanbao*) set lunch; after paying they receive an order card. At noon, the students turn in the cards to collect their lunches. The teacher reported: "Only five or six of the 40 students in my fifth grade class order their lunches this way. The rest bring their own lunch boxes from home. A few mothers deliver lunch to the school every day. In our class there is one girl who is an only child. Her mother, who is devoted to her, delivers a home-cooked lunch for her every day. Some of our kids refuse to eat the hamburgers ordered from the *fulishe* because they are not as tasty, or as prestigious as McDonald's. They demand that their mothers buy from McDonald's and deliver these hamburgers to school at lunch time. The kids think hamburgers ordered from McDonald's are better, and they come with a Coke and french fries. On Wednesdays and Saturdays, kids have only a half day of school. On those days many of them spend all their pocket money at the local McDonald's before going home."

A 1989 news article reporting on the early invasion of hamburgers into Taipei's primary schools blamed "lazy mothers" for the phenomenon.[15] The enormous expansion of primary schools in Taipei during the past decade has seen enrollments increasing from 2,000 to 6,000 students per school in some cases. Surprisingly, none of these schools have built cafeterias to serve students, as one would find in American schools of comparable size. Since the late 1940s, students have been required to bring their own lunch boxes or have a hot meal delivered (by mothers or servants) to school at lunch time. School kitchens usually provide steamers, which, for a fee, keep the boxes hot, especially during the winter. Unlike their counterparts in mainland China, Taiwan's school authorities do not allow students to go home for lunch, fearing the drain on children's energy and study time.

In 1987, the Taipei Municipal Bureau of Education initiated a free "nutritious lunch" project, subsidizing the cost of providing hot meals in school. Had it been implemented in all schools, the project would have covered nearly 300,000 primary school children; but only a handful of schools decided to participate. The burden of shopping for food, designing the menu, supervising the cooking, and serving thousands of children every day was designed to fall on the teachers, most of whom were unwilling to take on the extra work without overtime pay.

As noted earlier, many parents simply ordered a fast food lunch to be delivered to their children at school. This created mêlées and confusion at the school entrance, with hundreds of students struggling to get their hamburger or fried chicken lunches. A few private schools eventually decided to allow parents (or children) to order directly from McDonald's, Wendy's, and Lotteria (a Japanese fast food chain). The actual number of deliveries is not great, averaging approximately 200 lunches per school, accounting for fewer than 10 percent of the lunches eaten in most Taipei schools. According to Bill Rose, McDonald's began catering arrangements with 20 schools in 1994, with plans for expansion in the future. A school principal credited the fast food industry with promoting hygiene and etiquette. She said: "There is nothing wrong with encouraging students [to] eat fast food, especially hamburgers, at school. [Her school allows McDonald's lunch sets to be delivered to the school every day.] Every set lunch is neatly packaged in a box, and every food item is wrapped in a clean bag. Students become accustomed to using a napkin during meals. They learn hygienic behavior and proper etiquette by eating hamburgers. What is bad about fast food?"[16]

Conclusion: Globalization and Localization

The arrival of McDonald's in Taiwan set new standards for operation, competition, and management within the local catering industry. "From raw material, to processing, to distribution, we are upgrading the standards of the food industry in Taiwan. We set the standard, others follow," said Bill Rose. A tour of modern Taipei confirms his view; McDonald's is clearly the leader in the fast food sector, along with Hardee's, Wendy's, and Pizza Hut. But its unquestioned success does not mean that McDonald's has, in any real sense, replaced "traditional" cuisines in Taiwan. The competition the company has engendered may have had the ironic and unintended effect of helping to revitalize indigenous foodways.

Transnational food chains have placed local (and once ubiquitous) street vendors under intense competitive pressure; many food hawkers have disappeared. Meanwhile, local food companies have responded to the challenge by setting up fast food–style restaurants that serve fried rice, steamed dumplings, congee, spring rolls, and turnip cakes (a Taiwanese snack made of rice flour, once sold primarily by hawkers). By the early 1990s, restaurant chains were introducing Taiwanese-style dishes that were reputed to have medicinal effects, such as duck soup with ginger root. These "local" foods appeal to people who do not enjoy Western-style fast foods but do appreciate convenience, cleanliness, and speedy delivery.

One of the hallmarks of the worldwide McDonald's system is attention to sanitation and hygiene. In East Asia, as Watson notes in his Introduction to this volume, McDonald's is commonly regarded as having started a revolution in consumers' awareness of public sanitation. This certainly appears to have been the case during the first few years of the McDonald's franchise in Taiwan. The provision of clean toilets was much discussed in middle-class circles and soon became the general expectation in Taipei. Prior to McDonald's entry into the Taiwanese market, local restaurants did not consider it a high priority to provide customers with clean toilets. Standards in the mid-1990s have improved greatly in major urban areas; however, the "revolution" in consumer expectations has not yet affected smaller cities or towns. It is also clear, from my own observations, that the vigilance of McDonald's own staff may have slipped. Many toilets in Taipei outlets were far from clean (by any standard) during the summer of 1994.

By the mid-1990s McDonald's had become a routine feature of "ordinary" life among the growing number of upper-middle-class families that identify with the cosmopolitan culture emerging in urban Taiwan. An entire generation of young people have grown up eating hamburgers, fries, pizza, fried chicken, and hot dogs—together with Coke, Pepsi, 7-Up, and Sprite. To Taiwanese youth, these products are most assuredly "local."

Meanwhile, other forms of consumption that have no connection to transnational firms are also flourishing in Taiwan. Perhaps the best example is betel-nut chewing, which has if anything increased during the past decade. As noted earlier, a taste for betel nuts has come to be equated with Taiwaneseness—expressed in its most down-to-earth form. It is therefore ironic that the betel nut and the Big Mac have emerged as symbols of "local" culture for different, but not necessarily opposed, categories of consumers in Taiwan. The two symbols represent the need to be at once Taiwanese and cosmopolitan, to be of this place—the island of Taiwan—but also part of the world beyond. To outsiders (and to many insiders as well) the two modes of consumption—hyperlocal versus transnational—appear irreconcilable. But in today's Taiwan, they coexist and, to a surprising extent, reinforce each other. Both the betel nut and the Big Mac are expressions of Taiwan's pursuit of a national identity in a political environment that has never encouraged such concerns.[17]

Until the politics of identity cease to be an urgent matter for local people, food will never be just food in Taiwan. Meanwhile, the choices consumers make will continue to provide us with important clues to the competing symbols that constitute identity in Taiwan.

CHAPTER 4

McDonald's in Seoul: Food Choices, Identity, and Nationalism

Sangmee Bak

In this chapter I explore the relationship between food and national identity, taking McDonald's as a primary point of departure. In what ways do Koreans accept—and, more important, refuse to accept—American-style fast food as part of their culinary culture?[1]

Field research for this project was conducted in Seoul during the summer of 1994, a time when many Koreans were debating issues of food consumption and nationalism. From the outset, then, this was not simply a study of hamburgers. The research took me, of course, to McDonald's restaurants, but I also had to consider the impact of foreign foods on rural and urban communities, and the role of organizations such as the National Agricultural Cooperative Federation (NACF, or Nonghyŏp in Korean) in the public discourse on food. In the eyes of many Koreans, hamburgers, especially hamburgers identified with American-owned restaurants, stand in symbolic opposition to locally produced, Korean rice.

In Korea today, McDonald's remains immersed in public debates regarding dietary choice, protectionism, and national identity. These controversies are closely linked to a Korean dilemma: people wish to be, simultaneously, nationalistic and global. In recent years the Korean government has been negotiating the terms of its trade agreements with other countries, and the removal of an import ban on rice has been at the forefront of the confrontation between potential rice exporters (notably the United States) and local producers. The government has tried not to alienate the farming population, but has had a hard time justifying its ban on foreign rice now that Korea has become the twelfth-largest trading nation in the world.[2]

In 1992, when trade negotiations were under way, the Ministry of Agriculture, Forestry, and Fishing and NACF jointly produced a poster to promote the consumption of local agricultural produce. The slogan read "Healthy eating = Eating our Rice," and the poster depicted a large grain of rice trampling a greasy hamburger. American trade representatives complained that the poster was insulting and blamed the Korean government for blocking free trade.[3] As this incident indicates, rice and hamburgers are clearly understood symbols representing indigenous Korean food versus imported American food.

My concern is not to predict whether or not McDonald's will prove to be a successful business venture in Korea; I am interested in the historic and symbolic meanings Koreans associate with McDonald's. Most of my informants, business people and consumers alike, agreed that an ever-increasing number of people are eating American-brand fast foods, either because they wish to sample Western cuisine or because fast foods are convenient. As the domestic economy expands, more and more people will see McDonald's food as an affordable choice. Koreans' attitudes toward American fast food vary with their gender, economic condition, and political viewpoint.[4] There are also dramatic generational differences: it may be hard to convince a Korean child, whose favorite venue for birthday parties is McDonald's, that hamburgers are not part of her indigenous food culture.

The symbolic conflict between hamburgers and rice sheds light on contemporary society in Korea. As Arjun Appadurai has noted, in every society certain objects or commodities carry powerfully loaded social messages, much as cloth did in the context of Gandhi's resistance to British imperialism in pre-1947 India.[5] Foods, especially staple foods, often become intertwined with a group's identity, as Emiko Ohnuki-Tierney shows in her discussion of the central role of rice throughout Japanese history.[6] She argues that food is literally subsumed into the bodies of human beings and, given that it is shared with one's family, colleagues, or friends, that eating together unifies people. Consuming the staples that grow in one's native soil further reinforces the idea of oneness with fellow diners.

In his discussion of special commodities in particular cultural contexts, Appadurai argues that those items most saturated with social messages (e.g., cloth or rice) are "likely to be least responsive to crude shifts in supply or demand, but most responsive to political manipulation."[7] Despite careful presentation and planning, many Korean critics perceived McDonald's as the vanguard of encroaching American capitalism, the inevitable accompaniment to U.S. political and cultural influence. McDonald's found itself caught in the middle of a political debate that turned into a popular campaign against imported food. As rice symbolizes Korean indigenousness, so McDonald's hamburgers carry the burden of symbolizing Americana—regarded with deep ambivalence by many Koreans. In contrast to the situation in China, described by

Yunxiang Yan in Chapter 1, this direct link with American culture did not necessarily increase McDonald's popularity in Korea.

A Brief History of McDonald's in Korea

Even before McDonald's restaurants appeared in Korea, many Koreans recognized the brand name; McDonald's was frequently mentioned in the media as the quintessential giant American fast food chain. In the 1970s the United States headquarters of the McDonald's Corporation commissioned a market survey to investigate the prospects for expanding into Korea. To the company's disappointment, the survey found that Koreans were strongly anti-American, a reflection of the uneasy relationship between the two countries since the end of World War Two.[8]

By the 1980s, however, the McDonald's Corporation determined that the Korean business environment had changed. Cultural symbols associated with internationalization and globalism were rapidly gaining popularity during the preparation for the 1986 Asian Games and the 1988 Olympics, both held in Seoul. McDonald's took advantage of this opening, which came at a time when the overloaded market for fast food in the United States encouraged the company to expand internationally.

In 1986, a joint venture called McAnn was established between a Korean partner, Mr. Ann, and McDonald's International, headquartered in the United States.[9] In 1988, the first McDonald's restaurant opened in Apkuchŏng-dong, one of the most exclusive districts of Seoul, known for its cafes and boutiques, which are frequented by affluent, trendy members of the younger generation.[10] McDonald's occupied a newly opened two-story building, and was immediately identified by the local clientele as a modern, chic place to eat. The founding site still serves as the symbolic representation of McDonald's in Korean popular consciousness.

Soon after McAnn opened its seventh restaurant, Ann himself died. Wishing to boost the expansion rate of its Korean outlets, McDonald's International sought additional partners. ShinMc, another joint venture, was established in Seoul, followed by McKim, the third joint venture, in Pusan, Korea's second-largest city. In July 1994, ShinMc bought out the seven stores originally opened by McAnn, leaving only two partners in Korea.[11]

By July 1994, McDonald's had 26 restaurants in Korea and was planning to build five or six more by the end of the year. While the number of McDonald's restaurants has increased, the chain's rate of expansion in Korea has been much slower than in the other East Asian markets discussed in this book, and slower than that anticipated by the first Korean partner. Ann originally planned to open three restaurants in 1986 and 58 more by the end of 1990.[12]

Both the media and the general public have taken a keen interest in the fact that McDonald's involvement in the Korean market has been conducted with multiple business partners, which has not been the case in other East Asian countries. In Hong Kong and Taiwan, McDonald's International chose one entrepreneur and placed this person in charge of business in the entire country. Certain elements of the Korean mass media were very critical of local arrangements, accusing McDonald's of forcing its Korean partners to compete among themselves for a bigger share of business, resulting in their paying higher fees to the United States headquarters.[13] Since the issue of profits is especially sensitive for a multinational firm, this accusation created considerable negative publicity. Two examples of the newspaper headlines exemplify local coverage: "The tyranny of American fast food companies in the Korean market," and "McDonald's joint venture scheme."[14]

McDonald's as a "Local" Institution

In 1994 a marketing manager for ShinMc made a strong case to me that the local McDonald's was in fact a *Korean* business. He pointed out that McDonald's International held a 50 percent ownership stake in its Korean operations, while Korean citizens owned the other 50 percent.[15] That McDonald's is Korean is an interesting argument when one considers the company's ongoing efforts to represent its products as authentically American, and hence different from the hamburgers sold at local, supposedly less prestigious, restaurants. The marketing manager I interviewed also emphasized that business in Korea is conducted exclusively by Koreans. This is necessary, he said, because of the complex banking system in Korea and the need to negotiate with numerous government bureaucracies.

Without exception the employees I encountered during my 1994 research expressed positive feelings about their jobs and the restaurant company. As Korean citizens working for a multinational corporation, they certainly did not feel that they were helping foreigners siphon money out of Korean pockets, a common allegation of critics. Employees considered McDonald's a model company, one that donates money to local charitable causes and reinvests a substantial proportion of its profits in Korea. My informants argued that many native Korean firms would do well to emulate McDonald's system of efficient management and social responsibility. Women employees, in particular, expressed considerable satisfaction with the company's openness and relative lack of hierarchy, which in their view led to greater gender equality than is normally the case in Korean business circles.[16]

McDonald's and Its Rivals

In representing and differentiating itself in the Korean restaurant market, McDonald's has emphasized that it sells *the* authentic American hamburger. Since most Koreans have long believed that McDonald's does indeed make the "real" thing, competitors were forced to change their marketing strategies when the company began operation in Korea. Lotteria, a restaurant chain that opened in Korea prior to McDonald's, initially claimed that it sold authentic American hamburgers made from pure beef. There was some justification for this: until Lotteria opened in 1979, most local hamburgers were greasy patties made from meat of suspicious origin—as I recall vividly from my youth. To bolster its image of American authenticity, Lotteria's employees spoke basic English when transmitting orders among themselves. (Lotteria was owned by a Korean entrepreneur, who started the company in Japan; he was allowed to expand to Korea prior to other "foreign" food chains primarily because of his ethnic origin.) After the introduction of McDonald's and other American chains, the authenticity contest was largely conceded; Lotteria began to represent itself as a purveyor of delicious hamburgers, catering to specifically Korean tastes. The chain developed *pulgogi* burgers (Korean-style barbecued beef) and teriyaki burgers (Japanese-style marinated and grilled beef) which sold well. Meanwhile, Lotteria employees stopped speaking English among themselves and stopped talking about their "American" hamburgers.

Lotteria is currently expanding into China, where products from Japan or Korea appeal to those who want to participate in the new consumer-oriented culture.[17]

Another chain, Uncle Joe's Hamburger, invented the *kimchi* burger, which was popular among consumers who did not think a meal was complete without the traditional and ubiquitous condiment, made from spicy pickled cabbage. The owner, an American who has moved to Korea, found that many Korean adults expressed strong skepticism that hamburgers could be eaten as a meal and not a snack. But once he substituted *kimchi* (which is eaten only at regular mealtimes) for cucumber pickles, more people were willing to accept hamburgers as the basis of a full meal.[18] Although still a small chain, Uncle Joe's is considered an "enfant terrible" by its competitors, largely because of its readiness to adapt to Korean culinary preferences.[19]

Yet another hamburger chain, with the unambiguous name Americana, is in fact owned entirely by Koreans. It opened in 1980 as a spin-off of an American firm, JBS Big Boy Company, which provided technology and training.[20] This chain was initially successful; in 1989 it ranked second only to Lotteria in sales volume. However, in 1991, when the better known and perceivedly more prestigious American hamburger chains (notably McDonald's) were taking hold, locally produced hamburgers were no longer considered "real" American products and hence became less popular.[21] McDonald's thus began with a definite advantage in the authenticity battle. But as will be discussed below, the chain has paid a high price for becoming a symbol of American culture.

Creating a Market for McDonald's

To understand how McDonald's fits into the Korean culinary system, it is important to know what bread and meat—the two basic components of hamburgers—mean to Koreans. Since its introduction in the nineteenth century, bread has never been incorporated into the standard meal system; instead it is perceived as a snack food. The Korean term for snack is *kansik*, literally "in-between food." Meat, on the other hand, has always been a highly valued, desirable food, and it is eaten almost exclusively at mealtime. To attract a steady flow of customers who would make substantial purchases, McDonald's had to represent itself as a place where one ate a full meal, as opposed to a snack bar where people spend little money but stay for hours chatting. To the dismay of local management, most Koreans considered McDonald's restaurants to be snack bars.[22] Hamburgers were more readily categorized by their bread (*ppang*), than by their meat (*kogi*). To change this perception, the "value meal" was introduced: McDonald's offered a 10 percent discount on four combinations that included a burger, french fries, and a soft drink. The intention behind this campaign was to attract customers who would eat an entire set of foods and, in so doing, realize that hamburgers can form the basis of a filling meal.

At the company headquarters in Seoul, there was serious discussion regarding the proper Korean name for a "value meal."[23] The chain wanted to emphasize the concept of "meal," but the equivalent Korean term, *siksa*, was unsuitable because it is not ordinarily used in the sense that McDonald's managers had in mind. The more colloquial term *pap* was even less appropriate because it is used interchangeably for a meal and cooked rice. In the absence of an appropriate local term, they decided to use the English word "set." Most Koreans would recognize the English as referring to something complete in several parts.

McDonald's management concluded that there was no equivalent for the American idea of value in the Korean business context, where anything recognized as inexpensive is usually deemed inferior to its more costly counterparts. A high-level executive in McDonald's Seoul office told me that the chain hoped to educate Koreans about the concept of value, meaning high quality for low price, in the expectation that consumers would appreciate this aspect of McDonald's meals. In the meantime, the concept of value was translated as *alch'an*, which means something good packed inside a protective shell (such as a ripe pomegranate inside its tough skin, or a chestnut inside its hull). The "*alch'an* set menu" was successful and has helped the company redefine its restaurants as places to have a meal. According to the average transaction count (abbreviated as TC, registering every 1,000 sales) of the chain's restaurants, the set-meal sales rose from 400–500 out of every 1,000 transactions to 600–700 once the campaign was launched.[24]

When McDonald's enters a new market, the restaurants generally begin by offering standard menu items such as hamburgers, fries, and milk shakes. After several years, when local managers think their business is well established, new items are introduced to suit local tastes in order to boost sales.* In 1994, McDonald's in Korea was still selling the basic items, which did not include breakfast fare. Local managers were making their first plans to augment the menu with items designed to appeal to Korean tastes, such as melon-flavored milk shakes.

*Ed. Note: This strategy was followed for all the cases examined in this book; see Chapter 5 for a discussion of this process in Japan.

Prices of McDonald's food in Korea are relatively high when compared to those charged in other countries. In 1994, for instance, a Big Mac cost close to US$3. Each year when *The Economist* publishes its Big Mac index, the comparative prices are instantly quoted in every major newspaper in Korea.[25] Although the intent of *The Economist*'s survey is to compare the cost of living in various countries, using the price of the ubiquitous hamburger as an index, Koreans read the article in a very different way. Local headlines proclaim: "McDonald's Hamburgers Cost More Here!"

Negotiating Gender, Space, and Meanings of Fast Foods

The ratio of male to female customers in a Korean McDonald's is about 3:7.[26] Eating a hamburger in what is perceived primarily as a children's place is not appealing to most grown men. The food-ordering process at fast food restaurants, where people have to order and pay for the food before they sit down and eat it, makes some Korean men feel uncomfortable. In traditional restaurants, customers pay after the meal is eaten, which usually results in everyone's competing to pay for the whole table. Some men told me that they feel awkward and stingy paying for just their own food. Even before the introduction of fast food, women generally felt more comfortable about dividing up the check. Another reason women like McDonald's is that, like most fast food chains and unlike most conventional restaurants, it does not serve alcoholic beverages. An alcohol-free and child-friendly environment is perceived as an appropriate and safe place for women unaccompanied by male family members or friends. McDonald's hopes to increase the number of male customers while retaining its female clientele. Men who do enter the premises tend to buy a full set meal and spend less time in the restaurant; this makes them highly desirable customers. Given the high rent in urban Korea, and the fact that most McDonald's restaurants are located in central commercial districts, full profitability is only possible when restaurants are packed with paying customers who do not linger, thereby making possible a high turnover rate.

Korean consumers on the whole, however, treat "fast" food restaurants as leisure centers and tend to stay longer than do most Americans. According to a survey conducted at a New Jersey Burger King in 1978, the average customer sat down at the table for only 11 minutes.[27] According to my 1994 field observations at two separate McDonald's restaurants in Seoul, the average "sitting time" was 35 minutes. The total number of examples observed was 90: among these, 44 were groups of women (sometimes accompanied by their young children), 14 were groups of men, while 13 were mixed groups (nine of these 13 appeared to be dating couples). Families accounted for six examples, while eight women and five men ate alone. On average, groups of women stayed much longer (33 minutes) than did groups of men (20 minutes). Men eating alone and families with children purchased the largest amount of food per person; they left, on average, within 17–18 minutes. Dating couples stayed longest—46 minutes on average. When one considers that American McDonald's restaurants do a significant amount of business at their drive-through windows, an option that is not feasible at most Korean outlets, one can understand the management's concern for controlling eating time at the Seoul restaurants.

To alleviate the space problem McDonald's has introduced hostessing: women employees circulate to assist customers and put subtle pressure on people to leave when they have finished eating. People who do not buy food from the restaurant and use the space for other purposes are also made uncomfortable by hostesses, who among other ploys will seat strangers at the offenders' tables, thus maximizing use and making loiterers uneasy. Korean customers find it less awkward to be conducted to a seat by an employee than to ask a stranger for permission to share a table. Many customers feel uncomfortable lingering at a table if they are next to a stranger and will leave as soon as they are finished. In their desire for a speedy turnover, employees will go so far as to clean off the tables where customers are still seated. The degree of pressure depends on the neighborhood where the restaurant is located. In more affluent areas, where the traffic is relatively light, staff intrusion is less evident.

Young people (especially women college students and dating couples) often convert McDonald's restaurants into cafes where they chat over coffee or soft drinks. During my field investigations I observed many young women touching up their makeup, writing letters, reading books, and even holding reading-club meetings or study groups in McDonald's. The restaurants are a more economical choice than cafes or coffeehouses because they offer clean, comfortable, and air-conditioned spaces for US$1–2 per person, half or one-third what they would have to pay in a cafe. The courteous service, which is somewhat unusual by Korean standards for a moderately priced restaurant, is another reason why young people feel comfortable at McDonald's.

Holding birthday parties at McDonald's is currently one of the most popular and prestigious ways of entertaining children.[28] Moving birthday celebrations from the child's home to a public place has also changed the form of the parties, and children now expect to celebrate with their friends rather than family members, a break from accepted tradition. McDonald's provides party paraphernalia (such as paper crowns) and complimentary gifts that children take home in plastic bags. (In the summer of 1994, when the weather was unusually hot, the gifts were paper fans shaped and printed like Big Macs.) Without question, these gifts are very effective in making other children want to have their birthday parties at McDonald's. For managers who are trying to create a family atmosphere, the parties are a way to reach customer groups who represent future business. There is thus a constant negotiation between management and customers on the one hand, and between various groups of customers on the other, regarding the definition and use of restaurant space. McDonald's has tried hard to politely "educate" its consumers in the rules of *fast* food restaurants—not only is the service fast, but customers are expected to eat fast and leave fast, too.

Many customers I spoke with said that they were willing to pay the slightly higher prices at McDonald's instead of eating at a locally owned fast food restaurant because they preferred a clean, air-conditioned environment. For this reason, take-out is not an attractive option. Korean consumers have the clear idea that they are paying for *space*, and they wish to enjoy themselves in a pleasant environment. To alleviate the space problem, however, local management has promoted take-out options, featuring this style of consumption heavily in television commercials. Managers I spoke with agreed that it will take some time to convince the Korean public that take-out is a convenient and enjoyable way to eat McDonald's food.

Since most McDonald's restaurants in Korea are located in central commercial areas where transportation is convenient, the Golden Arches have become an easily recognizable landmark for meetings and rendezvous. There are usually many people standing in front of the bustling restaurants, waiting for friends or colleagues. The restaurant management accommodates these people by installing bulletin boards in the lobbies so customers can leave messages for one another on special memo paper, also provided by the management. Many people who use McDonald's restaurants as meeting places purchase only drinks, or buy nothing at all, going elsewhere as soon as they have met their friends. Those who decide to eat in the restaurant tend to wait for the other parties to arrive before purchasing anything. These local customs aggravate the problem of crowding, but the management seems to have accepted this as the price of their restaurants' popularity.

Another group of people who frequent the restaurants but do not purchase food are those who enter simply to use the rest rooms. Given the lack of public toilets in Korea, the relatively clean and convenient facilities provided by McDonald's encourage heavy traffic. Although the management does not explicitly discourage casual visitors from using their rest rooms, most restaurants display signs saying, "Please order before going upstairs" (where the toilets and most of the tables are usually located).

Consumption, Resistance, and Foreign Imports

During my interviews, many people seemed concerned that the Korean economy would be adversely affected if they patronized foreign-based restaurant chains. It is commonly believed that a preference for foreign goods is a sign of conspicuous consumption and vanity. For example, in an article on the government's plan to allow local companies to produce foreign brand-name merchandise under a license from the foreign company, to which they would pay royalties, one of the nation's two largest newspapers commented, "This change in policy might prove to be problematic considering our trade deficit, people's tendency to prefer foreign brands, and the trend of [over]consumption."[29] Ordinary Koreans are concerned about the percentage of profit going to foreign headquarters.

Newspaper and television journalists keep close track of multinational corporations, including fast food chains. Most of the coverage by the mass media has been negative. Price-gouging and profiteering, low nutritional and sanitary standards, and social irresponsibility are often cited as the main reasons to avoid foreign foods. One newspaper article stated, "Foreign franchise restaurants leave their lights on all night to draw attention to their restaurants despite the nationwide movement to save energy."[30] Another article maintained that, "Foreign fast foods are not hygienic, . . . they use bacon and ham that already are past their expiration dates."[31] Yet another newspaper article claimed that, "Fast food is full of fecal bacilli. . . . The Association of Housewives found as many as 100 million fecal bacilli in one gram of sandwich."[32]

American cultural imperialism—defined as the encroachment of cultural practices and values that reflect American political and economic power—is also frequently cited as a reason for Koreans to shun McDonald's restaurants. When McDonald's is mentioned in the mass media, it is usually referred to as "McDonald's, the largest American multinational restaurant chain."[33]

The Korean government has also been responsive to public concerns about imports. Transnational corporations have had to operate within the constraints of the "Fair Competition

Law," which is designed to prevent large businesses from taking advantage of smaller competitors.[34] The government can severely punish firms that are deemed to have violated fair trading practices, as defined by the general ethos of the business community in Korea. Local managers of McDonald's have found, for instance, that many of the standard promotional tools used in other countries (prizes, special sales) are not feasible in Korea, where such practices might be perceived as unfair competition—especially since small-scale, indigenous food purveyors do not routinely offer similar inducements. The mass media's close scrutiny of foreign fast food restaurants guarantees that government officials will watch every move McDonald's makes.

According to the Korean Fair Competition Law, companies cannot give away more than 1,000 Won (US$1.30) worth of gifts for purchases lower than 10,000 Won (US$13). For more expensive purchases, the gift's value cannot exceed 10 percent of the purchase price, or 50,000 Won (US$65), whichever is smaller. For sweepstakes gifts, the prize cannot exceed 10,000 Won for purchases costing less than 1,000 Won, or 50,000 Won for purchases of 1,000–100,000 Won.

In 1993 McDonald's restaurants in Korea gave out sweepstake tickets to their customers who bought the *alch'an* set menu (priced at 2,250–3,750 Won), with a grand prize of two tickets to Disneyland in California, clearly violating the local Fair Competition Law. Pizza Hut had a similar promotion that awarded winners personal computers.[35] American trade officials maintained that rigid enforcement of the Fair Competition Law was keeping American firms from expanding further into the Korean market, and asked the Korean government to amend the law.[36]

Management personnel I spoke with in Seoul were confident that McDonald's could overcome the inherent difficulties of operating in such a complex environment. They were convinced that their company's efficiency and capacity to deliver good food at reasonable prices would overcome the anti-American and anti-import sentiments that inhibit business; they expected customers to put aside political concerns and make purely economic, "rational" choices. Consumers are therefore courted as individuals, not as representatives of political factions or interest groups. Choosing McDonald's hamburgers over local foods, the management argued, should be taken as an economic decision on the part of an individual consumer rather than as symbolic behavior representing an overarching political ideology. Emphasizing McDonald's good value and convenience as a family restaurant is thus in line with the company's overall marketing strategy in Korea.

Another way to alleviate people's concerns about the "American" identity of McDonald's is to emphasize the Koreanness of the firm. In addition to highlighting the fact that Koreans own 50 percent of local operations, the management also makes it known that many ingredients—such as milk, ketchup, and hamburger buns—are supplied by Korean firms. These suppliers, in turn, sometimes make use of McDonald's reputation to enhance their own. Maeil Milk, a primary supplier to the chain, carries an ad on its milk cartons proclaiming, "Maeil Milk is of such high quality that it has met McDonald's strict standards." This ad supports McDonald's agenda of being portrayed in the Korean popular consciousness as a company that exemplifies cleanliness and pure, fresh food.

Rice Versus Hamburgers

The focal point of the debate regarding imported food and its relation to national identity is Korean rice and rice producers. An argument that seems to convince many Koreans of the need to protect domestic producers is that it is important to be self-sufficient in staple crops for national security reasons. Given that only half a century ago, Koreans experienced a devastating war during which they lacked the basic means of subsistence, this argument is an effective means of answering economists and business people who advocate the theory of comparative advantage in international trade. Koreans would be better off, according to proponents of open trade, if the country focused on developing high-tech industries while importing agricultural produce because Korea has a scarcity of land and an abundance of well-educated labor power. In national politics, rice farmers still constitute a significant voting bloc. Furthermore, many urbanites maintain close ties to relatives in rural areas, which means that urban and rural constituencies are not clearly divided. For many Koreans, the argument that every citizen should eat native produce to protect their compatriots in the countryside has considerable persuasive power—even though the price of Korean products may be higher. The general belief that Korean agricultural goods are superior in quality and nutritional value makes the argument even more convincing.

A slogan heard almost everywhere in Korea during the 1990s is: *Sint'oburi*, literally "body, earth, not, two." Translated more freely, this slogan means that human bodies and their native environments are so closely linked that people should eat what is produced locally in order to maintain cosmic harmony. Understandably, this rhetoric is promoted by the NACF, as well as by grass-roots environmental groups and housewives' associations, all of which oppose foreign food imports. According to the philosophy of *Sint'oburi*, eating American hamburgers made from imported beef destroys people's harmony with their environment in the most radical way, and through this process Korean identity is lost. Popular sympathy toward farmers and native rice is fostered by the Korean media, notably television documentaries dealing with agricultural issues. The intention behind these documentaries is clearly shown by their titles, such as: "American rice waiting for our doors to open,"³⁷ "Thailand and Australia, keeping their eyes on the Korean rice market!"³⁸ and "Our rice, our survival."³⁹ All these programs emphasize the seemingly limitless capacity to produce low-cost rice in foreign countries, and the threat this presents to Korean farmers. The programs stress the higher quality of native rice and the need for Koreans to eat what is produced in their own country, for both the physical health of consumers and the economic health of the nation.

The Korean mass media often frame the issue in terms of the survival of farmers, while downplaying the fact that Korean consumers would benefit from the lower price of imported rice. Despite this economic reality, urban industrial workers are often among the most active participants in anti-import campaigns, which are organized by farmers' associations and allied organizations.

Commensality and Individualism in Korea's Culinary Culture

In Korean, as in Chinese and Japanese, the term for "meal" is the same as the term for "cooked rice." Rice is definitely the most popular source of carbohydrates when compared to barley, corn, millet, and sweet potatoes. Traditionally there has also been a close association between eating rice and enjoying the good life. Korean folklore represents the affluent person as someone who lives in a tile-roofed house (shaped like a whale's back) while enjoying a steady diet of cooked rice and beef soup. For example, the story of Hŭngbu, one known to all Koreans, is about an extremely poor yet virtuous man whose children craved snow-white cooked rice (as opposed to low-grade brown rice) and meat broth.[40] Rice is thus more than a simple grain; it is imbued with symbolic meanings and is perceived as sacred by many Koreans. Women are instructed not to waste a single grain lest they anger the gods and ruin the household's luck.

Only in the 1980s did Koreans finally grow enough rice to meet the domestic demand without imports. In the 1970s the government implemented a number of aggressive policies to promote rice production, including a price support system as well as a research and development program. These policies proved successful, and by 1992 rice production, which had accounted for only 53.7 percent of the total grain output in 1965, had risen to 85.9 percent. As a result, rice farming has become almost synonymous with farming in general. Once Korea achieved self-sufficiency in rice production, the government changed its emphasis to producing tastier rice.[41]

Paralleling cultural patterns outlined in Ohnuki-Tierney's discussion of the Japanese diet in the next chapter, eating rice in Korea promotes commensality. People share rice that has been cooked in the same pot and usually share side dishes, except during special banquets. Sharing a residence is often called "eating rice from the same cooking pot." At McDonald's and other fast food restaurants, by contrast, customers pursue their own individualistic tastes. Although groups of people may eat together, they do not ordinarily share the food—except for french fries. In Korea, even when friends purchase separate packets of fries, they often pour the contents onto a tray and together eat from the resulting pile. This does not, however, create the same powerful sense of commensality as sharing a rice-based meal. One can eat alone in McDonald's and not feel strange; eating in isolation at a Korean-style restaurant, on the other hand, generates feelings of loneliness and self-pity. The dominant view of McDonald's food, according to my informants, is that it facilitates personal choice and promotes individuality, themes which appeal to the new generation (*sinsedae*), who regard uniqueness as an important quality.

In my view, one reason why McDonald's has not been more readily accepted by adult Koreans is that the style of food does not fit easily into the existing Korean food system. Hamburgers, in particular, have not found a "niche" in the preexisting hierarchy of food. Other foreign products, such as instant coffee, Spam, processed cheese, and Coca-Cola, have not presented a direct threat to the rice-based, "proper" Korean meal. Rather, these items have been subsumed into recognizable food categories. For instance Spam, which happens to be extremely popular in Korea,[42] is treated as a gift item during traditional holidays. It is often sliced and covered with an egg batter and fried, much like minced beef or pork in traditional cuisine. These Spam dishes are eaten with rice and other side dishes, thus fitting comfortably into traditional food categories. Hamburgers, by contrast, constitute an entirely new category. Spam has been thoroughly "localized" in Korea, whereas the Big Mac is still "foreign," not only as a trade-marked brand name but also as a category of food.

Perhaps as a consequence of recent economic growth and the rising consumption level, McDonald's hamburgers are not considered haute cuisine by most Korean consumers. This has made it difficult for the company to find a niche in the local market. On the one hand, managers realize that it is important to portray McDonald's as the "authentic" American hamburger restaurant; on the other, attempts are under way to become "local" and thereby fit into the class of ordinary purveyors of everyday food.

Conclusions

In this chapter I have outlined what might be called a series of negotiations and contestations regarding the meanings, demand for, and consumption of McDonald's hamburgers in Korea. Demand, as I have tried to show, is not a "natural" economic force, nor is it a constant and universal state.

All the parties examined in this chapter—Korean consumers, McDonald's managers and employees, farmers, media analysts, and Korean government officials—would no doubt agree with Sidney Mintz's point about food: Use implies meaning.[43] It is obvious that in Korea, the consumption of hamburgers communicates a variety of often contradictory messages. The farmers who promote the consumption of local produce argue that eating McDonald's hamburgers is tantamount to treason and the loss of Korean identity. Meanwhile, those who work for McDonald's convey the message that the consumption of hamburgers is a matter of rational choice, an ideologically neutral exercise based on personal tastes. Nonetheless, the current political environment in Korea encourages individuals to make consumption choices based on the perceived interest of Koreans as a group, rather than relying on personal preferences or economic self-interest.

The perceived seriousness of eating foreign-based foods is related to a general ambivalence toward achieving a globalized lifestyle and in the process losing one's identity as a Korean. In a study of British eating patterns, Mary Douglas notes that "whenever a people are aware of encroachment and danger, dietary rules controlling what goes into the body would serve as a vivid analogy of the corpus of their cultural categories at risk."[44] The fact that many children prefer foreign foods (pizza, hamburgers) to traditional dishes (*kimchi*, beef soup) is taken as a warning sign about the impending loss of Korean identity, since what is consumed is literally converted into the bodies of this next generation.

In addition to the essential role food plays in the formation of the body, consuming foreign items also poses a threat to the social body. In Korean society, sharing food promotes solidarity not only among the living, but also between the ancestors and their descendants. The symbolic eating of food that first has been offered in ancestor worship ceremonies (*ŭmbok*, or "partaking of luck") is a vivid example of how food connects various family members, both living and dead. The items used in these ceremonies must be familiar to the ancestors; their consumption, both spiritual and corporal, assures the continuity of Korean descent lines. The contestations regarding the consumption of foreign foods must be understood, therefore, in the context of social practices that involve far more than personal taste.

Korean consumers as a group and Koreans as individuals have been actively creating and redefining the transactional terms that condition acceptance of McDonald's hamburgers. Most customers I interviewed told me that their food choices do not simply reflect government guidelines or the agendas of interest groups that play on patriotic themes. Nor do they think that they are blindly influenced by the sophisticated marketing strategies of multinational restaurant chains. The young people who use the pleasant environment of McDonald's to socialize and study are fully aware that the management's intended use of this space is at odds with their own. Many customers even feel that they are taking advantage of the company by not spending enough money to compensate for the service received. Korean women have also found their own way to convert the space provided by McDonald's into a retreat from the stress of urban life. These consumers are creatively transforming the restaurants into "local" institutions, a process that is paralleled by McDonald's experience in China, Taiwan, Hong Kong, and Japan. But what makes the Korean process of localization different from its counterparts in these other East Asian cases is the dominant role of politics. McDonald's in Korea is not simply a corporation; it is a highly loaded symbol of American culture, and as such reflects all the complications and contradictions that have characterized Korean-American relations over the past fifty years.

CHAPTER 5

McDonald's in Japan: Changing Manners and Etiquette

Emiko Ohnuki-Tierney

The Golden Arches, a ubiquitous symbol of "late capitalism"[1] and the fragmentation of life in the fast lane in the United States, have found a home in Japan—another society where the apparently unlimited growth propelled by capitalism has given rise to an explosive rate of change in daily life. In this chapter I will re-examine some of the assumptions implicit in current discussions of the globalization process by focusing on the introduction and growth of McDonald's in Japan. In particular, I think we must shift our attention from the obsession with consumer behavior and focus instead on how new commodities become *embedded* in culture. Throughout Asia, for example, fast food is not simply a commodity; it is also a representation of "the West" or "America." How does McDonald's stand for Americana as perceived by the Japanese? Also, what are the unanticipated effects of a particular commodity, such as the McDonald's hamburger, as it becomes part of Japanese culture? My focus in this chapter, therefore, is not confined to the nature of McDonald's as a particular form of food, but also with the effects of fast food on Japanese table manners and lifestyles in general.

McDonald's in Japan

McDonald's was introduced in Japan in 1971 by Den Fujita, then a University of Tokyo student. He began with five restaurants and a $1.3 million investment during an economic boom in Japan. By 1985 the business had grown to such an extent that on New Year's Day a McDonald's near the Tsurugaoka Shrine in Kamakura set what was then a single-day, single-outlet, world sales record of $47,871.[2] In that same year, McDonald's was ranked number one in total sales among Japan's service companies.[3] By 1986, the chain had expanded to 556 restaurants, amounting to a $766.5 million empire. Every month that year the Japanese consumed 12,000 tons of American beef and 15,000 tons of Idaho potatoes;[4] in 1991, annual sales rose to $1.6 billion, with 860 restaurants.[5] By 1994, when the fieldwork for this study was conducted, McDonald's Japan had expanded to 1,048 outlets, with its branch below the Hanshin Department Store in Umeda, Osaka, at the top in terms of sales.[6]

McDonald's has made a practice of targeting locations noted for high real estate value, such as Ginza in Tokyo, where the first outlet opened.[7] Other restaurants are situated near major train stations and often have very little frontage space and limited seating space. The premium in such locations is on convenience, not comfort.

The Japanese menu includes the standard fare one would find in any American McDonald's, but, in an effort to increase sales, Japanese McDonald's restaurants have experimented with different food items such as Chinese fried rice (*MacChao*), curried rice with chicken or beef, fried egg burger (called *tsukimi-bāgā*, or "moon-viewing burger"), rib burgers, hotdog burgers, shrimp burgers, and chicken-*tatsuta* (a soy-sauce-flavored chicken sandwich).[8] Bacon-lettuce burgers were the featured item during the summer of 1994. So far, the only locally inspired item that has become a permanent feature of the McDonald's menu is the teriyaki burger. (In July 1994, on a flight to Tokyo, I interviewed a man who worked for the Mitsubishi Automobile Company and was returning from a tour of branch offices in the United States; he insisted that food in the Japanese McDonald's was much tastier than its American counterpart. After some discussion it became clear that, to him, McDonald's meant teriyaki burgers and the taste he craved was soy sauce.) Other items served in Japan that are not found in most American outlets include iced coffee, iced oolong tea, hot oolong tea, corn soup, café au lait, and bacon-potato pie.

McDonald's as a Snack

In Japan there is a vast array of foods served with rice that may qualify as "fast foods," although it is not always easy to determine which items fit this classification since Japanese cuisine has two characteristics that make it possible for almost any dish to become a fast food. First, except for soup, Japanese foods are usually served at room temperature. Although rice must be piping hot at the dinner table, it is eaten at room temperature in lunch boxes or in the form of rice balls. Second, the Japanese characteristically serve their "courses" all at once. Therefore, lunch boxes (*bentō*) are a natural extension of meals eaten at the table. *Bentō* are enormously popular and are sold in department stores, supermarkets, and grocery stores, as well as by vendors who sell them from minivans and cars parked in busy office areas. Prices range from ¥250 to ¥2,500;* decent-tasting *bentō* average around ¥500.[9] Because of the popularity of *bentō*, some foreign fast food companies have begun selling boxed lunches. For example, in the fall of 1992, Kentucky Fried Chicken started an expensive line of *bentō* lunches, claiming that they contained "the best" rice (*akitakomachi*) and fish.[10] Even railway stations sell their own *ekiben* (station lunches), ranging in price from ¥350 to ¥2,000.[11]

McDonald's has not posed a serious challenge to this lunch market. Despite its phenomenal success, my interviews as well as published magazine articles all testify that McDonald's food is considered a "snack" and not a full meal. Even Den Fujita concedes: "McDonald's has gained ample recognition among Japanese consumers. However, our image is that of a light-meal restaurant for young people. We are not regarded as a place for adults to have dinner." [12]

A young man from Mino, near Osaka, explained the situation. Any food with bread is not considered "filling," and so for lunch he and his university friends look for *donburi tei-shoku*—a large bowl of rice topped with various ingredients. He prefers rice burgers (a slice of meat, fish, or vegetable sandwiched between bun-shaped rice patties) to hamburgers. In his opinion, hamburgers are only a snack to be eaten between meals. An article in a popular magazine, entitled "Hamburgers as a Habit and *Gyūdon* [a large bowl of rice with beef and sauce on top] for a Full Stomach," develops this theme.[13] The author points out that young working men are not lured by the prospect of lunchtime hamburgers. On Sundays, when the same young men take their families out for a light meal, they often end up at McDonald's for lunch.

*During the period of this research (summer 1994) the exchange rate was US$1 = ¥103.

In this sense, therefore, McDonald's is competing with only a limited number of traditional fast foods, those made with noodles and other nonrice items. *Udon* (noodles made from wheat flour) are considered the original fast food of Japan, and were enjoyed by city dwellers of Osaka and Edo (Tokyo) some 200 years ago.[14] The second most popular type of noodle are *soba* (buckwheat noodles). The first *soba* shop appeared in the mid-seventeenth century in Edo as a snack place.[15] *Soba* shops boomed in popularity during the Teikyo period (1684–88).[16] In 1860 there were 3,763 *soba* shops in Edo, excluding street vendors.[17] *Rāmen*, made from wheat and originally introduced from China, rank third in popularity among Japanese noodle dishes.[18]

Udon and *soba* are not just fast food; they can even be haute cuisine if the noodles, the sauce, the seaweed, and the garnishes are of high quality and served in exquisite containers. At exclusive restaurants, the price can go as high as ¥2,500. *Rāmen*, however, remain low-class, regardless of the quality of noodles or sauce.[19]

Other recently imported foreign foods, such as Kentucky Fried Chicken, are treated more like meals than snacks, perhaps because chicken seems less alien than hamburgers to the Japanese. Pizza is also treated differently from McDonald's standard fare. Japanese pizzas—topped with octopus, squid, corn, and pineapple—are considered a party food for young people. It is also significant that pizza can be shared, a feature conspicuously absent in McDonald's fare. The chain known as Mos Burger, which has become popular in recent years, is McDonald's strongest competitor. Mos Burger serves its own version of burgers—a sloppy-joe-style concoction of meat and chili sauce on a bun. The chain also introduced rice burgers, which consist of meat, fish, or vegetable sandwiched between bun-shaped wedges of pressed rice. The Mos Burger chain is especially popular among Japanese young people. Outlets are located in busy areas, often near universities, but not, for example, in the fashionable Ginza district of Tokyo.[20]

Why Is McDonald's Food Considered a Snack?

The perception that McDonald's hamburgers are a snack and not a meal is a phenomenon that contributors to this volume discovered not only in Japan but also in Beijing, Hong Kong, Taipei, and Korea. Before we jump to the conclusion that these are identical cross-cultural parallels we must examine the meanings conveyed by meat and bread, the two basic ingredients of McDonald's hamburgers, in Japanese culture as compared to other Asian cultures. The Japanese share the basic rice diet of all East Asian peoples, but have been unique in their abstemious attitude toward meat, at least officially, until quite recently.

Shortly after the introduction of Buddhism (from India via Korea) in the sixth century, the doctrine of mercy for all living beings was translated into a legal prohibition against the consumption of land-dwelling animals. Since then the "official" diet of the Japanese has consisted of fish and vegetables.[21] With the development of an agrarian cosmology that became hegemonic during the early modern period (1603–1868) and extended through the Meiji period (1868–1912), rice and the paddies it grew in became metaphors for Japanese cultural identity, and later, for Japanese national identity.[22]

In contrast, Westerners were represented in the Japanese imagination as meat eaters. From a Japanese perspective, meat was *the* distinguishing characteristic of the Western diet, and thus of "barbarian" cultures. Japanese discourse about "the other" took the following form: *self* is to *other* as *rice* is to *meat.* Certain reformers favored an unabashed imitation of the West and advocated the abandonment of rice agriculture and the adoption of raising animals for meat. They argued that as long as the Japanese continued to eat only rice, fish, and vegetables, their bodies would never become strong enough to compete with meat-eating Westerners.[23] Advocates of this radical view also associated a diet dominated by rice with country bumpkins and uncivilized habits.[24] The Japanese even gave the name "a civilized bowl of rice" (*kaika donburi*; *kaika* = civilized) to a new dish consisting of beef or pork pieces sauteed with onions, added to a sauce made with eggs, and served over a large bowl of rice.[25]

Other Japanese leaders opposed imitating the West and argued for the superiority of the rice diet and the importance of rice agriculture. In 1854 an event was staged for the second visit of Commodore Perry, during which *sumō* wrestlers lifted heavy sacks of rice (*komedawara*) in front of these delegates, one of whom had asked why "the Japanese" were so strong. A wrestler named Hitachiyama replied that the Japanese were indeed physically powerful because they ate rice grown on Japanese soil.[26] Even though the Japanese began to eat meat during the Meiji period, it was never consumed in quantity until after World War Two. A rapid increase in meat consumption occurred during the 1970s and 1980s, especially among younger people. McDonald's thus appeals primarily to this postwar generation.[27]

Bread, by contrast, was introduced at the end of the nineteenth century in Yokohama and has been enormously popular in Japan. Japanese consumers have become as discriminating about bread as they are about rice.[28] Those who can afford the highest-quality foods buy bread only from well-known bakeries with German or French names. When it was first introduced, however, the hamburger bun itself was entirely new to the Japanese, in shape, taste, and use.

The first Japanese meal to be "invaded" by foreign foods was breakfast, with bread replacing rice. Ronald Dore argues that this takeover began in 1951, when housewives welcomed the idea of having bread for breakfast, which freed them from the necessity of rising early to cook morning rice. Today many urban Japanese would not think of eating rice at breakfast.[29] The popularity of bread is remarkable given that baking is not a traditional method of cooking in Japan (indeed, most Japanese do not own ovens). Furthermore, bread is consumed primarily at breakfast; even sandwiches are not popular.

While most other Japanese meals still include rice, the quantity has gradually declined. This is due to an increase in the consumption of side dishes—meat, fish, vegetables—rather than a substitution of bread for rice.[30] Nonetheless, an evening meal without rice would be the Japanese equivalent of having sandwiches for dinner in the United States. McDonald's efforts to incorporate new dishes, such as MacChao (Chinese fried rice) and curried rice, are no doubt due to the realization that "many Japanese just don't feel satisfied unless they eat rice with their dinner."[31]

The deciding factor that makes hamburgers a snack in Japanese eyes is therefore the absence of rice. In both Chinese and Japanese cultures, rice stands for food in general and is of enormous symbolic value, in the same way that bread is in the United States (as exemplified by such expressions as "breadwinner" and "bread-and-butter issue"). But Japan differs from the rest of Asia in that the presence of meat acts as an additional deterrent to considering hamburgers a true meal, especially for older Japanese.

Food and Commensality

One of the most important aspects of food is its role, both in ritual and in daily life, in bringing people together, in giving them a sense of community. By sharing food, and especially by eating the same kinds of food together, people form the bonds of social relationship. In this respect the role of rice in the Japanese diet is paramount. While all other dishes are served individually, cooked rice is delivered to the table in a common container (usually wooden) and ladled out to each diner, usually by the female head of household. The symbolic importance and power of this server is expressed by the wooden spatula, which belongs to her alone.[32] The phrase *onaji kama no meshi o kuu* (to eat from the same pot of rice) succinctly expresses the idea that those who share rice become "we."

In this respect, McDonald's hamburgers are the opposite of rice, since they are meant to be eaten individually and are difficult to share. (It is for this reason that pizza, another food that is designed for sharing, is popular as a party food for young people but hamburgers are not.) The physical arrangement of most McDonald's restaurants further de-emphasizes commensality: The original outlet at Ginza 4-chōme had neither tables nor seats. Although it has moved to larger accommodations at Ginza 8-chōme, it still has only 22 seats. Attached to both side walls are narrow counters, one with seven seats, the other with five. Here clients eat facing the wall—in fact, the counters are so narrow and the wall so close it is difficult not to bump one's forehead against the wall when eating. In the center is another narrow counter with ten stools. During my two visits in August 1994, only one young couple sat at the center counter, talking and enjoying each other's company; the remaining customers were alone, eating in silence. The McDonald's at Hankyū Umeda in Osaka is wedged into a small storefront containing a long, narrow counter against the back wall with no seating whatever. Customers in this facility must stand to eat. Most are alone, eating as fast as possible, although a sign states that there is seating upstairs. If not in meaning, then in form, these McDonald's are exact counterparts of the stand-up noodle shops (*tachisoba*) located on the platforms of busy train stations, providing quick meals to people who dash in, slurp down a bowl of noodles, and then run for the train. In fact, adjoining the McDonald's in Osaka is a *tachisoba* shop. McDonald's is also a popular venue for young men who bolt breakfast on their way to work.[33]

Other McDonald's restaurants in Japan provide more eating space for consumers. These are often designed with a relatively small area on the first floor for ordering and service, with seating provided on the second and third floors. Even in these settings, however, there are more stools (facing narrow counters against walls or facing windows) than chairs and tables. During one of my site visits (to the McDonald's in Roppongi, a fashionable Tokyo neighborhood), several young men of high-school age were eating on the second floor. Although they were sitting on stools overlooking the street, they managed to create a sense of commensality in spite of the physical arrangements. Other customers, however, ate alone—including one woman who sat with her back to the room and talked on the phone throughout her entire meal. (Public phones have been installed at many McDonald's restaurants.) In short, young people may convert McDonald's into a place to enjoy each other's company, but for the majority of adult Japanese, McDonald's is simply fast food, "fuel" for a busy workday. During an interview with a Japanese sociologist, I was told that McDonald's also caters to high-school and middle-school students, as well as to mothers with small children. He explained that there are no other restaurants where these customers can spend two or three hours together talking.[34] It is also obvious that many elementary-school children treat McDonald's as snack centers where they relax between their regular school and cram school; they, too, sit and talk for long periods. There appear to be few efforts by management to move these students out in favor of other customers.

McDonald's is decidedly not a venue for an upscale clientele. The only men in business suits I observed in Japanese outlets were foreigners. In fact, the aforementioned interviewee who works for Mitsubishi said that it would be awkward for him to enter McDonald's while he is wearing a business suit; if he wants a hamburger at work, he sends an *onnanoko* (office "girl") to get it for him. Similarly, he would not eat in a "stand-up noodle shop" while dressed for work.

One of the most radical changes in Japanese society during the past two decades is the growing economic power of young people, without whom McDonald's could not have made such inroads into the food market. Young people—up to high-school age—once ate exclusively at home; today even children as young as seven or eight frequently eat out. Students now have spending money, acquired from parents, part-time jobs, or both. In the past decade, part-time work for extra money has become commonplace among Japanese youth.[35] Most important, dating—a postwar phenomenon—now begins in middle school. To give but one example to illustrate the pervasiveness of the youth culture, I noticed a counter selling beepers, called "pocket bells" (*poke beru*), at the Takashimaya department store in Osaka in September 1994. They also transmit short messages, such as the name and telephone number of the caller. To my astonishment, the primary customers for beepers were not doctors or brokers but young people who did not want to miss a telephone call from their friends. Although the purchase of a beeper officially requires parental consent for buyers under the age of 18, beepers are extremely popular among teenagers. The ownership of "pocket bells" symbolizes not only the economic power of Japanese youth today, but also their changing culture. Despite the much-touted "examination hell" that begins in kindergarten, many children are no longer as enslaved to schoolwork as their parents were. A powerful peer-group culture has emerged, and McDonald's success is due, in part, to this new phenomenon.[36]

Constructed Americana

Despite founder Den Fujita's claim that McDonald's was not promoted as an import ("from America"),[37] the company has clearly capitalized on the fact that it is associated with American culture. Fujita did, however, depart from the "suburban approach" that characterizes McDonald's in the United States by locating his first restaurant on Ginza, the most fashionable street in Japan. He placed another outlet in the Mitsukoshi department store, which is not only the oldest but also the most prestigious of all Japanese department stores.[38] The location of these two restaurants helped create an image of McDonald's as a prime example of Americana, as imagined by Japanese people whose understanding of United States culture is limited. Furthermore, the fact that McDonald's opened in fashionable locations helped convince young people that eating while standing—an act that violates Japanese table manners—is chic. During the summer of 1986, in an extra effort to dramatize McDonald's American identity, Fujita sponsored a visit by the full troupe of the Broadway musical "42nd Street," which played a one-month run in Tokyo.[39]

How do Japanese consumers perceive McDonald's? Some of them identify the restaurant with American culture, or, to be specific, with *Americana as constructed* by the Japanese. A good example of this phenomenon is *McJoy*, a Japanese-language magazine produced by McDonald's for local customers; it publishes cover illustrations sent in by readers.[40] The October 1994 cover depicts a woman with blonde hair, green eyes, star-shaped sunglasses and earrings, and flesh-colored stars on her cheeks. The male artist, Morito Masahiko (a 39-year-old shop owner) attempted to "create the image of an American-type woman with stars and pop [culture]."

It is worth noting here that the mental image most Japanese conjure up when they think of *gaijin* (foreigners) is a person with blonde hair and blue eyes.[41] A popular children's song contains the line "My blue-eyed doll was born in America and came to a port in Japan." This representation, which emerged during the early twentieth century, continues to be *the* dominant image of Westerners, despite the fact that millions of Japanese have come into contact with Westerners of varying physical types. The picture on the cover of *McJoy* thus epitomizes Americana—a cultural image filtered through the lens of popular Japanese consciousness.

The Catburger Saga

While both managers and millions of Japanese consumers associate McDonald's with the positive aspects of American culture, there is a negative side as well, as exemplified by *nyan-bā gā-densetsu* (the lore of the catburger). The story, a form of *toshi densetsu* (urban folklore), first emerged in 1973 and spread among female high-school students in Tokyo: several girls allegedly saw the skins of cats being dried behind a McDonald's restaurant.[42] In 1975, another version circulated on Tokyo and Yokohama college campuses; it told of a boy who had wandered into a kitchen at McDonald's where he saw numerous cat heads, the implication being that hamburgers are made from cat meat. The apocryphal story concludes with the boy being bribed with a ¥10,000-note to keep quiet about his discovery.[43] This urban legend circulated among students for a while, but soon died out.

McDonald's is not the only target of this type of urban lore. Earthworms were supposedly seen in Mos Burger's buns. Kentucky Fried Chicken and the local fast food chains, Lotteria and Domdom, have all been similarly targeted. Animals associated with these foods include not only cats and worms but frogs and South American rats. A recent story circulating among Japanese youth claims that there is a factory in Australia which grows earthworms as a food export. In fact almost all *foreign* fast foods have been the victims of these kinds of rumors, including Chinese convenience foods such as dumplings (*gyōza*) and even *rāmen*, which are of Chinese origin but have been thoroughly "domesticated" in Japan. One urban legend has it that the reason *rāmen* taste so good is that the broth is made from crows.[44] The negative aspects of McDonald's association with the United States persist among many Japanese consumers. A woman in her late twenties, with whom I struck up a conversation on a train from Tokyo to Yokohama in August 1994, said that she rarely eats at McDonald's. She explained that McDonald's was "not nutritious," and one "cannot trust" what the company puts into the hamburgers, as evidenced by their "chemical taste."

Her emphasis on "chemicals" in McDonald's food makes an uncanny parallel to the views fostered by the opponents of foreign rice importation during the early 1990s. Pressured by the United States and the inevitable conclusion of GATT negotiations, the Japanese rice lobby argued that foreign grain was contaminated by insecticides and processing chemicals. Consumer groups became intensely involved in checking foreign rice for such contaminants and demanded that the government investigate the processing methods for all imports.[45] They also opposed the government's plan to mix imported and domestic rice, which would, in their view, adulterate "pure" Japanese rice with "impure," chemically tainted, foreign rice.[46] These campaigns had a wide-ranging effect on Japanese consumers, who were moved to defend domestic rice and local agriculture; many people equated Japanese rice with their self-identity, which is assigned the value of "purity." Rice plants were said to purify Japanese air and water.[47] It is little wonder that McDonald's, the quintessence of foreign food in many eyes, would find itself drawn into these symbolic duels.

McDonald's and Changes in Table Manners

So far my discussion of McDonald's in Japan has been confined to its reception and cultural associations. I would now like to consider not just what the food represents, but how it is eaten. When food consumption is a social act, manners are of paramount importance. Perhaps the most striking element of McDonald's introduction to Japan is that it encouraged the Japanese to eat differently—that is, to change their table manners.

The famous Latin treatise by Erasmus, *De civilitate morum puerilium* (On civility in children), published in 1530, warns: "It is impolite to greet someone who is urinating or defecating. . . . A well-bred person should always avoid exposing without necessity the parts to which nature has attached modesty. If necessity compels this, it should be done with decency and reserve."[48] The civilizing process in Japan took a quite different turn: urination in public places was quite commonly practiced by people from different social classes. In eighteenth-century Kyoto, even women urinated in public quite freely.[49] Prior to the 1964 Olympics, the Japanese government issued a plea to men not to urinate in public and to women not to breastfeed in open settings because "foreigners are coming, and they might think the Japanese are uncivilized." Unlike the Euro-American culture in which male genitals and women's breasts are at all times charged with religious and erotic meanings, the Japanese dissociate the sexual function of these body parts at other times. But with government pressure, breastfeeding in public has virtually disappeared. The male habit of urinating in public has not, although it is less common than it used to be.

Of much more significance to the Japanese concept of *civilité* are table manners, which have proved far more resistant to change. The traditional rules of the game are as follows: One must not touch food with one's hands when eating, and one must not eat while standing. The first rule derives from the notion that hands are, by definition, dirty, even after washing.

Hands touch all sorts of things and thus are always contaminated. Symbolically, hands stand for a liminal space demarcating the clean inside—the body, the self—from the dirty outside.[50] Chopsticks, used since the early Heian period (794–1185),[51] are by definition clean and thus, except for a few culturally identified foods, one must use chopsticks, even when eating soup noodles. Many Japanese find it difficult to eat sandwiches with their bare hands. To accommodate these sensibilities, sandwiches are often served cut into small pieces, with toothpicks for handling.

Conversely, there are culturally prescribed foods that Japanese *must* eat with their hands. For example, *nigirizushi* (vinegared rice balls with raw fish), although usually eaten with chopsticks, are handled with the fingers when they are of especially high quality. *Onigiri* (rice balls), eaten primarily for lunch, are commonly eaten with the hands. Note, however, that when most Japanese use their hands for eating, they cleanse them (culturally speaking) first with *oshibori*, or wet towels. In fact, Japanese food outlets often include *otefuki* (hand-cleaning towelettes) with their packaged products, irrespective of the nature of the food. Concerns about the ritual impurity of hands, especially the left hand, are almost universal.[52] In the United States, too, people who handle food for a living are required to wear rubber gloves. Conrad Kottak points out that the fast food chain he studied in New York City assured customers that "their food was never touched by human hands."[53]

McDonald's impact on the taboo against eating with one's hands has been limited. Most Japanese I observed during the summer of 1994 still ate their hamburgers in the paper wrapping, in such a way that their hands did not directly touch the food. Some people explained this practice as simply a means of keeping ketchup and other liquids from dripping on them, but the effect is still that their hands do not directly touch the food. Furthermore, I did not see a great increase in the use of hands when eating other foods. The first rule of Japanese table etiquette, therefore, seems to have been affected little by the introduction of McDonald's.

The second taboo, thou shalt not eat while standing, has received a direct hit from McDonald's. "Eating while standing," called *tachigui*, has had negative connotations in Japanese culture for centuries. It derives from the notion that one of the main distinctions between humans and animals is that the latter eat while standing. Also, the ban is part of a more general taboo against performing various acts while standing. Kumakura cites a passage from a classic, *Nihonshoki*, dated 720 A.D., in which putting things down, talking to a superior, pouring wine, etc., while standing were considered an extreme breach of etiquette, requiring the offender to commit suicide.[54] During the tea ceremony, in which the most elaborated form of manners is observed, one must kneel even to open a door. The term *tachigui* first appeared in 1898 in the novel *Genmu Shujaku* by Izumi Kyoka (1873–1939), a well-known writer. Nagai Kafu (1879–1959), another famous novelist, characterized Chicago as "the place where people grab food and eat while standing" in his *Amerika Monogatari* (Stories about America), published in 1908.[55] Kafu's observation clearly indicates how the custom of *tachigui* is seen as a marker of foreigners, "the other," in contrast to the Japanese. Proper Japanese table manners include sitting on one's legs on the floor (*seiza*) and eating at a low table. McDonald's hamburgers and french fries, as well as pizza and Kentucky Fried Chicken, are "finger foods" that require neither plates nor tables. In fact, as noted above, the first McDonald's in Japan had no seats.[56] In short, fast food restaurants, as epitomized by McDonald's, fostered table manners that are the polar opposite of traditional Japanese etiquette.

Other changes in public manners can be traced to the introduction of foreign products. For instance, Coca-Cola and rival soft drinks inspired the cultural sanction against *rappa nomi*, or drinking like one is blowing a trumpet (*rappa*)—imbibing directly from the bottle or can. Like *tachigui*, "trumpeting" was a negatively marked form of public behavior. Today, however, people do occasionally drink directly from the bottle or can, although this behavior is confined to young people in certain contexts, notably in fast food restaurants.

Another change in eating habits stems from the large-scale intrusion of ice cream into the fast food scene. Ice cream consumption was limited in prewar Japan, in part because many Japanese are lactose-intolerant, but also because of the Japanese taboo against cold foods and drinks, even in summer. These disadvantages were compounded by the fact that people must eat ice cream cones by opening their mouths wide and licking with their tongue. Traditional Japanese etiquette calls for the consumption of food in small amounts, opening one's mouth as discreetly as possible. Women especially are expected to cover their mouths with their hands when eating or laughing. Although many women use spoons to eat ice cream, younger people today often consume it like Americans, with their tongues—much to the distress of traditionalists.

All the modifications in table manners mentioned above have been inspired or reinforced by American-style fast food. But these changes did not occur overnight; even before Mc-Donald's, manners had become increasingly informal. What paved the way for this transformation in behavior was the introduction of chairs—a foreign importation that eroded the foundation of traditional etiquette, the practice of sitting on one's legs.[57]

Global Versus Local Cultures

As Daniel Miller points out, "the global" includes "everything from full gospel black churches and Miami brand names to youth music" that originates in Africa and the Caribbean.[58] More often than not, however, the cultural phenomena that are considered global are those that originate in the United States or Western Europe. In the traffic of the global and the local, all societies are not equal.

The academic preoccupation with consumer culture has blinded us to other significant dimensions of the globalization process. Goods are embedded in their culture of origin; their introduction into a different culture is more than a simple importation of commodities. In the case of McDonald's, the local (Japanese) construction of American culture has had a significant impact on how hamburgers are perceived. Despite nationalism, which feeds on various manifestations of anti-Americanism, almost every country in the world looks toward "America" as a model to emulate. But the Americana that is created for this purpose often bears little resemblance to the cultural system(s) prevailing in the United States.

I continue to be amazed by the image of America and Americans held by many of my fellow countrymen and countrywomen. Even intellectuals who are attuned to world affairs believe that the United States is a country where social hierarchies do not exist and individuals can achieve high status simply through the exercise of their own ability. The myth of a classless society, held dear by many Americans as well, is widely accepted in Japan. "America" is seen as an alternative to the hierarchical local society, which is characterized by conformity and the need to exploit personal connections to succeed. Thus the image of America as a social paradise persists in Japan, especially among young people—the segment of the population that frequents McDonald's most often.

From the perspective of the "civilizing process," McDonald's and other transnational food chains have helped to create an entirely new concept of manners. The transformation process was a complex one: manners and fashion began to merge. The new manners appeared first in fast food outlets—away from home—where it was fashionable to behave in new, iconoclastic ways. At home, traditional manners remained paramount and changed at a much slower pace. In the public sphere the "new" forms of etiquette gradually became the norm; the fashionableness of eating fast food wore thin as the restaurants became a routine feature of everyday, working life. The search for fashion—the new, the exciting, and the exotic—moved to other domains of Japanese popular culture. Meanwhile, McDonald's has become curiously "local." Fujita relishes the story of Japanese Boy Scouts who, when traveling abroad, were pleasantly surprised to find a McDonald's in Chicago.[59]

The irony in this story of cultural interchange is that the impact of McDonald's *food* has been minimal. McDonald's remains, in the eyes of most consumers, a "snack"; it has most assuredly not replaced traditional Japanese dinners or even lunches. And yet, McDonald's and its many rivals and imitators have had a profound impact in the revolution of public manners. This transformation is particularly significant in a society—present-day Japan—that cherishes interpersonal relationships and civil behavior.

McDonald's as Political Target: Globalization and Anti-globalization in the Twenty-First Century

James L. Watson

The first edition of this book was published in 1997, at the tail end of a worldwide economic boom. A great deal has happened during the intervening years. In the late 1990s pundits told us that digital technology would undermine the power of autocratic governments and that people everywhere would benefit from the "rising tide" of globalization. These optimistic projections seem hopelessly naive, today, in the aftermath of the Enron fiasco, the dot.com crash, and the post-9/11 war on terrorism.

Investors in East Asia were hit by devastating market setbacks in 1997. Hong Kong's property market imploded, leaving thousands of middle-class residents with mortgages on apartments that were suddenly worth less than half their purchase price. Japan's economy fell into a long slump in the 1990s and has yet to rebound. South Korea and Taiwan encountered serious setbacks as exports of high-technology products reached a plateau while competition from China was increasing. China has not experienced the same level of economic distress as its immediate neighbors, but the cost of maintaining growth has been high: in terms of personal income, China is rapidly becoming one of the world's most unequal societies.[1] Urban centers like Beijing and Shanghai flourish while vast stretches of the countryside stagnate.

All these countries are heavily dependent on exports—to the United States and Europe—to sustain the high standards of living attained in the 1990s. The people most directly threatened ·by global recession are the emerging middle classes discussed in *Golden Arches East*: entrepreneurs, office workers, teachers, and technology specialists. McDonald's promised an essential set of services to this generation of dual-income, stressed-out parents. This unbeatable formula consisted of hot food, fast delivery, security, safety, and entertainment—in one, "friendly" package. Will this formula work in the twenty-first century? Will Ronald McDonald (aka Uncle McDonald) be a superstar for the next generation of Chinese, Japanese, and Korean youngsters?

The Global Anti-Globalization Movement

In concert with economic developments, attitudes toward globalization have changed dramatically since *Golden Arches East* first appeared. The five core chapters (focusing on China, Hong Kong, Taiwan, Japan, and Korea) are based on fieldwork conducted during the mid-1990s, and as such they invoke economic and political conditions that no longer prevail. In retrospect, the final decade of the twentieth century was a period of global optimism, occasioned by the collapse of the Soviet empire and a "softening" of state communism in China. World peace no longer seemed to be an impossible dream, and many governments (notably in Europe) made drastic cuts in military spending. Globalization was welcomed and encouraged by new political elites that emerged in postsocialist societies. It was a heady time for people who had grown up during the dark days of the Cold War. The euphoria lasted exactly one decade—from the collapse of the Soviet Union in 1991 to the attack on the World Trade Center in 2001.

McDonald's benefited greatly from late-twentieth-century global optimism and became one of the world's most successful—and ubiquitous—multinational corporations. At the turn of the millennium the Golden Arches had spread to 119 counties with over 27,000 restaurants worldwide.[2] The corporation's future depends increasingly upon international (i.e., non-United States) sales.

By the early 2000s, young people all over the world began to question the rising-tide premise of globalization. Neoliberal theorists maintain that globalization is not a zero-sum game because the whole world wins in the end.[3] Other observers are more pessimistic and argue that, on balance, globalization benefits the metropolitan elites who control the flow of world capital and information: the rich get richer.[4] Until recently this debate was largely ignored by most Americans, who benefited from early-stage globalization of the 1980s and 1990s. Anti-globalists of that era were preoccupied with the power of American popular culture and the apparent inability of "weaker" cultures to resist. This was the heyday of *cultural imperialism* as a reigning paradigm in Western intellectual circles.[5]

Today, by contrast, the average American sees the world through very different lenses. Starting in 2003, news media began to focus on the problems caused by the outsourcing and offshoring of American jobs to China, India, and Mexico. Ironically, these are the same countries that an earlier generation of anti-globalists sought to protect from the ravages of

American cultural encroachment. Outsourcing and offshoring have become code words for the boomerang effects of globalization. During the 2004 U.S. presidential campaign, one of the candidates denounced "Benedict Arnold CEOs," who profited by sending American jobs abroad.[6] Newspapers throughout the country were suddenly filled with accounts of high-tech jobs moving from Palo Alto to Bangalore, where highly educated workers were readily available for less than half the cost. As the CEO of Infosys Technologies, an Indian outsourcing company, put it during a talk at the 2004 World Economic Forum, "Everything you can send down a wire is up for grabs."[7] Accountants in New York and Los Angeles regularly e-mail client tax data—including scanned receipts—to firms in India, where IRS forms are completed and returned for signature and submission.[8] American loan companies, banks, insurance agencies, and credit-card firms also outsource much of their routine data-entry and evaluation work—primarily to English-speaking India.[9]

McDonald's as Political Target

By the late 1990s McDonald's had become *the* primary target of the worldwide antiglobalization movement. Try the following exercise: Type "McDonald's" in the subject window of any Internet search engine and watch as thousands of anticorporate, anticapitalist, anti-obesity, antiglobalist, and anti-animal exploitation sites appear on the screen. It would take several days to surf through all of them (I tried and finally gave up after six hours). A central conclusion of the first edition of *Golden Arches East* is that McDonald's means different things to different people. Today those meanings are more likely to be negative than positive, a dramatic shift in public perception since the mid-1990s.

The list of world cities that have experienced violent anti-McDonald's demonstrations during the past decade seems endless: a partial list includes Antwerp, Athens, Beirut, Belgrade, Caracas, Changsha (China), Dammon (Saudia Arabia), Garden City (New York), Genoa, Istanbul, Jakarta, Karachi, Lima, London, Macau, Melbourne, Merksem (Belgium), Mexico City, Moscow, Mumbai (Bombay), Paris, Prague, Quevert (French Britanny), Quito, Riyadh, Rio de Janeiro, Rome, Seattle, and Xian (China).[10]

In Oaxaca, Mexico, plans to build a McDonald's restaurant in the historic central plaza mobilized local preservationists: "This is the center of our city, a place where people meet, talk politics, shop and spend time," said an artist. "[We] are drawing the line here against what the arches symbolize."[11] French farmer-turned-activist Jose Bove caused an international sensation by driving his tractor into a McDonald's restaurant in southern France. Mr. Bove subsequently became a global superstar as a result of his actions and tours the world as a public speaker, denouncing McDonald's in particular and American-instigated globalization in general.[12]

Perhaps the greatest blow to McDonald's international image occurred during the now infamous "McLibel" trial in London. The corporation's U.K. leadership made the fatal error of suing two demonstrators who had distributed anti-McDonald's leaflets outside several local restaurants (the leaflets can be found on the McSpotlight web site, see below). The trial lasted from June 1994 to June 1997; the proceedings attracted international media attention from the outset. The defendants, vegetarian activists Dave Morris and Helen Steel, were eventually found guilty of libel, but the judge also ruled that McDonald's was "culpably responsible" for animal cruelty and the exploitation of children.[13] It was a Pyrrhic victory that exposed the company to worldwide ridicule and vilification—a David and Goliath story in modern corporate guise. The trial spawned a popular web site, www.McSpotlight.org, that has become a staging ground for anti-McDonald's movements on a global scale. Organizers established a World Anti-McDonald's Day (October 16) that is coordinated through this and other web sites.[14]

Other national branches of the transnational corporation may have learned from the British disaster. McDonald's officials in France have been quick to respond to demonstrations in their country. Following an attack on its restaurants in 1999, a spokeswoman for McDonald's noted that 30,000 French citizens were employed by the company and that "80 percent of the products we serve are made in France." A counter-publicity campaign was launched with the slogan: "Born in the USA but made in France."[15] The owner of the McDonald's franchise in Jakarta, Indonesia, reacted in a similar fashion when his restaurants were threatened following the U.S. bombing of Afghanistan in 2001. "In the name of Allah, the merciful and gracious, McDonald's Indonesia is owned by an indigenous Muslim," read a green banner hanging outside Jakarta restaurants. Posters in Arabic noted that all food served at local McDonald's is *halal* ("lawful" according to Koranic strictures), guaranteeing that no pork products had entered the premises. Photos of the owner, Bambang Rachmadi, and his wife wearing Islamic dress during their pilgrimage to Mecca were prominently displayed.[16]

Why McDonald's?

Why should McDonald's be such a popular target of political protest? Other corporations (Coca-Cola and Disney, for instance) are regularly attacked, but no other company rivals McDonald's in the frequency and sheer intensity of anti-globalist, anti-American denunciations. If the United States Embassy is unapproachable, the nearest McDonald's restaurant is an acceptable, and for many demonstrators, a preferable, alternative.[17]

There is a good reason why food corporations attract so much political attention in contrast to automobile manufacturers, software designers, or media conglomerates (all of which, it could be argued, have a "deeper" impact on local economies). Food is serious business for all humans. As foodways change, notions of national identity are threatened, especially when American corporations are involved.[18] It is no coincidence that France and Italy, two societies where globalization is regularly equated with McDonaldization, are the epicenters of the rapidly growing "slow food" movement.[19]

The French response to American fast food is especially intriguing. By spring, 2004, there were 1,040 McDonald's restaurants in 750 French cities and towns.[20] While the Golden Arches sputtered in Germany during the same period, a new McDonald's was opening somewhere in France every six days, making it the company's most profitable European venture. These figures highlight a growing gap between the French intelligentsia and their working-class compatriots.[21] Time is money everywhere in today's world, which means that even in Paris the two-hour, multi-course lunch is, alas, a thing of the past, except perhaps for a handful of intellectuals and politicians.

McDonald's has fared less well in other parts of the world. Expansion plans in India were slowed by the announcement that beef extract (a flavor additive) was used in the United States for french fries billed as vegetarian. Although the extract was never exported to India, Hindu nationalists seized upon the scandal as evidence that the corporation was plotting to undermine the sacred vegetarian traditions of Hinduism.[22]

In 2003, McDonald's shocked the financial world by closing its restaurants in Bolivia, Paraguay, and Trinidad—three countries that had experienced severe economic problems. This was the corporation's first-ever retreat from a market. Middle-class customers in Bolivia reacted with outrage; they felt betrayed by a company they had associated with modernity and progress since it opened in their country in 1997.[23] McDonald's also closed restaurants in Japan, Denmark, Taiwan, and Britain.[24] Even more alarming to investors was the news that the Japanese franchise had suffered its first net loss since its opening in 1973.[25] Meanwhile, the corporation has become embroiled in a new controversy, this one potentially more serious than any it has yet encountered.

Obesity Politics

In August 2002, two New York teenagers sued McDonald's for, in essence, making them fat. Almost overnight obesity became the hot-button issue among anti-McDonald's organizations and interest groups. The politics associated with this controversy will have profound consequences for global food industries and their future development.

Robert Sweet, the judge in charge of the New York case, eventually dismissed the suit, as well as a follow-up action. His 64-page opinion reads, in part: "If consumers know . . . the potential ill effects of eating at McDonald's, they cannot blame McDonald's if they, nonetheless, choose to satiate their appetite with a surfeit of supersized McDonald's products." Further, "It is not the place of the law to protect [consumers] from their own excesses."[26] This ruling did not put an end to the controversy. Encouraged by the suit, the first of its kind, many trial lawyers, nutritionists, and anti-corporate activists are now arguing that purveyors of food should be held responsible for the long-term health consequences of their products, just as tobacco firms were called to account for cigarette damage.[27] The Center for Science in the Public Interest, for instance, has asked the U.S. Food and Drug Administration to put tobacco-style warning labels on sugary beverages, notably sodas and fruit drinks.[28] No action has yet been taken on the petition, but the pressure for regulatory action will certainly continue.

Similar campaigns are spreading to Europe and East Asia. In Korea a citizens' group attacked fast-food chains from "fatty nations" for encouraging obesity among Korean children. Anti-globalization movements in Hong Kong have seized the obesity issue and are making it a centerpiece of their publicity. And, of course, European media sources gave saturation coverage to the New York case; many commentators expect similar legal actions in England, France, and Italy.[29]

Defenders of the American food services industry responded quickly. The Center for Consumer Freedom (an industry-sponsored organization) launched a television advertising campaign featuring Seinfeld's "soup nazi"; the iconic character is seen refusing to serve overweight customers. Other ads in the series take aim at what industry supporters call the "food police."[30] Meanwhile the U.S. House of Representatives voted, 279 to 139, to support a Personal Responsibility in Food Consumption Act (popularly known as "the cheeseburger bill") in March 2004. As one Representative put it: "Look in the mirror because you're the one to blame." The act was designed to ward off what House Majority Leader Tom DeLay called the "Ronald McDonald made me do it defense." This legislation was backed by the National Restaurant Association and was endorsed by the White House; at this writing (fall 2005) the United States Senate has not considered the bill.[31]

Critics of the American food industry, such as Tufts University nutritionist James Tillotson, note that there "are no legal requirements for [the mega-eight food companies] to consider the weight implications of their marketing and product activities." He questions whether U.S.-government policies—which "are based on the belief that a person's weight is his or her sole responsibility"—are enough to prevent the human suffering caused by obesity. "Only Congress," he concludes, "has the power to mobilize our nation to solve this health plague."[32] Kelley Brownell, a Yale psychologist and well-known critic of the food industry, points to the saturation of advertising aimed at children: "the average [American] child sees 10,000 food advertisements a year," and these ads are often produced "in a pernicious way," he claims.[33]

McDonald's thus finds itself, once again, at the center of a controversy that extends well beyond the United States. Obesity is indeed a growing menace to world health, particularly for the next generation of consumers who are, on average, heavier than their parents—especially in East Asia.[34] McDonald's, which makes the 560-calorie Big Mac and the 730-calorie Double Quarter Pounder with Cheese, is by no means the only purveyor of fattening food. Hardee's produces a sandwich—the Monster Thickburger—that packs 1,420 calories.[35]

Burger King sells the Double Whopper with Cheese (1,040 calories) and Wendy's offers the Big Bacon Classic (580 calories). And a large Coca-Cola Classic (32 ounces) weighs in at 310 calories. Why should McDonald's take the rap for obesity? The omnipresence of the Golden Arches is, no doubt, primarily responsible for its popularity as an obesity target; it is, after all, the world's largest fast-food chain. In my view, however, there is another reason why McDonald's attracts so much attention. The archetypical meal at McDonald's consists of the big four items on any weight-conscious hit list: fried meat, deep-fried potatoes, sugar-laden drink, and an ice cream dessert. It is also notable that McDonald's is a *restaurant* where the offending items are served—ready-to-eat—in a clean, safe, air-conditioned, and reasonably quiet setting. Unlike the products of most other food companies that find themselves in the obesity spotlight (e.g., Coca-Cola and Kraft Foods), McDonald's aspires to be a home away from home, a nurturing environment that serves *hot* meals—not the cold makings of a meal prepared elsewhere. It is the successful creation of a substitute home that may account for the high level of vitriol directed at McDonald's.[36] The very attractiveness of McDonald's restaurants, and the seemingly unbeatable combination of its foods, has become the company's Achilles' heel.[37]

McDonald's has, of course, made efforts to change its public image as a purveyor of fat- and calorie-laden foods. In March 2003, following the New York obesity suit, McDonald's announced it was cooperating with Newman's Own (established by the Hollywood actor Paul Newman) to introduce a new line of salads. This was not the first attempt by the company to produce a healthier line of products (recall the McLean Deluxe[38] episode of the early 1990s), but it was certainly the most successful.[39] McDonald's also announced that it would eliminate supersized french fries and soft drinks at the end of 2004. The very term "supersize" had become a magnet for antiobesity attacks and appeared in the title of a popular anti-McDonald's film.[40] Other innovations included a shift to all-white-meat in Chicken McNuggets and the promotion of a fruit and walnut salad. The company has also taken the lead in buying antibiotic-free chicken, pork, and beef—a move that has had a serious impact on the American meatpacking industry.[41] Anti-obesity activists are not impressed by these transformative efforts,[42] but consumers in the United States seem to be responding favorably, to judge from McDonald's recent market rebound. It is unclear whether these healthy trends will affect business in other countries.

Family Revolutions: The Gray Challenge

The first edition of *Golden Arches East* demonstrated that McDonald's owed much of its success, particularly in East Asia, to a general transformation in family values. Earlier modes of kinship organization emphasized the importance of horizontal relations that cut across generations (sons worrying about parents before considering their own offspring); the nuclear family (husband, wife, and their minor children) was often an afterthought. Grandparents depended upon their adult children (especially sons) for financial and social support in old age.[43] This was the hallmark of the Confucian family system that East Asian leaders often tout as their answer to globalization and "Western" consumerism.[44] As outlined elsewhere in this book, McDonald's could never have succeeded in East Asia without appealing to youth and, equally important, the stressed-out parents of young children. Confucianism, at least as it relates to family values, was long dead by the time McDonald's arrived on the scene. The conjugal family, which highlights the needs of children and de-emphasizes support for the elderly, now reigns supreme throughout East Asia.[45] Today the post-Confucian societies of East Asia face yet another family revolution, this one potentially more significant than the conjugal transformation of the late twentieth century. In 1998, 10 percent of China's population was over age 60; projections for 2020 boost this figure to 16 percent. Japan faces even more dire prospects: 17 percent of Japanese citizens were 65 or older in 2000, but by 2020, 26 percent will be aging retirees. Korean figures are similar, with approximately 13 percent over 65 in 2000, rising to 21 percent by 2020.[46] The Japanese and South Korean governments have implemented social security programs for seniors—even though, as in the United States, future funding is uncertain. Beijing, by contrast, has made few efforts to create a modern social security system, which means that the burden continues to fall on families, not the state.[47] Meanwhile, the locus of consumer power will soon shift to a new generation as the parents of China's only children, products of the single-child family policy, retire en masse.[48] Unlike earlier generations of retirees, China's boomers will not be content with minimal (Maoist-era) pensions; they will expect their singleton offspring to help them maintain a comfortable lifestyle—and they will live a lot longer than their predecessors.

Do McDonald's and other child-centered industries have a future in this new demographic environment? If recent developments in the Hong Kong franchise are any indication, the answer is resoundingly affirmative. During the 1980s and 1990s it was young people, ages 10 to 20, who turned the Golden

Arches into urban hot spots and after-school clubs. Today, by contrast, Hong Kong's McDonald's restaurants are fast becoming havens for retirees.[49] The full ramifications of China's demographic transformation will not be felt until the 2020s, but it is obvious that elder-friendly industries are the Next Big Thing—in East Asia as in the United States and Europe.[50]

Conclusion: McDonald's as a Political Symbol

It is obvious that, in spite of all the company's efforts, McDonald's carries the baggage of globalization—the good, the bad, and the downright ugly. McDonald's is unique among its rivals in the sense that it is regularly singled out for special attention by activists worldwide. It is difficult, in fact, to find a protest movement that does *not* target the Golden Arches.

To comprehend the full extent of cultural change in the modern world it is important to distinguish between *form* and *content*. Initial impressions are almost always deceptive, especially when judging the impact of globalization. First-time visitors to shopping malls in Beijing or Seoul are always struck by the visual images of Americana: Nike shops, Starbucks outlets, Dunkin Donut stalls, Disney posters, Coca-Cola coolers, and— of course—the Golden Arches. It is little wonder that novice observers (a category that includes many journalists, pundits, and business-class globalists) jump to the conclusion that globalization has changed the "essential" core of non-Western cultures. What they see is the *form*, the outward appearance, of globalization; the internal meaning (i.e., the *content*) that people ascribe to these cultural innovations cannot be appreciated without knowledge of the local language, history, and customs. The perceived "sameness" of world cultures is an illusion, a mirage that masks a vast panoply of local responses to globalization. This, in turn, helps explain how McDonald's—along with the ubiquitous Golden Arches—has become *the* symbol of globalization. The content of that symbol (i.e., the meanings people attach to it) varies according to political, economic, and social circumstances. During the 1990s the majority of consumers in China, Korea, Russia, and other emerging markets saw McDonald's as a symbol of modernity, freedom, affluence, and new family values. Today, midway through the first decade of the twenty-first century, perceptions of globalization have darkened. McDonald's, in turn, has found itself implicated in all the leading "anti" movements that are so characteristic of the post-9/11 era.

This essay reflects social conditions in 2005—which happens to be McDonald's fiftieth anniversary. Will Ray Kroc's fabled corporation last another fifty years? Anthropologists are notoriously bad financial prognosticators, so it is best to seek such advice elsewhere. What does seem clear, from an anthropological perspective, is that McDonald's will continue to carry the baggage of globalization well into the twenty-first century. Other corporate targets are emerging—notably Wal-Mart and Starbucks—but, as yet, they have not overshadowed McDonald's in respect to activist attention. This could change, but the nature of McDonald's core product (hot, "comfort" food) and the rise of a global anti-obesity movement mean that the Golden Arches are unlikely to fade from the center stage of world politics any time soon. Stay tuned: We have only seen the previews. The big show—obesity politics—has just begun.

Reference Matter

Notes

BOOK EPIGRAPHS: Daphne Berdahl, *Where The World Ended: Identity, Differentiation, and Re-Unification in the German Borderland* (Berkeley: Univ. of California Press, 1997); John Zubrzycki, "To Curry Favor in India Debut, McDonald's Sells Maharaja Macs," *Christian Science Monitor*, Oct. 16, 1996, Clarinet.biz.industry.food: 5421.

Introduction

1. On opening day, April 23, 1992, the Beijing restaurant registered 13,214 transactions (representing 40,000 customers), setting a new one-day sales record for McDonald's. *New York Times* (NYT), Apr. 24,1992.

2. *Wall Street Journal* (WSJ), Nov. 22, 1994, p. A16. See also *Business Week* (BW), Dec. 5, 1994, p. 46; *Tampa Tribune*, Nov. 21, 1994, p. 2; NYT, Jan. 8, 1995, p. 19; *Newsweek*, Dec. 12, 1994, p. 54; *South China Morning Post* (SCMP), Dec. 3, 1994, p. 2. This restaurant finally closed down on December 2, 1996, and was relocated to new premises only 150 meters away (NYT, Dec. 2, 1996, p. D2.).

3. Rubie S. Watson, "Making Secret Histories: Memory and Mourning in Post-Mao China," in Rubie S. Watson, ed., *Memory, History, and Opposition Under State Socialism* (Santa Fe, N.M.: School of American Research, 1994).

4. "First Quarter Results," McDonald's Investor Release, Apr. 18, 1996, p. 10 (restaurant and country figures); *1995 Annual Report*, McDonald's Corp., McD6-3030, p. iii (sales figures); *Welcome to McDonald's*, 1996 Student Information Packet, McD5-2940, pp. 13–14 (customers served and hourly rate of new restaurants). Belarus and Tahiti were the 100th and 101st countries to open McDonald's res-

taurants, in December 1996. (Clarinet.biz.industry.food:5850, Dec. 9, 1996)

5. BW, May 8, 1995, p. 8, announcing that the chain's operating revenues from non-U.S. sales had passed 50 percent.

6. Headline in *Boston Globe*, Dec. 15, 1994, announcing the opening of McDonald's in Mecca, Saudi Arabia.

7. Headline in *The Sunday Times* (London), June 25, 1995, reporting on libel action taken by Britain's McDonald's against two unemployed activists who had accused the company of environmental degradation. The 314-day trial (Britain's longest ever) began in 1990 and ended in December 1996. In an article appearing in *The Independent* (London, June 10, 1995, p. 13), the author notes that "a million Britons will eat at McDonald's today." Given its obvious commercial success, why, he asks "has the burger chain become the focus of so much middle-class distaste?"

8. See Lana Wong, "Noodles Take on Sesame Seed Buns," SCMP *International Weekly* (SCMPIW), July 13, 1996, p. B3. Ma Zhiping reports that the first "national development plan for fast food production . . . will soon be announced by the State Council" (*China Daily*, Mar. 14, 1996).

9. For a discussion of this theme, see John Tomlinson, *Cultural Imperialism: A Critical Introduction* (Baltimore: Johns Hopkins Univ. Press, 1991). Ester Reiter's book *Making Fast Food* (Montreal: McGill Queen's Univ. Press, 1991) focuses on Burger King's "invasion" of Canada; for another view, see Phil Lyon et al., "Is Big Mac the Big Threat?" *International Journal of Hospitality Management* 14(2): 119–22 (1995).

10. See John Huey, "America's Hottest Export: Pop Culture," *Fortune*, Dec. 31, 1990, pp. 50–60.

11. See, for example, Ariel Dorfman and Armand Mattelart, *How To Read Donald Duck: Imperialist Ideology in the Disney Comic* (New York: International General, 1975).

12. Ronald Steel, "When Worlds Collide," NYT, July 21, 1996.

13. Marshall McLuhan and Bruce R. Powers, *The Global Village: Transformations in World Life and Media in the 21st Century* (New York: Oxford Univ. Press, 1989). For a critique of globalism as a homogenizing process, see Mike Featherstone, "Introduction," in

Mike Featherstone, ed., *Global Culture: Nationalism, Globalization and Modernity* (London: Sage, 1990), pp. 1–14.

14. Benjamin R. Barber, *Jihad vs. McWorld* (New York: Times Books, 1995), p. 4.

15. See, e.g., James Der Derian, "Speed Pollution," *Wired* 4.05 (May 1996), pp. 120–21; Robert Rossney, "Metaworlds," *Wired* 4.06 (June 1996), pp. 140–46, 202–21; Po Bronson, "On the Road to Techno-Utopia," *Wired* 4.05 (May 1996), pp. 122–26, 186–95. The Executive Editor of *Wired*, Kevin Kelly, has produced the clearest statement of the digital revolution in his *Out of Control: The New Biology of Machines, Social Systems, and the Economic World* (Reading, Mass.: Addison-Wesley, 1995). For another view, see Richard Rosecrance, "The Rise of the Virtual State," *Foreign Affairs* 75(4): 45–61 (1966).

16. Patty Jo Watson, "Archaeology, Anthropology, and the Culture Concept," *American Anthropologist* 97(4): 683–94 (1995).

17. Robert Redfield's definition was perhaps the most widely accepted among anthropologists until the 1970s. For Redfield, culture is "that complex whole which includes knowledge, belief, art, morals, law, customs, and any other capabilities and habits acquired . . . as a member of society" (1940, as quoted in P. J. Watson, "Archaeology," p. 683).

18. Roy D'Andrade, *The Development of Cognitive Anthropology* (Cambridge, Eng.: Cambridge Univ. Press, 1995), pp. 182–217; see also James Boster, "Requiem for the Omniscient Informant," in J. Dougherty, ed., *Directions in Cognitive Anthropology* (Urbana: Univ. of Illinois Press, 1985).

19. The notion of "taste" as an expression of refined social status is reflected most clearly in consumption patterns. See Pierre Bourdieu, *Distinction: A Social Critique of the Judgement of Taste* (Cambridge, Mass.: Harvard Univ. Press, 1984); Daniel Miller, *Modernity—An Ethnographic Approach: Dualism and Mass Consumption in Trinidad* (Oxford: Berg Publishers, 1994), pp. 203–56; and Daniel Miller, "Consumption as the Vanguard of History," in Daniel Miller, ed., *Acknowledging Consumption: A Review of New Studies* (London: Routledge, 1995).

20. See, e.g., Daniel Miller, "The Young and the Restless: A Case

of the Local and the Global in Mass Consumption," in Roger Silverstone and Eric Hirsch, eds., *Consuming Technologies: Media and Information in Domestic Spaces* (London: Routledge, 1992).

21. Arjun Appadurai, "Disjuncture and Difference in the Global Cultural Economy," in Featherstone, ed., *Global Culture.*

22. Featherstone, "Introduction," *Global Culture*, p. 6; see also Ulf Hannerz, *Cultural Complexity* (New York: Columbia Univ. Press, 1992), pp. 217–67.

23. Christopher A. Bartlett and Sumantra Ghoshal, *Managing Across Borders: The Transnational Solution* (Boston: Harvard Business School Press, 1991).

24. "The Post-National Economy: Goodbye Widget, Hello Nike," *Far Eastern Economic Review* (FEER), Aug. 29, 1996, p. 5.

25. Saskia Sassen, *The Global City: New York, London, Toronto* (Princeton, N.J.: Princeton Univ. Press, 1991).

26. John Love, *McDonald's: Behind the Arches* (New York: Bantam Books, 1986), p. 431.

27. Scott Pendleton, "Giving Golden Arches Global Span," *Christian Science Monitor*, May 21, 1991, p. 8, emphasis added.

28. Love, *McDonald's*, p. 431. Critics of McDonald's will note that the definition of "control" is at issue here. The corporation sets out very clear guidelines, within which all franchisees must operate, down to the exact placement of the pickles on the bun and the design of crew uniforms. Local operators do not "control" this dimension of their business, but, as Love and Cantalupo point out, franchise holders often own up to 50 per cent of the business and make decisions about the disposition of profits. They also have considerable control over local advertising, restaurant location, and (limited) menu innovation.

29. In China, 95 percent of McDonald's raw materials is sourced locally; see Emily Thornton, "McManaging Supplies," FEER, Nov. 23, 1995, p. 76.

30. As Daniel Ng puts it: "When we started up [in Hong Kong], a very famous restaurateur declared that 'Chinese don't eat hamburgers.' Everyone had reasons why it wouldn't work." FEER, Jan. 11, 1996, p. 30.

31. See Love, *McDonald's*, pp. 425–30 on Fujita, pp. 431–33 on Ng. See also "Den Fujita: Bringing Big Macs to Japan," BW, Sept. 8, 1986, p. 53; "Daniel Ng: Asian Achievement," FEER, Jan. 11, 1996, p. 30; and "Ng Sells Stake, but Sticks with Burgers," *Asian Wall Street Journal*, Apr. 13, 1995, p. 10. For the Ray Kroc legend, see his *Grinding It Out* (Chicago: Regnery, 1977).

32. V. Snegirjov, "The Hero of Capitalist Labor: McDonald's Is Not a Mere Restaurant Chain, It Is an Entire Philosophy," *Pravda*, July 31, 1991, pp. 1, 4 (translation courtesy McDonald's Canada).

33. Richard Robison and David Goodman, eds., *The New Rich in Asia: Mobile Phones, McDonald's, and Middle-Class Revolution* (London: Routledge, 1996); see also Roger Janelli with Dawnhee Yim, *Making Capitalism: The Social and Cultural Construction of a South Korean Conglomerate* (Stanford, Calif.: Stanford Univ. Press, 1993), pp. 89–123.

34. On women's work and changing gender roles, see Jean C. Robinson, "Of Women and Washing Machines: Employment, Housework, and the Reproduction of Motherhood in Socialist China," *China Quarterly* 101: 32–57 (1985).

35. See Sangmee Bak, "Professional Woman's Work, Family, and Kinship: A Case Study of a Taiwan Television Station." Ph.D. diss., Harvard Univ., 1994, pp. 37–73.

36. On the nature of conjugality and its consequences, see Yunxiang Yan, *The Flow of Gifts: Reciprocity and Social Networks in a Chinese Village* (Stanford, Calif.: Stanford Univ. Press, 1996), pp. 193–206; and Charlotte Ikels, *The Return of the God of Wealth: The Transition to a Market Economy in Urban China* (Stanford, Calif.: Stanford Univ. Press, 1996), pp. 118–39.

37. See, e.g., Jing Jun, "Children as Consumers: Links of Population Policy and Economic Reform in China," in David Wu, ed., *Changing Diet and Foodways in Chinese Culture* (Hong Kong: Chinese Univ. of Hong Kong, in press).

38. Merry White, *The Material Child: Coming of Age in Japan and America* (Berkeley: Univ. of California Press, 1994), p. 112.

39. SCMPIW, Dec. 2, 1995.

40. Ezra Vogel, *Japan's New Middle Class* (Berkeley: Univ. of California Press, 1963).

41. White, *The Material Child.*

42. Theodore Bestor, "Lifestyles and Popular Culture," in R. Powers and H. Kato, eds., *Handbook of Japanese Popular Culture* (Homewood, Ill.: Greenwood Press, 1989).

43. Janet W. Salaff, *Working Daughters of Hong Kong: Filial Piety or Power in the Family?* 2d ed. (New York: Columbia Univ. Press, 1995), pp. xviii–xx.

44. Fai-ming Wong, "Industrialization and Family Structure in Hong Kong," *Journal of Marriage and the Family* 37: 985–1000 (1975).

45. Bak, "Professional Woman's Work."

46. Charles Stafford, *The Roads of Chinese Childhood* (Cambridge, Eng.: Cambridge Univ. Press, 1995), p. 61.

47. Janelli, *Making Capitalism*, pp. 207–10; see also Okpyo Moon, "Urban Middle Class Wives in Contemporary Korea," *Korea Journal* 30(11): 30–43 (1990).

48. Interviews with colleagues at Seoul National Univ., 1990. One mother, a left-wing intellectual, said: "My kids insist on eating at McDonald's and KFC. They won't eat *kimchi* [pickled cabbage], no matter how hard I try to force them. When it comes to food, they always win and I always lose."

49. Reuters, Aug. 6, 1996, Clarinet.biz.industry.food:3476.

50. On the origin of fast food see, e.g., Holly Chase, "The *Meyhane* or McDonald's? Changes in the Eating Habits and the Evolution of Fast Food in Istanbul," in Richard Tapper and Sami Zubaida, eds., *Culinary Cultures of the Middle East* (London: I. B. Tauris, 1994), p. 76; Paul H. Noguchi, "*Ekiben:* The Fast Food of High-Speed Japan," *Ethnology* 33(4): 317–30 (1994); John K. Walden, "Fish and Chips and the British Working Class, 1870–1930," *Journal of Social History* 23(2): 244–66 (1989). Walden calls fish and chips "the pioneer fast-food industry" (p. 244).

51. *Asian Wall Street Journal*, Dec. 28, 1995.

52. All franchise holders are required to take a two-week course on quality control and management procedures at Hamburger University. There are branches of the school in London, Munich, and Tokyo. See Robin Leidner, *Fast Food, Fast Talk: Service Work and*

Routinization of Everyday Life (Berkeley: Univ. of California Press, 1993), pp. 54–57; and Rhonda Reynolds, "The Dean of Fast Food's Harvard," *Black Enterprise*, Sept. 1994, p. 52.

53. Leidner, *Fast Food*, p. 82.

54. Ibid., pp. 48–58.

55. Alan B. Krueger, "Ownership, Agency, and Wages: An Examination of Franchising in the Fast Food Industry," *Quarterly Journal of Economics* 106(1): 75–101 (1991), p. 78.

56. Eric Berg, "An American Icon Wrestles with a Troubled Future," NYT, May 12, 1991, p. B6.

57. BW, Oct. 13, 1986, p. 80.

58. Thomas L. Friedman, "14 Big Macs Later . . . ," NYT, Dec. 31, 1995 (emphasis in original).

59. Medical researchers are only beginning to explore the mysteries of taste, perhaps the last of the human senses to receive serious attention. Linda Bartoshuk, a researcher at the Yale School of Medicine, notes that taste buds are not distributed evenly in human populations: some people have more, many more, than do others. The range of "taste worlds" varies accordingly, from supertasters (who can discern minute differences in flavor additives) to nontasters (who consume whole chili peppers without blinking). It should not be surprising, therefore, that opinions vary regarding the taste of McDonald's standardized fare. John Willoughby, "Taste? Bud to Bud, Tongues May Differ," NYT, Dec. 7, 1994, pp. C1, C11. See also Constance Classen, *Worlds of Sense: Exploring the Senses in History and Across Cultures* (London: Routledge, 1993).

60. When the son of a Japanese executive first spotted the Golden Arches while traveling with his family in North America, he exclaimed: "They even have McDonald's in the United States!" *Christian Science Monitor*, May 21, 1991, p. 8. Engineers and computer scientists who have returned to their native Taiwan with American-born children report the opposite response: "Look! They have McDonald's here!" (personal communication with colleagues in Taiwan). The February 22, 1995, *International Herald Tribune* carries a revealing photograph with the following caption: "[A returned scientist] having breakfast with his family [wife and three children] at a McDonald's restaurant in Hsin-chu, northern Taiwan" (p. 2).

61. Andrew Selvaggio, "Feeding Olympians and Other Fans of the Big Mac." NYT, May 29, 1996, pp. C1, C4. Olympic athletes consumed 150,000 Big Macs and double cheeseburgers in 22 days; McDonald's press release, July 31, 1996, http://www.mcdonalds.com.

62. Nuri Vittachi, "Gates to the Middle Kingdom," SCMPIW, Dec. 30, 1995, p. 11.

63. Reuters, "First Kosher McDonald's Opens in Israel," Oct. 11, 1995. Clarinet.biz.industry.food:3859. Earlier outlets in Israel were nonkosher and had sparked protests; see, e.g., Lisa Talesnick, "Rabbi Battles Golden Arches," *Boston Globe*, Mar. 23, 1995.

64. Jonathan Karp, "Food for Politics: McDonald's Opens in India's Prickly Market," FEER, Oct. 24, 1996, p. 72; Dan Biers and Miriam Jordan, "McDonald's in India Decides the Big Mac Is Not a Sacred Cow," WSJ, Oct. 14, 1996, p. A11. Given KFC's recent problems with Hindu nationalists and radical vegetarians, other fast food chains (including McDonald's) appear to have shelved expansion plans for India; see Miriam Jordan, "U.S. Food Firms Head for Cover in India," WSJ, Nov. 21, 1995, p. A14. On January 30, 1996, demonstrators broke through a police cordon in Bangalore and ransacked a KFC outlet (NYT, Jan. 31, 1996). Earlier a KFC restaurant was closed by New Delhi health inspectors after they spotted two flies in the kitchen; the "discovery" caused great hilarity in the local press (NYT, Nov. 25, 1995, p. 4).

65. John Oleck, "When Worlds Collide," *Restaurant Business* 92 (10): 48–56 (July 1, 1993), p. 50.

66. Holly Chase, "The *Meyhane* or McDonald's?" p. 75; Silvia Sansoni, "Big Macs Al Dente?" BW, Nov. 28, 1994, p. 8 (Italy); Harlan Byrne, "Welcome to McWorld," *Barron's*, Aug. 29, 1994, p. 25 (Netherlands); *Welcome to McDonald's*, 1996, McDonald's Corp., McD 5-2940, p. 29 (Philippines, Norway, Germany, Uruguay); and personal observations in Japan, Taiwan, and Hong Kong.

67. Richard Gibson, "McDonald's Decides to Trim the Low Fat in Menu Shake-Up," WSJ, Feb. 5, 1996, p. B5; Simon Midgeley, "Big Mac Gets a Mouthful of Abuse," *The Independent*, Oct. 28, 1994.

68. James Scarpa, "McDonald's Menu Mission," *Restaurant Business*, July 1, 1991, p. 4.

69. Julie Vorman (Reuters), "Burger King to Dish Up 'Stealth' Fries," Mar. 20, 1996. Clarinet.biz.industry.food:4562; see also, "America's Fry-Meisters Go to War," BW, Sept. 16, 1996, p. 8.

70. See, e.g., Martyn J. Lee, *Consumer Culture Reborn* (London: Routledge, 1993), esp. chap. 5, "The Political Economy of Fordism," pp. 73-85.

71. Allen Sheldon, "A Theater for Eating, Looking, and Thinking: The Restaurant as Symbolic Space," *Sociological Spectrum* 10: 507-26 (1990), p. 520.

72. Warren J. Belasco, "Toward a Culinary Common Denominator: The Rise of Howard Johnson's, 1925-1966," *Journal of American Culture* 2(3): 503-18 (1979), pp. 511-13.

73. Food chains were standardized and franchised after gasoline companies had shown the power of brand names; see John A. Jackle, "Roadside Restaurants and Place-Product Packaging," in George O. Carney, ed., *Fast Food, Stock Cars, and Rock 'n' Roll: Place and Space in American Pop Culture* (London: Rowan & Littlefield, 1995), p. 97.

74. *Welcome to McDonald's*, McDonald's Corp., McD 5-2940 (1996), pp. 8-10.

75. Elaine Louie, "Sushi, in Just Three Seconds," NYT, Jan. 4, 1995, pp. C1, C7.

76. *The Economist*, Jan. 15, 1994, p. 89.

77. Krueger, "Ownership," p. 83.

78. Dolores Whiskeyman, "Will You Take Your Order, Please?" *American Demographics* 13(1): 13 (Jan. 1991).

79. Ethnographic interviewing carried out in Moscow by Melissa Caldwell; tray liners and video of McDonald's opening day in Moscow ("A Taste of the West," 1994 Update, SCV 94-10, McDonald's Canada) provided by George Cohon. The tray liner explains the "Big Mak" as "Two chopped steaks made of fresh, wholesome beef with chopped lettuce, slabs of cheese, slices of pickled cucumber, and onions placed in a sliced bun covered with sesame seeds" (translation courtesy of Melissa Caldwell).

80. Melissa Caldwell observed many Muscovites disassembling Big Macs and eating them layer by layer; see Chap. 2 for a similar method of eating among novice consumers in Hong Kong.

81. Peter Stephenson, "Going to McDonald's in Leiden," *Ethnos* 17(2): 226–47 (1989), pp. 236–37.

82. Rick Fantasia, "Fast Food in France," *Theory and Society* 24: 201–43 (1995), pp. 221–22; Melissa Caldwell, "Consumption, Choice, and Fast Food in Moscow," research paper, 1995, Dept. of Anthropology, Harvard Univ.

83. Sheldon, "A Theater," p. 519.

84. Ron Harris, "Candlelight, Champagne and Two Big Macs, Please," *San Jose Mercury News*, Sept. 16, 1994, pp. E1–E2; Peter Wilson, "KFC Won't Chicken Out in Third Venezuelan Try," *Advertising Age*, Dec. 13, 1993, pp. 1–15.

85. Quoting from a tray liner distributed in Maine, 1994: "At McDonald's today, value means a lot more than just low prices. It means fast, courteous service. Clean restrooms. And a smile with your change. It's what you deserve."

86. Leidner, *Fast Food*, p. 68.

87. *The Economist*, Jan. 31, 1990, p. 74.

88. Japan may be an exception to this rule, given that "a smile is taken so seriously [in Japanese McDonald's] that it is often listed on the menu board. The price: ¥0." FEER, Jan. 5, 1995, p. 48.

89. Penny Moser, "The McDonald's Mystique," *Fortune*, July 4, 1988, p. 113.

90. Andrew Pollack, "Food-Poisoning Outbreak Alarms Japan," NYT, July 25, 1996, pp. A1, A8.

91. Personal communications: Jun Jing and Jeanne Shea. Fifty-six percent of small restaurants and 44 percent of the street stalls in Beijing failed a sanitary utensil test, according to China's Ministry of Health. Furthermore, over a quarter of the food products sold in Chinese shops do not meet general health standards. UPI, Nov. 4, 1996, Clarinet.biz.industry.food:5578.

92. Beverly Chao, "McDonald's to Sue Copycats," SCMPIW, May 7, 1994; personal observations by Sangmee Bak, Thomas Rawski, and J. L. Watson.

93. Donald McNeil, "Restoring Their Good Names: U.S. Companies in Trademark Battles in South Africa," NYT, May 1, 1996, p. B1; *Wired* 4.02 (Feb. 1996), p. 166 (Bangalore); Reuters, "McDonald's Wins Danish Ruling on Name," Aug. 24, 1995, Clarinet.biz.

industry.food:3570; David Lindley, "What's in a Name? Mc-Dharma's Natural Fast Food," *Mother Jones*, Jan. 1987, p. 15.

94. Oleck, "When Worlds Collide," p. 56; Seth Faison, "Razors, Soap, Cornflakes: Pirating in China Balloons," NYT, Feb. 17, 1995, p. D2; and SCMPIW, July 13, 1996, p. B3. A colleague returned recently from the interior of Hebei province, in north China, bearing a special gift: a pair of socks embossed with the Golden Arches and packaged like a typical packet of McDonald's fries. An entire museum could be filled with these knockoffs, all of which testify to the power of the brand name and its primary symbol.

95. Personal communications, Bernadine Chee and Eriberto (Fuji) Lozada.

96. Hamilton Beazley and John Lobuts, "Rational Teaching, Indentured Research, and the Loss of Reason," *Academe*, Jan.-Feb. 1996, p. 30 (McThink, McMyth); Douglas Coupland, *Generation X* (New York: St. Martin's, 1991) (McJobs); Eugene Kennedy, quoted in NYT, July 13,1996 (McSpirituality).

97. George Ritzer, *The McDonaldization of Society* (Thousand Oaks, Calif.: Pine Forge Press, 1991), p. 1.

98. Ibid.

99. "All the World's a McStage," BW, May 8, 1995, p. 8. Meanwhile McDonald's has become the world's leading brand name, according to Interbrand, a consultancy that specializes in consumer recognition; McDonald's has surpassed Coca-Cola, which was the number one brand name in 1990. See *The Economist*, Nov. 16, 1996, p. 72.

Chapter 1

This chapter is based on fieldwork in Beijing, August to October 1994, supported by a grant from the Henry Luce Foundation to the Fairbank Center for East Asian Research, Harvard University. I owe special thanks to Tim Lai, Zhang Ziyun, and several staff members at Beijing McDonald's for their cooperation and assistance during my research. I also wish to thank Wang Rui, Sheng Shuangxia, He Jie at Beijing University and Lian Dongyan at Guanhualu Primary School for research assistance. I am grateful to Selina Chan, Jun Jing, Sidney Mintz, James Watson, and Rubie Watson for their valuable comments on early drafts of this chapter.

1. *New York Times* (NYT), Apr. 24, 1992.
2. *China Daily*, Sept. 12, 1994; *Shijie ribao* (World Journal), Dec. 2, 1966.
3. *Fuwu zhiqiao* (Service Bridge), Aug. 12, 1994.
4. Ibid., Aug. 19, 1994.
5. With some differences in emphasis, McDonald's is recognized as a symbol of Americana in the United States as well as in many parts of the world. As Ritzer notes, "Many people identify strongly with McDonald's; in fact, to some it has become a sacred institution. On the opening of the McDonald's in Moscow, one journalist described it as the 'ultimate icon of Americana.'" See George Ritzer, *The McDonaldization of Society* (Thousand Oaks, Calif.: Pine Forge Press, 1993), p. 5.
6. Every time McDonald's opened a new restaurant in the early 1990s, it was featured in the Chinese media. See, e.g., *Tianjin qingnian bao* (Tianjin Youth News), June 8, 1994; *Shanghai jingji bao* (Shanghai Economic News), July 22, 1994; *Wenhui bao* (Wen Hui Daily), July 22, 1994. See also Han Shu, "M: changsheng jiangjun" (M [McDonald's]: the undefeated general), *Xiaofei zhinan* (Consumption Guide) 2: 10–11 (1994).
7. See, e.g., *Shoudu jingji xinxi bao* (Capital Economics Information), Nov. 28, Dec. 3, 1993.
8. Xu Chengbei, "Cong maidanglao kan shijie" (Seeing the world from McDonald's), *Zhongguo pengren* (Chinese Culinary Art) 8: 3 (1993).
9. *Fazhi ribao* (Legal System Daily), Sept. 9, 1992.
10. *Gaige daobao* (Reform Herald) 1: 34 (1994).
11. See Xu Chengbei, "Kuaican, dacai yu xinlao zihao" (Fast food, formal dishes, and the new and old restaurants), *Jingji ribao* (Economics Daily), Sept. 17, 1994.
12. See Rosemary Safranek, "The McDonald's Recipe for Japan." *Intersect* 2(10): 10 (Oct. 1986); and NYT, Apr. 13, 1994.
13. The figure was provided by Tim Lai, the General Manager, during my interview with him on September 28, 1994.
14. As China's best-informed group of young people, college students are generally fond of foreign food. In my survey of 100 students in a major university in Beijing, only three had not eaten at

McDonald's. In another Beijing college, when first-year students returned from a three-week stint of military training (a program designed to instill an appreciation of communist ideology), the first thing they did was visit their favorite restaurants, such McDonald's, KFC, and Pizza Hut.

15. K. C. Chang, "Introduction," in K. C. Chang, ed., *Food in Chinese Culture: Anthropological and Historical Perspectives* (New Haven, Conn.: Yale Univ. Press, 1977), p. 7. See also E. N. Anderson, *The Food of China* (New Haven, Conn.: Yale Univ. Press, 1988), p. 25.

16. Xu Chengbei, "Kuaican wenhua and wenhua kuaican" (The culture of fast food and the "cultural fast food"), *Zhongguo pengren* 10: 15–16 (1991).

17. *Zhongguo ripin bao* (Chinese Food News), Nov. 6, 1991.

18. *Jingji ribao*, Sept. 15, 1991.

19. Interview with Tim Lai, Sept. 28, 1994.

20. For an interesting study of eating etiquette in south China, see Eugene Cooper, "Chinese Table Manners: You Are How You Eat," *Human Organization* 45: 179–84 (1986).

21. For a critique of the social consequences of McDonald's fast food and its culture, see Ritzer, *The McDonaldization of Society*.

22. These figures were provided respectively by Tim Lai, the General Manager, and the Head of the Personnel Department in my interviews on September 28 and October 22, 1994. The presence of Communist Party branches within the restaurants also makes McDonald's distinctive from its counterparts elsewhere in the world. See NYT, Apr. 24, 1992.

23. *Far Eastern Economic Review*, Mar. 4, 1993, p. 50.

24. *Zhongguo jinkou bao* (China Import News), Sept. 13, 1994.

25. *Beijing wanbao* (Beijing Evening News), Sept. 10, 1994.

26. See, e.g., *Zhongguo qingnian bao* (China Youth News), Sept. 29, 1994; *Guangming ribao* (Guangming Daily), Sept. 29, 1994. News of the flag-raising ceremony was also broadcast on Beijing Radio Station.

27. A legal dispute occurred between McDonald's and Beijing's local government in late November 1994. The Beijing municipal office asked McDonald's to vacate its restaurant at the corner of Wang-

fujing Street, to make room for a large commercial office and residential complex planned by a Hong Kong billionaire. Because McDonald's believed it held a lease on the site for another 18 years, the case gained worldwide publicity. See *Wall Street Journal*, Nov. 22, 1994; *South China Morning Post*, Nov. 27, 1994; and *Newsweek*, Dec. 12, 1994. An agreement was finally reached in late 1996. McDonald's agreed to relocate its flagship restaurant so that the construction of the new commercial complex could proceed. The fast food chain was to receive compensation for the move from the Beijing government, and a new location emerged as a possibility, about 150 meters farther north on the same street (Wangfujing Street). See *Shijie ribao* (World Journal), Dec. 2, 1996.

28. See, e.g., *Beijing wanbao*, Feb. 10, 1994; and Ya Guanning, "Jingcheng kuaican yipie" (A glance at the fast food in Beijing), *Fuwu jingji* (Service Economy) 4: 24–25 (Apr. 1994).

29. Conrad P. Kottak, "Rituals at McDonald's," *Journal of American Culture* 1(2): 372 (1978).

30. According to Ritzer, replacing human workers with technology is one of the four basic features of the McDonaldization process. See Ritzer, *The McDonaldization of Society*, pp. 10–11.

31. In the restaurant at Changan Shopping Mall, a retired head nurse performed her new role as Aunt McDonald so well that when she was promoted and transferred to another outlet in Shanghai, customers continued to ask about her.

32. The concepts of *renqing*, *guanxi* (personal networks), and *mianzi* (face) dominate Chinese patterns of social behavior. For a detailed discussion, see Yunxiang Yan, *The Flow of Gifts: Reciprocity and Social Networks in a Chinese Village*, esp. chaps. 6 and 9 (Stanford, Calif.: Stanford Univ. Press, 1996).

33. *Beijing wanbao*, Mar. 14, 1994.

34. Since the late 1970s the Chinese government and experts from various fields have agreed that, without a strict plan for population control, China would eat up whatever resources it had. In 1979 couples of childbearing age were encouraged to have only one child per family, and this became a national policy in 1980. After the 1982 national census, which revealed that China's population was over one billion, the single-child policy was implemented rigorously nation-

wide and some 20 million people (most of them women) underwent sterilization. The policy was relaxed in the mid-1980s, however, and rules about second children were liberalized slightly in 1984. For complex social and economic reasons, the single-child policy encountered more resistance in the countryside than in urban areas, and it was most effectively carried out in major cities such as Beijing and Shanghai. For detailed studies, see Judith Banister, *China's Changing Population* (Stanford, Calif.: Stanford Univ. Press, 1987); and Susan Greenhalgh, "The Evolution of the One-Child Policy in Shaanxi, 1979–88," *China Quarterly* 122: 191–229 (1990).

35. *China Daily*, Sept. 12, 1994.

36. Jack Goody, *Cooking, Cuisine and Class* (Cambridge, Eng.: Cambridge Univ. Press, 1982), p. 181. The rise of "children's power" seems to be a modern phenomenon, which has occurred in many countries, including the United States. I am grateful to Sidney Mintz for pointing this out to me and pushing me to consider the link between parent-child interactions and the influences of modernity.

37. See John F. Love, *McDonald's: Behind the Arches* (New York: Bantam Books, 1986), p. 449.

38. *Zhongguo xiaofeizhe bao* (China Consumer News), Sept. 12, 1994.

39. See, e.g., Gao Changli, "Woguo jiushi niandai chengxian duoyuanhua xiaofei qushi" (Consumption trends have diversified in China during the 1990s), *Shangpin pingjie* (Commodity Review) 10: 6 (1992); and Dong Fang, "Zhongguo chengshi xiaofei wuda redian" (The five hot points in Chinese urban consumption), *Jingji shijie* (Economic World) 1: 22 (1994).

40. Gong Wen, "Guonei gaoxiaofei daguan" (Hyperconsumption in China), *Xiaofei zhinan* (Consumption Guide) 2: 1–12 (1993); and Zhao Bo, "Xingxing sese yang xiaofei" (Varieties of consumption of foreign goods), *Market Price* 3: 9 (1994).

41. Luo Jufen, "Gaoxiaofei: buke yizhi de chaoliu" (Luxury consumption: an irresistible trend), *Shangpin pingjie* 6: 5 (1993).

42. Lin Ye, "Xiaofei lingyu xin sanjian" (The new three big items in consumption), *Zhongguo shicang* (China Market) 7: 28 (1994).

43. For details of this survey, see Pian Ming, "Beijing qingnian rezhong gaodang shangpin" (Beijing youth are keen on expensive

commodities), *Zhongguo gongshang shibao* (China Industrial and Commercial Times), July 16, 1994.

44. See *Xiaofeizhe bao* (Consumer News), Aug. 22, 1993.

45. See news reports in *Zhongguo xiaofei shibao* (China Consumption Times), Feb. 3 and Mar. 3, 1993.

46. Gu Bingshu, "Waican: dushi xin fengshang" (Eating out: a fashion in cities), *Xiaofeizhe* (Consumers) 3: 14–15 (1994).

47. *Beijing wanbao*, Jan. 27, 1993.

48. *Beijing qingnian bao* (Beijing Youth Daily), Dec. 18, 1993.

49. Mian Zhi, "Xishi kuaican fengmi jingcheng, zhongshi kuaican zenmoban?" (Western fast food sweeps Beijing; what will Chinese fast food do?), *Aiqing, hunyin yu jiating* (Love, Marriage, and Family) 6: 11 (1993).

50. Yan Zhengguo and Liu Yinsheng, "Zhongguo kuaican shichang shui zhu chenfu?" (Who will control the fast food market in China?), *Shoudu jingji xinxi bao*, Dec. 8, 1992.

51. See, e.g., *Shichang bao* (Market News), Nov. 10, 1992; Xiao Hua, "Da ru zhongguo de yang kuaican" (The invasion of foreign fast food in China), *Jiating shenghuo zhinan* (Guide of Family Life) 5: 6–7 (1993); and Yang Guangzeng, "Yang kuaican chi shenme?" (What do we get out of foreign fast food?), *Gaige daobao* (Reform Herald) 1: 34 (1994).

52. See, e.g. *Beijing wanbao*, Jan. 27, 1993; and Huang Zhijian, "Yige juda de qingnian xiaofei shichang" (A huge consumption market among youths), *Zhongguo qingnian yanjiu* (Chinese Youth Studies) 2: 13 (1994).

53. Sidney Mintz, "Time, Sugar and Sweetness," *Marxist Perspectives* 2: 65 (1979). In his well-known book *Sweetness and Power: The Place of Sugar in Modern History* (New York: Penguin Books, 1985), Mintz offers an excellent analysis of how sugar, which was initially an imported foreign luxury good, was transformed by capitalism into an everyday necessity for working-class Europeans during the seventeenth and eighteenth centuries.

54. See *Beijing wanbao*, Sept. 13, 1992; and Mar. 15, 1993.

55. You Zi, "Jingcheng zhongshi kuaican re qi lai le!" (Chinese-style fast food is getting hot in Beijing!), *Jingji shijie* 6: 60–61 (1994).

56. See *Beijing wanbao*, Mar. 15, 1993.

57. Personal interview, Sept. 28, 1994.

58. See *Jingji ribao*, Sept. 17, 1994. For a detailed study of the responses of the local restaurant industry to the challenge posed by foreign fast food chains, see Yan Yunxiang, "Beijing de kuaican re jiqi dui chuantong yinshi wenhua de yingxiang" (The fast food fever and its impact on local dietary culture in Beijing), in Lin Qinghu, ed., *Di si jie yingshi xueshu wenhua yantaohui lunwenji* (Proceedings of the 4th symposium on Chinese dietary culture) (Taipei: Foundation of Chinese Dietary Culture, 1996), pp. 47–63.

59. See R. N. Adams, "The Dynamics of Societal Diversity: Notes from Nicaragua for a Sociology of Survival," *American Ethnologist* 8: 2 (1981). For further discussions of transnationalism and local responses, see Chadwick Alger, "Perceiving, Analysing and Coping with the Local-Global Nexus," *International Social Science Journal* 117: 321–40 (1988); Jonathan Friedman, "Being in the World: Globalization and Localization," *Theory, Culture & Society* 7: 311–28 (1990); and Ulf Hannerz, "Cosmopolitans and Locals in World Culture," *Theory, Culture & Society* 7: 237–51 (1990).

60. See Daniel Miller, "The Young and the Restless in Trinidad: A Case of the Local and the Global in Mass Consumption," in Roger Silverstone and Eric Hirsch, eds., *Consuming Technologies: Media and Information in Domestic Spaces* (London: Routledge, 1992), pp. 163–82.

Chapter 2

Funding for this project was provided by the Chiang Ching-kuo Foundation through a grant administered by the Chinese University of Hong Kong (summer 1994) and by the Henry Luce Foundation in association with the Fairbank Center for East Asian Research, Harvard University. The author thanks the following people who helped in various ways but are not in the least responsible for the conclusions or interpretations drawn: Joseph Bosco, Sidney Cheung, Chiao Chien, Hsu Cho-yun, Stella Kao, Liu Tik-sang, Gordon Mathews, Teng Tim-sing, Elaine Tsui, Rubie Watson, and David Wu. I am grateful to Elia Wong and Jessy Tsang for helping with field surveys at a McDonald's restaurant in the Hong Kong New Territories (Yuen Long, Castle Peak Road). Special thanks go to Daniel Ng,

Chairman of McDonald's Hong Kong, and to Jeffrey Wai, Franchise Owner of the Yuen Long restaurant, both of whom were generous enough to share their extensive knowledge of the Hong Kong food scene and changing popular culture.

1. K. C. Chang, "Introduction," in K. C. Chang, ed., *Food in Chinese Culture* (New Haven, Conn.: Yale Univ. Press, 1977), p. 14.

2. Each of these seven outlets had over two million transactions per year. In 1992 McDonald's was feeding 250,000 Hong Kong residents every day, representing 4 percent of the population (*Forbes*, Mar. 16, 1992, p. 156); see also *The Economist*, Dec. 4, 1993. The value of fast food receipts in Hong Kong increased from HK$55 million in 1987 to HK$712 million in 1992 (*Hong Kong Monthly Digest of Statistics, March, 1994* [Hong Kong Census and Statistics Dept.], p. 95).

3. "McDonald's Reports Strong Global Results," news release, McDonald's Corp., Jan. 23, 1997, http://www.mcdonalds.com. Census figures for McDonald's in the United States are from *McDonald's Investor Highlights*, McD3-1775, 1993, p. 2. Hong Kong's estimated population was 6,218,000 at the end of March 1996; see Clarinet.WORLD.Asia.Hong-kong (Reuters, Nov. 5, 1996); by January 1997, the figure had grown to nearly 6,400,000. The *Asian Wall Street Journal* (AWSJ) (Apr. 13, 1995, p. 10) estimated McDonald's 1994 sales in Hong Kong at approximately US$130 million.

4. The most influential model from this era is that of Immanuel Wallerstein and his colleagues. See Wallerstein's *The Modern World System* (New York: Academic Press, 1974); and Walter L. Goldfrank, ed., *The World-System of Capitalism: Past and Present* (London: Sage, 1979).

5. Louise do Rosario, "Hong Kong's Café de Coral Fights to Stay on Top," *Far Eastern Economic Review*, July 28, 1994, pp. 69–70.

6. Records and photos on file, Archives Dept., Coca-Cola Company, Atlanta, Georgia.

7. According to a 1994 international survey, Hong Kong was the world's most stressful place to work (see *South China Morning Post International Weekly* [SCMPIW], Nov. 20, 1994, p. 3). Hong Kong workers averaged 2,375 hours of work per year (9.7 hours per day),

outranked only by South Korea and Chile (SCMPIW, Sept. 18, 1994, p. B2).

8. From 1990 to 1994, Hong Kong residents spent on average 55.5 percent of their food budgets on meals outside their homes (data from *Consumer Price Index Report, April, 1994* [Hong Kong Census and Statistics Dept.], p. 29). Comparable figures for U.S. consumers are strikingly different: 38.3 percent of the average American household's food budget in 1988 was devoted to food eaten outside the home (David Smallwood et al., *Food Spending in American Households, 1980–1988* [Statistics Bulletin no. 824, Economic Research Service, U.S. Dept. of Agriculture, 1991], pp. 5, 15).

9. See, e.g., John Love, *McDonald's: Behind the Arches* (New York: Bantam Books, 1986), pp. 431–33; and "Daniel Ng: Asian Achievement," *Far Eastern Economic Review*, Jan. 11, 1996, p. 30. In April 1995, Mr. Ng sold his 33 percent stake in the Hong Kong business to McDonald's Corp. (Oak Brook); Don Dempsey was appointed the new Managing Director. Mr. Ng was named Chairman of McDonald's Hong Kong unit (AWSJ, Apr. 13, 1995, p. 10).

10. Interview with Daniel Ng, Jan. 14, 1993, Hong Kong.

11. KFC's initial entry into the local market ended in failure, but after a second attempt it rebounded and soon became one of Hong Kong's leading fast food chains. The full story of this remarkable transformation has yet to be told.

12. The dichotomy between rice and toppings (in Mandarin, *fan* versus *cai*) is the core feature of Chinese cuisine; see Chang, "Introduction," pp. 7–8.

13. Hong Kong consumers have become more conscious of health concerns during the past decade and fast foods are increasingly associated with a rise in childhood obesity there. Children in Hong Kong have the world's second-highest cholesterol rates (following Finland) and are ingesting 30 percent of their daily calories from fat—double the amount of people who consume a "traditional Cantonese diet." (SCMPIW, Apr. 27, 1996; see also "Life in the Fast Food Lane," *Sunday Hong Kong Standard*, Oct. 15, 1995, special report.)

14. See Love, *McDonald's*, p. 431.

15. A recent menu innovation is the Shogunburger, a sausage

patty doused with teriyaki sauce and served in a bun; this item is also sold by McDonald's outlets in Japan and Taiwan.

16. Interview with Daniel Ng, June 16, 1994. McDonald's has subsequently become a breakfast institution in Hong Kong, offering newspapers and free refills of hot drinks. McDonald's was cited as Hong Kong's top venue for fast breakfasts in *Next*, a popular magazine serving upwardly mobile consumers (*Next* 166: 102–4 [May 14, 1993]).

17. This approach is usually associated with Max Weber, who stressed the role of personality factors in explaining the rise of capitalism; see his *The Protestant Ethic and the Spirit of Capitalism* (New York: Scribner's, 1958 [1904–5]). For interesting ethnographies of the East Asian business world see Rodney Clark, *The Japanese Company* (New Haven, Conn.: Yale Univ. Press, 1979); Roger Janelli with Dawnhee Yim, *Making Capitalism: The Social and Cultural Construction of a South Korean Conglomerate* (Stanford, Calif.: Stanford Univ. Press, 1993); and Robert H. Silin, *Leadership and Values: The Organization of Large-Scale Taiwanese Enterprises* (Cambridge, Mass.: Harvard Univ. Press, 1976).

18. I compared prices for equivalent items at the following chains: Café de Coral, Fairwood, Golden Fastfood, Hardee's, KFC, Maxim's Fast Food, McDonald's, and Wendy's.

19. AWSJ, Apr. 13, 1995, p. 10. The Big Mac in Hong Kong is approximately one-third the price of the equivalent in Tokyo. *The Economist* (Apr. 2, 1997, p. 75) notes that the Big Mac in Beijing is now the cheapest in the world; Hong Kong is second-lowest and Poland third-lowest in price.

20. *Fourth Quarter Report*, McDonald's Corp., 1990. This record, in turn, was broken two years later when McDonald's first Beijing outlet was opened; see Introduction, n. 1.

21. Interview with Daniel Ng, Jan. 14, 1993.

22. McDonald's was awarded the top Restaurant Hygiene Award, conferred by the Hong Kong Urban Council, three years in a row—1991, 1992, 1993.

23. The company continues its campaign to maintain clean restrooms, but the heavy traffic makes this increasingly difficult. McDonald's has been overtaken in the cleanliness sweepstakes by other,

more expensive restaurants, but these establishments do not have a mass clientele and do not tolerate casual use.

24. Sample of 527 customers (306 women) in the outlet at Yuen Long, Hong Kong New Territories, Castle Peak Road; surveyed June 8 and 12, 1994.

25. There have been complaints about the lack of "friendly" service in Hong Kong McDonald's, primarily from Filipina maids who congregate in Central District on Sundays and patronize fast food restaurants in that area (see *South China Morning Post* [SCMP], letters to editor, Oct. 26 and Nov. 2, 1992). McDonald's management has made efforts to address these concerns (see SCMP, letter to editor, Nov. 5, 1992). Chinese customers, by contrast, seem to care little whether they receive service with a smile when visiting McDonald's.

26. E. Christine Jackson, "Ethnography of an Urban Burger King Franchise," *Journal of American Culture* 2(3): 534–39 (1979), p. 537.

27. The average eating time in this restaurant was 25.9 minutes, timed from the moment of sitting (with food) and departing from the table. Periods surveyed were Wednesday, June 8, 1994, 11:30 A.M.–2:30 P.M., 3:30 P.M.–5:00 P.M., and Sunday, June 12, 1994, 11:00 A.M.–3:00 P.M.

28. That honor probably goes to the Kowloon Motor Bus Company, which introduced a crash barrier system to channel passengers to buses at its Star Ferry concourse in the early 1970s. It was only later, however, that queuing became an accepted practice at bus stops and taxi stands throughout Hong Kong.

29. A survey of the Yuen Long McDonald's shows that the vast majority of customers (75.7 percent) arrived in groups of three or more. Observations in other outlets confirm that these figures are typical of most McDonald's restaurants in Hong Kong, except those in central business districts (Victoria and Tsimshatsui).

30. Pizza restaurants, including the Pizza Hut chain, do not allow hovering. It is doubtful, however, that these establishments fit into the local category of "fast food" because they tend to be more expensive and more formal than McDonald's and Café de Coral.

31. During particularly busy weekends, some outlets delegate one employee to stand in the center of the restaurant and hand out napkins to customers after they have received their food. One Sunday in

June 1994, I watched a young man hand out napkins with both hands, in rapid-fire fashion, for two straight hours until he was relieved by another worker. The routine continued most of the day, essentially removing the equivalent of one full-time employee from the crews behind the counter.

32. Riots occurred in 1967, and there was widespread fear of a communist takeover in the 1970s; for a discussion of this period in Hong Kong's history, see James L. Watson, "Living Ghosts: Long-Haired Destitutes in Colonial Hong Kong," in Barbara Miller, ed., *Hair in Asian Cultures* (Albany: State Univ. of New York Press, in press).

33. Chinese growers have begun to produce an elongated potato suitable for McDonald's french fries, but in the early 1990s Idaho potatoes were cheaper in Hong Kong than comparable products imported from central China. U.S. food exports to Hong Kong totaled US$4.8 billion in 1990, making it the fifth-largest Asian market for American produce (*Asian Business*, Dec. 1991, p. 26). The percentage of Chinese raw materials used by McDonald's in Hong Kong has been steadily increasing as supplies improve.

34. Maximizing local supplies is a standard practice for McDonald's; see Love, *McDonald's*, pp. 442–45.

35. *Oppose McDonald's*, 1st ed. (student newspaper), Chinese Univ. of Hong Kong Student Union, Oct. 15, 1993.

36. "We Treasure Rain Forests Too," Chinese-language leaflet, McDonald's Corp., Hong Kong, 1993.

37. McDonald's has been the target of regular demonstrations, often violent, in Mexico City; see "Protesters in Mexico City Ransack a McDonald's," *New York Times* (NYT), Nov. 9, 1994. For French reactions see Rick Fantasia, "Fast Food in France," *Theory and Society* 24: 201–43 (1995); and for protests in England see "Burger Protesters Take Their Beef to Ronald," *Independent*, June 6, 1995, pp. 1–2.

38. Hong Kong Earth Summit (Green Power), June 26, 1994, at Hong Kong University of Science and Technology; "Let's Get Growing" workshops, co-organized with the Hong Kong Council of Early Child Education and Services; sponsorship of "Green Sunday" and "Clean and Green" youth participation projects.

39. There were 168 Ronald McDonald Houses in 12 countries by the end of 1995 (*1995 Annual Report*, McDonald's Corp., McD6-3030, p. 13). The Hong Kong hostel is located in Shatin, a "new city" in the New Territories, and is associated with a university hospital that specializes in pediatric medicine. The story behind this charitable institution is interesting in its own right and will be recounted in a subsequent publication. Suffice it to note here that McDonald's found itself in the middle of a battle between the Hong Kong government and indigenous villagers whose ancestors had settled in the Shatin region several centuries before the British Crown Colony was established. Ronald McDonald House was, in effect, held hostage while landowners attempted to settle a long-standing dispute with the government over development rights in the New Territories.

40. "McDonald's Earth Effort," McDonald's Corp., Hong Kong; leaflet collected in May, 1994.

41. In May 1995, the Hong Kong branch of Friends of the Earth attacked McDonald's for using more styrofoam containers than comparable outlets in Australia and the United States; this protest was widely covered in the local press (see, e.g., SCMP, May 15, 1995).

42. In 1995 the average high school student in Hong Kong received HK$846 (US$107) per month in spending money, provided by parents (SCMPIW, Dec. 2, 1995).

43. Lineage villages located in Yuen Long district, New Territories. See James L. Watson, *Emigration and the Chinese Lineage* (Berkeley: Univ. of California Press, 1975), and Rubie S. Watson, *Inequality Among Brothers: Class and Kinship in South China* (Cambridge, Eng.: Cambridge Univ. Press, 1985).

44. Melissa Caldwell reports similar deconstructions of the Big Mac in Moscow's McDonald's, see Introduction, n. 80.

45. Personal communication, Dr. Maria Tam.

46. In one recent case, McDonald's television advertising backfired: "Parents were outraged over scenes showing [a] toddler lying to his mother by telling her his father wanted to eat at McDonald's—and then reversing the tale for his father." The Hong Kong Broadcasting Authority disapproved, calling the ad "unacceptable." SCMPIW, Jan. 20, 1996, p. 2.

47. Focus groups organized by Hong Kong McDonald's were asked what characteristics Ronald McDonald represented. The most common answers were "young, vigorous, generous, and socially responsible" (interview with Daniel Ng, Jan. 14, 1993). Independent interviews with Hong Kong children, conducted by two of my research assistants in June 1994, confirmed these findings.

48. See, e.g., Pierre Bourdieu, *Distinction: A Social Critique of the Judgement of Taste* (Cambridge, Mass.: Harvard Univ. Press, 1984).

49. Personal communication, Marie Wong, drawing on her field research in Tuen Mun. M.A. thesis in Anthropology, Chinese Univ. of Hong Kong, 1995.

50. Elisabeth Tacey, "TVB Gets Go Ahead for Satellite Broadcasts," SCMPIW, Oct. 23, 1994, p. 1.

51. Ruth Mathewson, "Induction Plan Under Way," SCMP, June 14, 1995.

52. SCMPIW, Mar. 12, 1995, p. 1.

Chapter 3

1. Fieldwork was conducted between the winter of 1993 and the spring of 1995, during visits to Taipei. Wei-lan W. Wu joined me in data collection, including observations and interviews: thus the first-person plural is used in the text to designate those parts of the study that are joint efforts.

2. One conspicuous example is the current president, Lee Teng-hui: he is most fluent in Japanese, and he speaks Taiwanese (Min-nan) better than Mandarin. His speech is so heavily accented and ungrammatical that when he speaks Mandarin on television, subtitles in Chinese characters are needed to make his speech comprehensible.

3. Kwang-chow Li, *Kengting National Park Prehistoric Culture* (Taipei: Commission for Cultural Development. Executive Yuan, 1987), p. 29.

4. Ching Yueh, "Consumption of Betel Nuts Climbs to an All-Time High" *Free China Review*, Jan. 6, 1996.

5. Ibid.

6. Interview (June 1994, Taipei) with Bill Rose, Chairman of the Board of Directors of McDonald's Taiwan. The following statements about the McDonald's operation are excerpts from this interview. I

am grateful to Mr. Rose for his willingness to discuss the history of McDonald's in Taiwan. I wish to emphasize, however, that neither he nor any of my other informants bears any responsibility for the interpretations and reconstructions presented in this chapter.

7. News release, McDonald's Corp., July 18, 1996, http://www.mcdonalds.com.

8. *Kongshang Shibao* (KS), Oct. 27, 1994, p. 33, has three short articles about McDonald's in Taiwan by Chen Chun-lin.

9. Fei Jia-qi, "Mai-Dang-Lau: zai tai zhide yiman" (McDonald's is so content in Taiwan), KS, July 13, 1994.

10. Fei Jia-qi, "Tai-wan Mai-Dang-Lau jiang chiao shequ tuo dian" (McDonald's will colonize communities), KS, July 13, 1994.

11. Julian Baum, "Extortion in Taiwan," *Far Eastern Economic Review*, May 14, 1992, p. 61.

12. Conrad P. Kottak, "Rituals at McDonald's," *Journal of American Culture* 1(2): 370–86 (1978).

13. See Eugene Anderson, *The Food of China* (New Haven, Conn., Yale Univ. Press, 1988) for a cultural conception of the essential two parts of a Chinese "meal"—*fan* and *cai* (rice and vegetable or meat dishes).

14. For a set meal of a McChicken or Filet-o-Fish, a Coke, and fries. In June–July 1994, the pricing in the McDonald's in Taipei was higher in absolute terms when compared with that in Cambridge, Mass., and Hong Kong's central district. A regular hamburger cost US$0.896, a Big Mac US$2.31, and a cheeseburger US$1.19.

15. Huang Yen-lin, "Jingguan hanbao zhengduozhan" (Quietly observe the hamburger wars), *Zhongyang ribao* (Central Daily News), May 12, 1989, p. 4.

16. Ibid.

17. Joseph Bosco, "The Emergence of a Taiwanese Popular Culture," *American Journal of Chinese Studies* 1(1): 51–64 (1993).

Chapter 4

This paper was presented at the Anthropology Departmental seminar, Harvard University, and at the 94th Annual Meeting of the American Anthropological Association in Atlanta, Georgia, in November 1994. The following people have given invaluable help at various stages in the preparation of this manuscript: Hoyt Alverson, Cho Im-chin, Michael Herzfeld, Kim Kwang-ok, Kim Young-pil, Lee Eung-chul, Lee Mun-woong, Sidney Mintz, James L. Watson, and Rubie S. Watson. I deeply appreciate the generous research grants from the Northeast Asia Council of the Association for Asian Studies, and the Goodman Foundation of the Anthropology Department at Dartmouth College.

1. Except in the sections describing Korean culture and traditions I use "Korea" or "Koreans" to refer only to South Korea and South Koreans. McDonald's was not doing any business in North Korea as of 1997.

2. *World Tables* (Baltimore: Johns Hopkins Univ. Press, 1995), published for World Bank.

3. *Chosun Daily*, Dec. 5, 1992.

4. A more detailed profile of McDonald's customers is provided in the following pages.

5. Arjun Appadurai, "Introduction: Commodities and the Politics of Value," in Appadurai, ed., *The Social Life of Things: Commodities in Cultural Perspective* (New York: Cambridge Univ. Press, 1986), pp. 3–63.

6. Emiko Ohnuki-Tierney, *Rice as Self: Japanese Identities Through Time* (Princeton, N.J.: Princeton Univ. Press, 1993).

7. Appadurai, "Introduction."

8. Interview, July 1994.

9. *Dong-A Daily (DD)*, Feb. 15, 1986.

10. *Han'guk Daily*, Oct. 19, 1992.

11. Interview, July 1994. 12. DD, Feb. 15, 1986.

13. DD, Mar. 14, 1992. 14. DD, May 22, 1992.

15. Interview, July 30,1994. 16. Ibid.

17. *Han'gyŏre News*, June 26, 1993.

18. *Kugmin Daily*, Mar. 31, 1992.

19. *Business Korea*, Aug. 1991, Seoul, Korea.

20. "Re-organizing the Fast Food Industry," *Food Industry* (June 1990), pp. 42–53.

21. DD, Mar. 13, 1991. 22. Interview, July 30, 1994.

23. Ibid. 24. Ibid.

25. *Han'guk Daily*, May 13, 1990; *Chosun Daily*, Apr. 24, 1993; *Han'guk Daily*, Apr. 12, 1994.

26. Actual numbers of customers and their food orders were counted regularly by the author and her research assistant during the summer of 1994 in two different McDonald's restaurants in Seoul. This sex ratio among the customers was confirmed later in an interview with the Marketing Manager at McDonald's Korean headquarters.

27. E. Christine Jackson, "Ethnography of an Urban Burger King Franchise," *Journal of American Culture* 2(3): 534–39 (1979), p. 537.

28. *Kyŏnghyang News*, Feb. 17, 1994.

29. DD, Jan. 10, 1986.

30. *Segye Daily*, June 28, 1992.

31. DD, June 23, 1992.

32. *Kyŏnghyang News*, Aug. 15, 1992.

33. DD, Feb. 15, 1986, and Mar. 14, 1992.

34. The law's stated goal is "to reduce the concentration of economic power and precipitate competition by regulating abuses of dominant large enterprises, *multi-national firms and monopolistic importers*" (emphasis added), in "Economy," *A Handbook of Korea* (Seoul: Korean Overseas Information Service, 1993).

35. *Kugmin Daily*, July 22, 1993; *Segye Daily*, July 23, 1993.

36. *Han'gyŏre News*, Feb. 6, 1994.

37. Korean Broadcasting System 1 (KBS), Feb. 24, 1992.

38. KBS, Feb. 25, 1992.

39. KBS, Feb. 28, 1992.

40. *Seoul News*, May 21, 1993.

41. "Agriculture, Forestry, and Fishery," in *A Handbook of Korea*, pp. 410–17.

42. *Wall Street Journal*, Sept. 20, 1989, pp. A1, A16.

43. Sidney W. Mintz, *Sweetness and Power: The Place of Sugar in Modern History* (New York: Penguin Books, 1985).

44. Mary Douglas, "Deciphering a Meal," in Clifford Geertz, ed., *Myth, Symbol, and Ritual* (New York: Norton, 1971).

Chapter 5

1. I use Fredric Jameson's term here in a nontechnical way and without all the attendant conceptual properties with which he endows it. Jameson, *Postmodernism; or, The Cultural Logic of Late Capitalism* (Durham, N.C.: Duke Univ. Press).

2. Marc Frons, "Den Fujita: Bringing Big Macs—and now Broadway—to Japan," *Business Week*, Sept. 1986, p. 53.

3. *Business Asia* 25(21): 6–7 (Oct. 1993).

4. Frons, "Den Fujita," p. 53.

5. Nagami Kishi, "Two Decades of Golden Arches in Japan," *Tokyo Business Today* 60(4): 38–40 (1992), p. 39.

6. Atsuo Tanaka, "Taiku auto to ieba hazusenai fāsūtohudo chein rupo" (The "must" list for takeouts: report on fast food chains), *Hanako West* 46: 45–47 (July 1994), p. 46.

7. Initially at Ginza 4-chōme, Mitsukoshimae, it has now moved near the Ginza 8-chōme, close to the subway station.

8. See *Business Asia*, 1993.

9. *Asahi*, Oct. 26, 1993.

10. Ibid.

11. Paul Noguchi, "Savor Slowly: *Ekiben*—The Fast Food of High-Speed Japan," *Ethnology* 33(4): 317–40 (1994), p. 319.

12. Quoted in Kishi, "Two Decades of Golden Arches in Japan," p. 40.

13. *Jiyū Jikan*, "Shūkan to shite no hanbāgā to manpukukan no gyūdon" (Hamburgers as a habit and *gyūdon* [a large bowl of rice with beef and sauce on top] for a full stomach), *Jiyū Jikan*, May 5, 1994, pp. 32–33.

14. Hisao Nagayama and Akihiko Tokue, "Udon," *Look Japan* (1994): 25.

15. Naomichi Ishige, *Shokutaku no bunkashi* (Cultural history of the dining table) (Tokyo: Bungei Shunjū, 1976), p. 223.

16. Saiichi Maruya, *Chūshingura towa nanika* (What is *chūshingura*?) (Tokyo: Kōdansha, 1984), p. 16.

17. Ishige, *Shokutaku no bunkashi*, pp. 223–24.

18. Emiko Ohnuki-Tierney, "The Ambivalent Self of the Contemporary Japanese," *Cultural Anthropology* 5: 196–215 (1990).

19. See ibid. for an interpretation of the film *Tampopo*, in which *rāmen* are the focal point.

20. They are not located right in the center of Tokyo, but they are close enough. For instance, there is an outlet at Ebisu and one at Itabashi.

21. Some people continued to eat meat dishes, however, although they "converted" them into flowers by renaming them. Thus the names of flowers were given to animal meats, such as cherry blossoms for horsemeat and peony for wild boar. Harada offers historical records to show that the Japanese ate meat more often than is generally assumed. Nobuo Harada, *Rekishi no naka no kome to niku: shokumotsu to tennō sabetsu* (Rice and meat in history: food, emperor, and discrimination) (Tokyo: Heibonsha, 1993).

22. See Ohnuki-Tierney, *Rice as Self: Japanese Identities through Time* (Princeton, N.J.: Princeton Univ. Press, 1993).

23. Tsuneharu Tsukuba, *Beishoku, nikushoku no bunmei* (Civilizations of rice consumption and meat consumption) (Tokyo: Nihon Hōsō Shuppankai, 1986 [1969]), pp. 109–12.

24. Ibid., p. 113. Some scholars view Tsukuba's work as too deeply embedded in *nihonjinron* (theories about the Japanese), a semischolarly, semi-journalistic genre of writings about the Japanese that is often chauvinistic. I use his work as an ethnographic source.

25. *Nihon kokugo daijiten* (Dictionary of the Japanese language), 5, p. 381.

26. Tsukuba, *Beishoku*, pp. 102–9. For details of this section, see Ohnuki-Tierney, *Rice as Self*.

27. A man in his late forties who is an editorial writer for the *Asahi* newspaper told me during a visit to New York that although he prefers McDonald's, his children prefer Mos Burgers.

28. For details of how the Japanese use bread, see Naomichi Ishige, *Shokuji no bunmeiron* (Eating and culture) (Tokyo: Chūokōronsha, 1982), pp. 22–23.

29. Ronald P. Dore, *City Life in Japan* (Berkeley: Univ. of California Press, 1958), p. 60; for details see Ohnuki-Tierney, *Rice as Self*, p. 41.

30. For details see Ohnuki-Tierney, *Rice as Self*, pp. 20–22.

31. Kishi, "Two Decades of Golden Arches in Japan," p. 40.

32. For details see Ohnuki-Tierney, *Rice as Self,* pp. 94–96.

33. In Japan today, most young, unmarried working women continue to live at home with their parents. This practice eliminates their need to breakfast outside their home. Young unmarried men, however, typically live in company dormitories, some of which do not provide breakfast. The ones that do usually offer the traditional Japanese breakfast, although for several decades many urban families have been eating toast, eggs, and salad (often made of shredded cabbage) and coffee or tea for breakfast. For those who prefer a "Western" breakfast, the alternative to eating in the company dorms is McDonald's or the many coffee shops. Breakfast often comes as a set meal for less than ¥1,000, and includes potato salad, hot dogs, hamburgers, and other items unfamiliar to Westerners as breakfast foods.

34. Dr. Imada is a professor of sociology at Tokyo Kogyo Daigaku.

35. This phenomenon incidentally relates to a more general one—changes in the system of cultural valuations of jobs. Some that used to be ranked as lower-class jobs, such as waiting tables, were never performed, even temporarily, by middle- or upper-class people. There have been many changes of this nature as the class structure has become less rigid and many more middle- and upper-class women have entered the job market.

36. Marian Burros, "Eating Well," *New York Times,* Apr. 13, 1994.

37. Rosemary Safranek, "The McDonald's Recipe for Japan," *Intersect* 2(10): 7 (Oct. 1986).

38. Many colleagues and friends told me that companies and individuals chose this store to send gifts from at annual gift-exchange times. Lately it has become customary to choose a store to send out gifts to designated individuals instead of delivering them in person.

39. Frons, "Den Fujita," p. 53.

40. Both McDonald's and Mos Burgers circulate these magazines, to which customers submit their essays.

41. My mother's family imported French food into Yokohama. My father was in the export business, so she came in contact with foreigners of various physical types throughout her life. Yet after I came to the United States, my mother kept writing to warn me against falling in love with a man with blue eyes.

42. Hikaru Saitō, "Nyan-bāgā densetsu no nazo" (The puzzle of the catburger lore), *Hanako West* 46: 47 (July 1994).

43. Kumakura Isao, Professor at the National Museum of Ethnology in Japan and Kindaichi Hideho, Professor at Kyōrin Univ.; both personal communications, May 1994.

44. Saitō, "Nyan-bāgā."

45. Hiroshi Shimogaito, *Zoku okome to bunka* (Rice and culture, cont.) (Osaka: Zen-Ōsaka Shōhisha Dantai Renrakukai, 1988), pp. 76–78; *Asahi,* Oct. 30, 1993; Nov. 12, 1993.

46. *Asahi,* Nov. 11, 12, 17–19, 1993. For more detailed treatment of this subject, see Ohnuki-Tierney, *Rice as Self,* and "Structure, Event and Historical Metaphor: Rice and Identities in Japanese History," *Journal of the Royal Anthropological Institute* 30(2): 1–27 (June 1995).

47. Inoue, "Kome no hanashi," p. 103; and Okabe Saburo. Saburo is Director of the Science and Technology Division of the Liberal Democratic Party and a member of the House of Councilors. Published in the Record of Sangiin Gaimu Iinkai Kaigiroku, No. 5 (during the 118th session of the Diet), p. 7.

48. Quoted in Norbert Elias, *The Civilizing Process* (Oxford: Blackwell, 1994 [1939]), p. 106.

49. Tadashi Inoue and Naomichi Ishige, eds., *Shokuji sahō no shisō* (Concepts behind eating manners) (Tokyo: Domesu Shuppan, 1990), p. 97.

50. Emiko Ohnuki-Tierney, *Illness and Culture in Contemporary Japan: An Anthropological View* (Cambridge, Eng.: Cambridge Univ. Press, 1984), pp. 28–31.

51. Chopsticks were recovered from the site of the imperial palace for the preceding Nara period (646–794), but not from the surrounding towns (Sahara's remarks in Inoue and Ishige, eds., *Shokuji,* p. 79).

52. Robert Hertz, *Death and the Right Hand* (Glencoe, Ill.: Free Press, 1960 [1907 & 1909 in French]).

53. Conrad Kottak, "Rituals at McDonald's," *Journal of American Culture* 1(2): 370–86 (1978), p. 374.

54. Isao Kumakura, "Zen-kindai no shokuji sahō to ishiki" (Table manners and their concepts before the modern period), in Inoue and Ishige, eds., *Shokuji,* p. 108.

55. *Nihon kokugo daijiten* 13, p. 67.

56. Motoko Murakami, "Gendaijin no shokuji manā-kan" (Thoughts on contemporary eating manners), in Inoue and Ishige, eds. *Shokuji*, p. 133.

57. What is called traditional Japanese etiquette usually refers to the "Ogasawara-ryū" or Ogasawara School, which originated in the early Muromachi period (1392–1603) (*Nihon kokugo daijiten* 3, p. 311); Murakami, "Gendaijin."

58. Daniel Miller, "The Young and the Restless in Trinidad: A Case of the Local and the Global in Mass Consumption," in Roger Silverstone and Eric Hirsch, eds., *Consuming Technologies: Media and Information in Domestic Spaces* (London: Routledge, 1992), pp. 163–82 (see especially pp. 179–80).

59. Rosemary Safranek, "The McDonald's Recipe for Japan," p. 7.

Update

1. Joseph Kahn, "China Hopes Economy Plan Will Bridge Income Gap," *New York Times* (NYT), Oct. 12, 2005, p. A5.

2. "McDonald's Plans," *Wall Street Journal.com* (WSJ.Com), May 18, 2000.

3. See, e.g., Jagdish Bhagwati, *In Defense of Globalization*. New York: Oxford University Press, 2004.

4. Joseph E. Stiglitz, *Globalization and Its Discontents*. New York: Norton, 2003.

5. See Introduction to this book.

6. Saritha Rai, "An Outsourcing Giant Fights Back," NYT, Mar. 21, 2004, p. BU1. Benedict Arnold was a patriot turned traitor during the American Revolution.

7. Steve Lohr, "Many New Causes for Old Problem of Jobs Lost Abroad," NYT, Feb. 15, 2004, p. 25.

8. Lynnley Browning, "Outsourcing Abroad Applies to Tax Returns," NYT, Feb. 15, 2004, p. BU12.

9. Saritha Rai, "Financial Firms Hasten Their Move to Outsourcing," NYT, Aug. 18, 2004, p. W1.

10. References can be found in a web search for "McDonald's protest" or "McDonald's bombing." See also David Barboza, "When

Golden Arches Are Too Red, White, and Blue," NYT, Oct. 14, 2001, pp. BU1, BU11.

11. Tim Weiner, "McTaco vs. Fried Crickets: A Duel in the Oaxaca Sun," NYT, Aug. 24, 2002, p. A2.

12. Suzanne Daley, "French See a Hero in War on 'McDomination'," NYT, Oct. 12, 1999, pp. A1, A4.

13. Dirk Beveridge, "Expensive Beef for McDonald's: Chain Wins Libel Suit, Loses British PR War," *Boston Globe*, June 20, 1997, p. A16. See also John Videl, *McLibel: Burger Culture on Trial*. New York: Free Press, 1998.

14. See, e.g., "World Anti-McDonald's Day Protest Begins," *AAP. com* (Australia), Oct. 16, 1999.

15. Patricia Ochs, "Trade Fight Has Flavor of France," *Boston Globe*, Sept. 7, 1999, p. A2.

16. Jay Solomon, "Amid Anti-American Protests, Mr. Bambang Invokes Allah to Sell Big Macs in Indonesia," WSJ.Com, Oct. 26, 2001.

17. Such views are sometimes reinforced by government officials in Europe. Berlin Mayor Eberhard Diepgen embarrassed the American ambassador to Germany, John Kornblum, during a public ceremony marking the opening of the 1,000th McDonald's restaurant in Germany: "Ah, I see the American ambassador is here," said the mayor. "Perhaps he should . . . build a McDonald's restaurant [near Brandenburg Gate in the center of unified Berlin] instead of a United States embassy." The comment sparked a diplomatic row during a tense time in U.S.-German relations; see Leon Mangasarian, "Hamburgers or Penstripes? U.S. Embassy Row in Berlin Roils Ties," *Deutsche Press-Agentur*, 3 Nov. 1999, on Lexus-Nexus.com.

18. On food and national identity, see Part 1, "Food and Globalization," of *The Cultural Politics of Food and Eating*, ed. by James L. Watson and Melissa Caldwell. Oxford: Basil Blackwell, 2005. See also Alison Leitch, "Slow Food and the Politics of Pork Fat: Italian Identity," *Ethnos* 68(4): 437–462, and Gordon Mathews, "Cultural Identity and Consumption in Post-Colonial Hong Kong," in *Consuming Hong Kong*, ed. by Gordon Mathews and Tai-lok Lui. Hong Kong: Hong Kong University Press (1999).

19. Leitch, Mathews, "Slow Food and Pork Fat"; Alexander Stille, "Slow Food," *Nation.com*, Aug. 20, 2001; Rebecca Tuhus-Dubrow, "Talking About Slow Food," *Nation.com*, June 1, 2004.

20. "Burgers and Fries à la francaise," *Economist*, Apr. 17, 2004, p. 60; on French resistance to McDonald's, see Rick Fantasia, "Fast Food in France," *Theory and Society* 24: 201–43 (1995).

21. This is also true in the United States, judging from the author's experience of speaking about this book since its release in 1997. American intellectuals find it difficult to be objective about McDonald's; see James L. Watson, "Interview on *Golden Arches East*," with Lucien Errington, *Education About Asia* 8(1): 7–9 (2003). The work of Pierre Bourdieu is particularly relevant to understanding social class and responses to food (see his *Distinction: A Social Critique of the Judgment of Taste*. Cambridge, Mass.: Harvard University Press, 1984.) For an American take on McDonald's and class, see Katherine Newman, *No Shame in My Game: The Working Poor in the Inner City*. New York: Vintage, 1999.

22. "They are playing with our religious sentiments in pursuit of profit. . . . We will shut down all McDonald's restaurants in [this] country," said a spokesman for Shiv Sena ("Army of Shiva"), WSJ.Com, May 4, 2001. Despite these protests, McDonald's continues to expand in India, with 47 outlets in 2003 and plans to open 50 more; see *BBC News.com*, Apr. 7, 2003.

23. Deborah Cohen, "McDonald's Posts First-Ever Quarterly Loss," *Reuters.com*, Jan. 23, 2003. One disgruntled Bolivian complained, "I guess Bolivia will never be a fully globalized and capitalized country like the United States." Another said, "I grew up with McDonald's, I celebrated my birthdays in McDonald's, I even wanted to work at McDonald's. I feel deceived, and most of all sad." See "McDonald's Leaves Bolivia for Good," *CNN.com*, Dec. 1, 2002.

24. McDonald's Corporation, *Annual Report, 2002*; "McDonald's Plans to Close 13 Restaurants in Denmark," *Associated Press.com*, Dec. 2, 2002.

25. Mariko Sanchanta, "McDonald's Japan Makes First Yearly Loss," *Financial Times.com*, Feb. 14, 2003.

26. Colleen DeBaise, "Don't Blame McDonald's For Supersized Kids—Judge," WSJ.Com, Jan. 22, 2003; see also, Shirley Leung,

"Obesity Suit Against McDonald's Is Dismissed by Federal Judge," *WSJ*, Sept. 3, 2003, p. B4.

27. Kate Zernike, "Lawyers Shift Focus from Big Tobacco to Big Food," *NYT*, Apr. 9, 2004, p. A15.

28. Betsy McKay, "Group Asks FDA [Food and Drug Administration] to Put Tobacco-Like Warning on Sodas, Fruit Drinks," *WSJ*.Com, July 13, 2005.

29. On Korea, see Seo Jee-yeon, "Anti-Fast Food Drive Raging," *Korea Times.com*, June 10, 2004; on Hong Kong's emerging antiobesity movement, see "Hong Kong Mulls Kids' Lunch Law to Fend Off Obesity," *Agence France Presse English.com*, May 15, 2005. European sources include Elisabeth Rosenthal, "Even the French Are Fighting Obesity," *International Herald Tribune.com*, May 4, 2005; Andrew Borowiec, "France Says 'non' to Child Obesity," *Washington Times.com*, Aug. 24, 2004; John Hooper, "Italy's Fasting Solution," *Guardian Unlimited.com*, Sept. 4, 2003; "NHS [British National Health Service] to Receive £3 Million for Training to Tackle Obesity," *Medical News Today.com*, Dec. 31, 2004.

30. http://www.consumerfreedom.com/advertisements_detail.cfm/ad/29.

31. Carl Hulse, "Vote in House Bars Some Suits Citing Obesity," *NYT*, Mar. 11, 2004, pp. A1, A21.

32. James Tillotson, "No Wonder We're Getting So Fat," *Boston Globe*, Sept. 17, 2004, editorial, p. A23.

33. David Barboza, "Rampant Obesity a Debilitating Reality for the Urban Poor," *NYT*, Dec. 26, 2000, p. D5; see also, David Barboza, "Barrage of Food Ads Takes Aim at Children," *NYT*, Aug. 3, 2003, pp. BU1, BU11.

34. "One-third of Hong Kong people are obese and half are overweight," according to research cited in Lydia Ho, "Fats of Life Revealed by New Index on Obesity," *South China Morning Post* (Hong Kong), Feb. 18, 2000, p. 3.

35. Bruce Horovitz, "Restaurant Sales Climb with Bad-For-You Food," *USA Today*, May 13, 2005, p. 1A. The Monster Thickburger contains two ground-beef patties, bacon, and cheese. It weights two-thirds of a pound and is 2 ½ inches thick.

36. On the social significance of fast food restaurants as substitute homes, see Katherine Newman, *No Shame in My Game* (op. cit.) In some American inner-city neighborhoods McDonald's is the only place where hot meals are available.

37. Jack Greenberg, former CEO of McDonald's, voiced similar views in a 2001 interview: "This kind of criticism [by anti-McDonald's activists] is the price of our success. There is no other retailer, no other service business that touches so many people every day in such a personal way." See "McAtlas Shrugged: FP Interview," *Foreign Policy*, May/June 2001, pp. 26–37.

38. The McLean Deluxe was introduced in 1991 and contained only nine grams of fat, with a total of 310 calories. It was never popular with McDonald's core customers and was discontinued in 1996; see, Cliff Edwards, "McDonald's Drops McLean Burger," Associated Press.com, Feb. 5, 1996.

39. Steven Gray, "McDonald's Profit Jumps 42%," WSJ, Apr. 22, 2005; on the salad venture, see "Newman's Own and McDonald's Announce Exclusive Alliance," McDonald's Corporation, *PRNewswire*, Yahoo.com, Mar. 10, 2003.

40. "Super Size Me," a 2004 independent film directed and written by Morgan Spurlock.

41. Marian Burros, "McDonald's Takes Steps On Its Antibiotic Promise," NYT, Jan. 12, 2005, p. D2.

42. See, e.g., the full-page ad in the NYT, Sept. 24, 2004, p. A19, "A Broken McPromise."

43. Charlotte Ikels, ed., *Filial Piety: Practice and Discourse in Contemporary East Asia*. Stanford: Stanford University Press, 2004.

44. Michael Barr, "Lee Kuan Yew and the 'Asian Values' Debate," *Asian Studies Review* 24(3): 317–28; see also, "Confucius and Confusion," special issue, *Far Eastern Economic Review*, Feb. 9, 1989.

45. See, e.g., Yunxiang Yan, "The Triumph of Conjugality: Structural Transformation of Family Relations in a Chinese Village," *Ethnology* 36(3): 191–212 (1997).

46. On China, see *Far Eastern Economic Review*, Dec. 10, 1998, citing World Bank figures; on Japan, see Gerard Anderson and Peter Hussey, "Population Aging: A Comparison Among Industrial

Countries," *Health Affairs*, May/June 2000, pp. 191–203; on Korea, see U.S. Bureau of Census International Database, 2000.

47. The Director of the Global Aging Initiative (Center for Strategic and International Studies, Washington D.C.), notes that "China has the distinction of being the first major economy to grow old before they grow rich," as quoted in Mark Fritz, "U.S. Birth Rates Remain High," WSJ.Com, Aug. 23, 2005. By 2040, China is expected to have a higher percentage of citizens over 60 than the United States, primarily because the U.S. birth rate (2.0 lifetime births per woman) is higher than China's birthrate (1.6), see data in Fritz article, "U.S. Birth Rates."

48. Vanessa L. Fong, *Only Hope: Coming of Age Under China's One-Child Policy*. Stanford: Stanford University Press, 2004; and Jun Jing, ed., *Feeding China's Little Emperors: Food, Children, and Social Change*. Stanford: Stanford University Press, 2000. See also Susan Greenhalgh, "The Peasantization of the One-child Policy in Shaanxi." In Deborah Davis and Stevan Harrell, eds., *Chinese Families in the Post-Mao Era*. Berkeley: University of California Press, 1993.

49. This is also true in parts of the American Midwest and South, where McDonald's outlets have become breakfast and lunch meeting places for retired people. In parts of Iowa and rural Illinois, people over 70 far outnumber children eating at the Golden Arches. The reasons are obvious: McDonald's are clean, air-conditioned, quiet, and relatively cheap. Furthermore, as local diners and cafes disappear from the rural American landscape (owing primarily to the retirement of local entrepreneurs and the absence of successors) fast-food outlets are the only eateries in town.

50. Sales of Happy Meals, specially packaged meals for children first introduced by McDonald's in 1976, have been steadily declining in recent years. The demand for adult foods (e.g., salads and chicken sandwiches) has been growing; see Shirley Leung and Suzanne Vranica, "Happy Meals Are No Longer Bringing Smiles to McDonald's," WSJ, Jan. 31, 2003, pp. B1, B4.

Select Bibliography

Alfino, Mark, John S. Caputo, and Robin Wynyard, eds. 1998. *Mc-Donaldization Revisited: Critical Essays on Consumer Culture*. London: Praeger.

Appadurai, Arjun. 1996. *Modernity At Large: Cultural Dimensions of Globalization*. Minneapolis: University of Minnesota Press.

————. 1995. "The Production of Locality." In Richard Fardon, ed., *Counterworks: Managing the Diversity of Knowledge*. London: Routledge.

————. 1996. *Modernity at Large: Cultural Dimensions of Globalization*. Minneapolis; University of Minnesota Press.

Applbaum, Kalman. 2000. "Crossing Borders: Globalization as Myth and Charter in American Transnational Consumer Marketing." *American Ethnologist* 27(2): 257–82.

————. 2004. *The Marketing Era: From Professional Practice to Global Provisioning*. London: Routledge.

Bak, Sangmee. 2005. "From Strange Bitter Concoction to Romantic Necessity: The Social History of Coffee Drinking in South Korea." *Korea Journal* 45(2): 37–59.

Barber, Benjamin R. 1995. *Jihad vs. McWorld*. New York: Times Books.

Belasco, Warren J. 1979. "Toward a Culinary Common Denominator: The Rise of Howard Johnson's, 1925–1966." *Journal of American Culture* 2(3): 503–18.

Berger, Peter L. 1997. "Four Faces of Global Culture." *The National Interest* 49: 23–29.

Bestor, Theodore C. "Supply-Side Sushi: Commodity, Market, and the Global City." *American Anthropologist* 103(1): 76–95.

————. 2000. "How Sushi Went Global." *Foreign Policy*, Nov./Dec. 2000, pp. 54–63.

Bhagwati, Jagdish. 2004. *In Defense of Globalization.* New York: Oxford University Press.

Boas, Max, and Steve Chain. 1976. *Big Mac: The Unauthorized Story of McDonald's.* New York: Dutton.

Bosco, Joseph. 1993. "The Emergence of a Taiwanese Popular Culture." *American Journal of Chinese Studies* 1(1): 51–64.

———. 1999. "The McDonald's Snoopy Craze in Hong Kong." In Gordon Mathews and Tai-lok Lui, eds., *Consuming Hong Kong.* Hong Kong: Hong Kong University Press.

Bourdieu, Pierre. 1984. *Distinction: A Social Critique of the Judgement of Taste.* Cambridge, Mass.: Harvard University Press.

Caldwell, Melissa. 2004. "Domesticating the French Fry: McDonald's and Consumerism in Moscow." *Journal of Consumer Culture* 4(1): 5–26.

Chase, Holly. 1994. "The *Meyhane* or McDonald's? Changes in the Eating Habits and the Evolution of Fast Food in Istanbul." In Richard Tapper and Sami Zubaida, eds., *Culinary Cultures of the Middle East.* London: I. B. Tauris.

Cohen, George. 1997. *To Russia with Fries.* Toronto: McClelland and Stewart.

Collins, Jane L. 2000. "Tracing Social Relations in Commodity Chains: The Case of Grapes in Brazil." In Angelique Haugerud, M. Priscilla Stone, and Peter D. Little, eds., *Commodities and Globalization: Anthropological Perspectives.* Boulder: Rowan and Littlefield.

Counihan, Carole M. 1999. *The Anthropology of Food and Body: Gender, Meaning, and Power.* London: Routledge.

Critser, Greg. 2003. *Fat Land: How Americans Became the Fattest People in the World.* Boston: Mariner Books.

Cutler, David M., Edward L. Glaeser, and Jesse M. Shapiro. 2003. "Why Have Americans Become More Obese?" *Journal of Economic Perspectives* 17 (3): 93–118.

Dorfman, Ariel, and Armand Mattelart. 1975. *How To Read Donald Duck: Imperialist Ideology in the Disney Comic.* New York: International General.

Douglas, Mary, and Baron Isherwood. 1978. *The World of Goods: Towards an Anthropology of Consumption.* London: Allen Lane.

Fantasia, Rick. 1995. "Fast Food in France." *Theory and Society* 24: 201–43.

Fong, Vanessa L. 2004. *Only Hope: Coming of Age Under China's One-Child Policy.* Stanford: Stanford University Press.

———. 2004. "Filial Nationalism among Chinese Teenagers with Global Identities." *American Ethnologist* 31(4): 631–48.

Freidberg, Susanne. 2004. *French Beans and Food Scares: Culture and Commerce in an Anxious Age.* New York: Oxford University Press.

Gillette, Maris B. 2000. "Children's Food and Islamic Dietary Restrictions in Xi'an." In Jun Jing, ed., *Feeding China's Little Emperors: Food, Children, and Social Change.* Stanford: Stanford University Press.

Goodman, David, and Michael J. Watts, eds. *Globalising Food: Agrarian Questions and Global Restructuring.* London: Routledge.

Goody, Jack. 1982. *Cooking, Cuisine and Class: A Study in Comparative Sociology.* Cambridge: Cambridge University Press.

Gries, Peter H. 2004. *China's New Nationalism: Pride, Politics, and Diplomacy.* Berkeley: University of California Press.

Hannerz, Ulf. 1996. *Transnational Connection: Culture, People, Place.* London, Routledge.

Harvey, David. 1989. *The Condition of Postmodernity.* Oxford: Basil Blackwell.

Hogan, David Gerard. 1997. *Selling 'em by the Sack: White Castle and the Creation of American Food.* New York: New York University Press.

Ikels, Charlotte. 1996. *The Return of the God of Wealth: The Transition to a Market Economy in Urban China.* Stanford: Stanford University Press.

———, ed. 2004. *Filial Piety: Practice and Discourse in Contemporary East Asia.* Stanford: Stanford University Press.

Jackle, John A. and Keith A. Sculle. *Fast Food: Roadside Restaurants in the Automobile Age.* Baltimore: John Hopkins University Press.

Jackson, E. Christine. 1979. "Ethnography of an Urban Burger King Franchise." *Journal of American Culture* 2(3): 534–39.

Jameson, Fredric. 1991. *Postmodernism, or The Cultural Logic of Late Capitalism.* Durham: Duke University Press.

Janelli, Roger with Dawnhee Yim. 1993. *Making Capitalism: The Social and Cultural Construction of a South Korean Conglomerate.* Stanford: Stanford University Press.

Jing, Jun, ed. 2000. *Feeding China's Little Emperors: Food, Children, and Social Change.* Stanford: Stanford University Press.

Kottak, Conrad P. 1978. "Rituals at McDonald's." *Journal of American Culture* 1(2): 370–86.

Kroc, Ray. 1977. *Grinding It Out: The Making of McDonald's.* Chicago: St. Martin's.

Krueger, Alan B. 1991. "Ownership, Agency, and Wages: An Examination of Franchising in the Fast Food Industry." *Quarterly Journal of Economics* 106(1): 75–101.

LaFeber, Walter. 1999. *Michael Jordan and the New Global Capitalism.* New York: Norton.

Leidner, Robin. 1993. *Fast Food, Fast Talk: Service Work and Routinization of Everyday Life.* Berkeley: University of California Press.

Leitch, Alison. 2003. "Slow Food and the Politics of Pork Fat: Italian Food and European Identity." *Ethnos* 68(4): 437–62.

Love, John F. 1986. *McDonald's: Behind the Arches.* New York: Bantam Books.

Lozada, Eriberto. 2000. "Globalized Childhood? Kentucky Fried Chicken in Beijing." In Jun Jing, ed., *Feeding China's Little Emperors: Food, Children, and Social Change.* Stanford: Stanford University Press.

Luxenberg, Stan. 1985. *Road Side Empires: How the Chains Franchised America.* New York: Viking.

Lyon, Phil, et al. 1995. "Is Big Mac the Big Threat?" *International Journal of Hospitality Management* 14(2): 119–22.

Mathews, Gordon. 1999. "Cultural Identity and Consumption in Post-Colonial Hong Kong." In Gordon Mathews and Tai-lok Lui, eds., *Consuming Hong Kong.* Hong Kong: Hong Kong University Press.

McLamore, James W. 1998. *The Burger King: Jim McLamore and the Building of an Empire.* New York: McGraw-Hill.

McLuhan, Marshall, and Bruce R. Powers. 1989. *The Global Village: Transformations in World Life and Media in the 21st Century.* New York: Oxford University Press.

Miller, Daniel. 1998. *A Theory of Shopping.* London: Polity Press.

———. 1992. "The Young and the Restless: A Case of the Local and the Global in Mass Consumption." In Roger Silverstone and Eric Hirsch, eds., *Consuming Technologies: Media and Information in Domestic Spaces,* pp. 163–82. London: Routledge.

Mintz, Sidney W. 1985. *Sweetness and Power: The Place of Sugar in Modern History.* New York: Viking.

Moon, Youngme, and Kerry Herman. 2003. "McDonald's Russia: Managing a Crisis." Harvard Business School, *Case Study,* no. 9-503-020.

Naim, Moises. 2001. "McAtlas Shrugged: McDonald's CEO Greenberg on Why Those Who Hate Globalization Should Learn to Love His Company." *Foreign Policy,* May/June, 2001: 26–37.

Newman, Katherine S. 1999. *No Shame in My Game: The Working Poor in the Inner City.* New York: Alfred A. Knopf and Russell Sage Foundation.

Noguchi, Paul H. 1994. *"Ekiben:* The Fast Food of High-Speed Japan." *Ethnology* 33(4):317–30.

Ohnuki-Tierney, Emiko. 1993. *Rice as Self: Japanese Identities Through Time.* Princeton: Princeton University Press.

———. 1999. "We Eat Each Other's Food to Nourish Our Body: The Global and the Local as Mutually Constituent Forces." In Raymond Grew, *ed., Food in Global History.* Boulder: Westview Press.

Oliver, Thomas. 1986. *The Real Coke, The Real Story.* New York: Penguin.

Ong, Aihwa. *Flexible Citizenship: The Cultural Logics of Transnationality.* Duke University Press, 1999.

Patico, Jennifer, and Melissa J. Caldwell. 2002. "Consumers Exiting Socialism: Ethnographic Perspectives on Daily Life in Post-Communist Europe." *Ethnos* 67(3): 285–94.

Pendergrast, Mark. 1993. *For God, Country, and Coca-Cola: The Unauthorized History of the Great American Soft Drink and the Company That Makes It.* New York: Scribner's.

Pereira, Alexius A. 2000. "McAunties and McUncles: Older Crew Members in Singapore's Fast Food Industry." *Research in the Sociology of Work* 9: 129–45.

Peterson, Peter G. 1999. "Gray Dawn: The Global Aging Crisis." *Foreign Affairs* 78(1): 42–55.

Raz, Aviad E. 1999. *Riding the Black Ship: Japan and Tokyo Disneyland.* Cambridge, Mass.: Harvard University Press, East Asian Monographs

Reiter, Ester. 1991. *Making Fast Food.* Montreal: McGill–Queen's University Press.

Ritzer, George. 1993. *The McDonaldization of Society: An Investigation into the Changing Character of Contemporary Social Life.* Thousand Oaks, Calif.: Pine Forge Press.

———. 1998. *The McDonaldization Thesis.* London: Sage.

Rosencrance, Richard. 1999. *The Rise of the Virtual State: Wealth and Power in the Coming Century.* New York: Basic Books.

Sassen, Saskia. 1991. *The Global City: New York, London, Toronto.* Princeton: Princeton University Press.

———. 1998. *Globalization and Its Discontents.* New York: New Press.

Schlosser, Eric. 2001. *Fast Food Nation: The Dark Side of the All-American Meal.* Boston: Houghton Mifflin.

Sheldon, Allen. 1990. "A Theater for Eating, Looking and Thinking: The Restaurant as Symbolic Space." *Sociological Spectrum* 10: 507–26.

Shell, Ellen Ruppel. 2002. *The Hungry Gene: The Inside Story of the Obesity Industry.* New York: Grove Press.

Smart, Barry, ed. 1999. *Resisting McDonaldization.* London: Sage.

Smith, Trenton G. 2004. "The McDonald's Equilibrium: Advertising, Empty Calories, and the Endogenous Determination of Dietary Preferences." *Social Choice and Welfare* 23: 383–413.

Stephenson, Peter. 1989. "Going to McDonald's in Leiden." *Ethnos* 17(2): 226–47.

Stiglitz, Joseph E. 2003. *Globalization and Its Discontents.* New York: Norton.

Tomlinson, John. 1991. *Cultural Imperialism.* Baltimore: Johns Hopkins University Press.

———. *Globalization and Culture*. 1999. Chicago: University of Chicago Press.

Traphagan, John W. and L. Keith Brown. 2002. "Fast Food and Intergenerational Commensality in Japan: New Styles and Old Patterns." *Ethnology* 41(2): 119–34.

Vidal, John. 1998. *McLibel: Burger Culture on Trial*. New York: New Press.

Walden, John K. 1989. "Fish and Chips and the British Working Class, 1870–1930." *Journal of Social History* 23(2): 244–66.

Waters, Malcolm. 1995. *Globalization*. London: Routledge.

Watson, James L. 1987. "From the Common Pot: Feasting with Equals in Chinese Society." *Anthropos* 82: 389–401.

———. 2000. "China's Big Mac Attack." *Foreign Affairs* 79(3): 120–34.

———. 2003. "Interview on Golden Arches East," with Lucien Ellington. *Education About Asia* 8(1): 7–9.

———. 2004. "Globalization in Asia: Anthropological Perspectives." In Marcelo Suarez-Orozco and Desiree Qin-Hillard, eds., *Minding the Global: Culture and Globalization in the New Millennium*. Berkeley: University of California Press.

Watson, James L. and Melissa L. Caldwell, eds. 2005. *The Cultural Politics of Food and Eating*. Oxford: Basil Blackwell.

White, Merry. 1994. *The Material Child: Coming of Age in Japan and America*. Berkeley: University of California Press.

Wilk, Richard R. 1999. "Real Belizean Food": Building Local Identity in the Transnational Caribbean." *American Anthropologist* 101(2): 244–55.

Wolf, Martin. 2001. "Will the Nation-State Survive Globalization?" *Foreign Affairs* 80(1): 178–90.

———. 2004. *Why Globalization Works*. New Haven: Yale University Press.

Yan, Yunxiang. 1997. "The Triumph of Conjugality: Structural Transformation of Family Relations in a Chinese Village." *Ethnology* 36(3): 191–212.

———. 2000. "Of Hamburger and Social Space: Consuming McDonald's in Beijing." In Deborah S Davis, ed., *The Consumer*

Revolution in Urban China. Berkeley: University of California Press.

―――. 2002. "Managed Globalization: State Power and Cultural Transition in China." In Peter Berger and Samuel Huntington, eds., *Many Globalizations: Cultural Diversity in the Contemporary World*. New York: Oxford University Press.

―――. 2003. *Private Life Under Socialism: Love, Intimacy, and Family Change in a Chinese Village, 1949–1999*. Stanford: Stanford University Press.

Yoshimoto, Mitsuhiro. 1994. "Images of Empire: Tokyo Disneyland and Japanese Cultural Imperialism." In Eric Smoodin, ed., *Disney Discourse*. London: Routledge.

Index

In this index an "f" after a number indicates a separate reference on the next page, and an "ff" indicates separate references on the next two pages. A continuous discussion over two or more pages is indicated by a span of page numbers, e.g., "57–59."

Adams, Richard, 75
Advertising, 19, 34, 43–44, 99, 223n46
Aging, 237nn47, 49, 50; of East Asian population, 195–96
Agriculture, 137, 154f
Air Max Penny, 11
Americana, 64–66, 72–73, 99, 122, 143, 161, 172–73, 180–81, 215n5
Amerika Monogatari (Nagai Kafu), 178
Animal cruelty, 188
Anti-Americanism, 139
Anti-globalization, 185–86, 191; McDonald's as target of, 186–90
Anti-McDonald's movement, 188, 234n22, 236n37
Apkuchŏng-dong, 139
Appadurai, Arjun, 138
Arby's, 27
Argonne National Laboratory, 26
Art exhibits, 57–58
Assembly-line production, 25–26
Aunt McDonald, x, 19, 61, 214n31
Australia, 121
Automation, 25–26

Bangalore, 34
Barber, Benjamin, 7
Beijing, vi, 1, 7, 12, 18, 28, 33f, 39, 40–41, 184, 193–94, 201n1, 212–13n14, 220nn19, 20; Aunt McDonald in, x, 19; yuppies in, 2, 9; service expectations in, 30, 44–45, 50–51; advertising in, 43–44; consumers in, 45–51, 53–57, 69–71; children in, 51–52, 64–65; behavioral changes in, 52–53; social interaction in, 53–54; localization in, 54–56, 58–59, 60–63, 75–76; art exhibits in, 57–58; restaurants in, 63–64, 74–75, 213–14n27
Beijing Fast Food Company, 74
Bentō, 163–64
Berson-Marsteller, 43
Betel-nut chewing: in Taiwan, 115–19
Big Bacon Classic, 193
Big Mac index, 146
Big Macs, 22ff, 45, 146, 157–58, 192, 209nn79, 80, 220n19
Birthday parties, 19, 57, 62, 64, 203–4, 148–49

Body language, x. *See also* Smiling
   service
Bolivia, 190
Bombings, 122–23
"Book of Little Honorary Guests,"
   61f
Bove, Jose, 187
Breakfast, 70, 85–86, 220n16, 230n33
Brownell, Kelley, 192
Buddhism, 166
Buffets, 95–96
Burger King, 25, 193

Café de Coral, 81, 221n30
Cake-rating system, 104
Caldwell, Melissa, 29
Cantalupo, James, 12
Capital, investment, 121–22
Capitalism, 161
Caracas, 30
Carr's, 12
Catering industry, 74
Celebrations, 57. *See also* Birthday
   parties; Rituals
Center for Consumer Freedom,
   191
Center for Science in the Public
   Interest, 191
Chiang Kai-shek, 113
Child-rearing, 14–15
Children, vf, 188, 214–15nn34, 36;
   as consumers, 16ff, 27–28, 51–52,
   70, 95, 100–102; localization
   process and, 19–20, 37–38, 60–61;
   identification by, 22–23; educa-
   tion of, 62–64; appeal to, 64–66;
   and fast food, 130–31, 206n48,
   219n13; and school lunches, 131–
   33
Children's Paradise, 62

China, 10, 25, 32, 36, 66, 98, 121,
   143, 202n8, 210n91, 211n94,
   212n6, 213–14nn22, 26, 27,
   220n20, 222n33, 237n47; cultural
   imperialism in, 4–5; single-child-
   family policy in, 16, 214–15n34;
   localization in, 38, 75–76; foreign
   cultural influences in, 39–40,
   212–13n14; modernization in,
   41–42; consumers in, 42–43; food
   preparation in, 44–45, 47; consumerism in, 67–70; meals in,
   77–78, 219n12; and Hong Kong,
   108–9; economic growth in, 183–
   84; demographic changes in, 195,
   196. *See also* Beijing; Hong Kong;
   Shanghai
Chinese Consumers Society, 68
Chinese National Day, 55
Chinese New Year, 59
Class, 2, 9–10, 18. *See also* Status
Cleanliness, 23, 33–35, 71–72, 153;
   in Hong Kong, 89–90
Coca-Cola, 12, 24, 35f, 81–82, 179,
   193, 211n99
Cohon, George, 14
Coke, *see* Coca-Cola
Cold War, 113
Commensality, 156–57; in Japan,
   169–72
Community centers: restaurants as,
   125–26, 128–29
Competition, competitiveness, 42,
   142
Computerization, 26f
Confucianism, 194–95
Conjugality, 15–16
Consumerism, viii, 17–18; in China,
   67–71
Consumers, *see* Customers

Consumption, ix–x, 11, 20, 206n48; in China, 67–70. *See also* Eating
Copenhagen, 34
Corporations, transnational, 11–12, 97–98, 151–52
Council for Economic Construction, 121
Courtship, 50–51
"Credit clubs," 131
Crowding, 94–95, 147–48
Cuisine, 70; local, 9, 10, 166–69; acceptance of, 35–37; American, 72–73; Chinese, 77–78, 219n12; in Taiwan, 110–12, 119. *See also* Food systems
Cultural imperialism, 5, 27, 151, 185
Culture, viii, 2, 8, 86f, 107, 203n17; popular, 5, 10–11, 14, 108, 119; local, 9, 135; American, 64–66, 72–73, 99, 122, 143, 161, 172–73, 180–81; globalism and, 79–80; public, 96–97; on Taiwan, 111–13; youth, 123–25; Japanese, 166–67
Customers, ix–x, 3–4, 14, 42; education of, 27–31, 92–93; in Beijing, 43, 48–50, 69–71; perceptions of, 45–47; children as, 51–52, 100–102; behavioral changes of, 52–53, 96–97; restaurant use by, 53–57, 94–95, 125–28, 129–30

DeLay, Tom, 192
Democratic Progressive Party, 117
Demographics: of aging, 195–96
Demonstrations: against McDonald's, 187, 188, 222n37
Deng Xiaoping, 32, 88
Denmark, 190
Deterritorialization, 10–11

Dietary habits: changes in, 6, 66
Donahue, Phil, 33
Dore, Ronald, 168
Double Quarter Pounder with Cheese, 192
Double Whopper with Cheese, 193
Douglas, Mary, 159
Durban, 34

Eateries, 70–71
Eating: and table manners, 175–76
Ecology camps, 99
Economy, 190; East Asian, 183–84
Edo, 165
Education, 89; consumer, 27–31, 52–53, 92–93, 102; of children, 62–64
Egalitarianism, 30–31, 42
Elderly, 194–95, 196
Elites, 10, 185
Employees, 55, 59, 60–61, 91–92, 124–25, 141–42
Entrepreneurs, 13–14
Environmental issues, 4, 98–99, 154–55, 223n41
Equality, 30–31, 42
Ethnic awareness, 118
Exports, 184, 222n33
Eye contact, 31–32

Fair Competition Law, 151–52
Families: changes in, 14–17, 18, 194–95, 214–15n34; and restaurant use, 57, 58–59, 126–28; appeal to 59–60
Fantasia, Rick, 29
Fast food, 18; use of, vi–vii, ix–x, 42; impacts of, 4–7, 133–34; in China, 47–48, 71, 73–74, 202n8; in Hong Kong, 79, 80–83; and socialization, 125, 130–31; as

school lunches, 131–33; attitudes toward, 137–38; in Korea, 142–43, 151; in Japan, 162–65; urban legends about, 174–75
Fast Food, Fat Talk (Leidner), 21
Fast food industry, 4, 20–21, 25–26, 208n64; obesity issues and, 191–92
Finger foods, 179
Food and beverage industry, 12, 191–92
Food preparation, 47, 72
Food production, 25–26, 41–42, 44–45
Food systems: in China, 47, 219n12; in Hong Kong, 80–81, 84–85; on Taiwan, 111–12, 134; and national identity, 136, 138, 154–55, 158; in Korea, 139, 144f, 155–57; in Japan, 163–64, 166–69, 177; commensality in, 169–72
Ford, Henry, 25
France, 29, 187ff
Franchises, franchising, 3, 21, 26, 204n28, 209n73
French fries, 6, 24–25, 26, 179, 222n33
Friedman, Thomas, 22
Friendliness, 31–32, 91, 221n25
Fujian, 111f
Fujita, Den, 13f, 162, 172f, 181

Gates, Bill, 23
Gender, 7, 14; and restaurant use, 55–56, 146–47; and business operations, 141–42
Genmu Shujaku (Izumi Kyoka), 178
Germany, 24, 189, 233n17
Gifts, 152, 230n38

Ginza district, 166, 169, 172
Globalism, globalization, 7–8, 139, 183, 234n23; and culture, 79–80; vs. localism, 115, 133–35; attitudes toward, 185–86; impacts of, 196–97
Goody, Jack, 66
Great Britain, 4, 24, 159, 190, 202n7; McLibel trial in, 187–88
Green Power workshops, 99
Guangdong, 78, 112
Guangzhou, 78

Hakka, 111–12
Hamburgers, 119–20, 157, 165–66; symbolism of, 137, 138–39, 154–55, 158–60; competition with, 142–43; as snack, 168–69; and commensality, 169–70; and table manners, 177–78, 179
Hamburger University, 12, 21, 206n52
Hankyū Umeda, 170
Hanshin Department Store, 162
Hardee's, 133, 192
Hard Rock Café, 48
Health, *see* Cleanliness; Nutrition; Sanitation
Heian period, 177
Heinz, 12
Hinduism, 190
Hitachiyama, 167
Honggaoliang, 34
Hong Kong, vf, x, 2, 6f, 9–10, 13, 17, 23f, 36, 52, 77, 121, 140, 183, 191, 204n30, 218–19nn3, 7, 219–20nn15, 19, 221–22nn25, 31, 32, 33, 223nn39, 41, 46, 224n47, 235n34; local culture in, 14, 107–8; children in, 16, 20, 27, 100–

102; birthday parties in, 19, 103–
4; consumer education in, 28–29,
92–93; service expectations in,
30, 32, 91–92 ; youth in, 37, 105–
7; cleanliness in, 33, 89–90; fast
foods in, 79, 80–83, 218n2,
219nn8, 11, 13, 220n16; food system in, 84–85; consumer culture
in, 86, 94–95; perceptions in, 88;
smiling in, 90–91; queuing in,
93–94, 221n28; buffets in, 95–96;
transnational corporations in,
97–98; protests in, 98–99; and
China, 108–9; demographic
changes in, 195–96
Hostessing, 147–48
Hovering, 94–95
Howard Johnson's, 25–26
Hungbu, 156
Hygiene, 33, 72–73, 133, 134

Ice cream, 179
Identity: and betel-nut chewing,
117–19; and cuisine, 135f, 138,
154–55, 158–59
Immigrants: to Taiwan, 111–12
Imperialism: American, vii, 38. See
also Cultural imperialism
India, 23, 138, 186, 190, 208n64
Individualism, 157
Indonesia, 188
Industrialization, 25–26, 41–42, 44–
45
Infosys Technologies, 186
Internationalization, 139
Internet, 8
Investment, 121–22
Islam, 23
Israel, 23, 208n63
Italy, 24, 189

Izumi Kyoka: *Genmu Shujaku*,
178

Jakarta, 188
Japan, 2, 6, 11, 24, 33, 37, 66, 108,
112, 121, 161–62, 181ff, 190, 195,
207n60, 210n88, 219–20n15,
228n7, 229nn20, 21, 230nn33, 35,
38, 41, 231n51; owner-operators
in, 12–14; children in, 16, 20;
food systems in, 163–64; snacks
vs. meals in, 166–69; commensality in, 169–72; urban legends in,
174–75; table manners in, 175–80
JBS Big Boy Company, 143

Kellogg's, 12
Kentucky Fried Chicken (KFC), 4,
12, 74, 83, 164f, 174, 179,
206n48, 208n64; in Beijing, 47–
48, 49, 73
Kinship, x, 16. See also Families
KMT, see Kuomintang
Korea, x, 2, 4, 13, 34, 36, 97, 121,
183, 191, 195, 218–19n7, 226n1;
food chains in, 18, 142–43; service expectations in, 30–31, 32;
localization in, 38, 141–42;
national identity in, 136–37,
154–55, 158–59; American fast
food in, 137–38, 139–41, 159–60,
206n48; market creation in, 144–
46; restaurant use in, 146–50,
227n26; foreign companies in,
150–54, 227n34; food system in,
155–58
Korean War, 36, 113
Kottak, Conrad, 59, 125
Kroc, Ray, 14, 33, 195–96, 197
Kuomintang, 112–14, 117

Kwan, Robert, 21
Kyoto, 176

Labor, 26–27, 42, 122, 124
Lai, Tim, 39
Lawsuits: libel, 187–88, 202n7; obesity, 190–91
Lee Teng-hui, 114, 224n2
Leiden, 29
Leidner, Robin: *Fast Food, Fast Talk*, 21
Leisure centers, 56, 147
Libel suits, 187–88
Lifestyles, 14–15
Little Emperor (Empress), 16, 62–63
Localism, localization, 13–14; and children, 19–20; process of, 35–36, 37–38, 125–26; in Beijing, 54–56, 58–59, 60–63, 72–73, 75–76; in Taiwan, 115–16; vs. globalization, 133–35, in Korea, 141–42, 157, 160
London: McLibel trial in, 187–88
Lotteria, 133, 142–43
Low-income families, 52
Lunches, boxed, 163–64

McAllan, 34
McAnn, 139f
MacChao, 168
McDharma's, 34
McDonaldization, 35, 214n30
McDonaldization of Society, The (Ritzer), 35
Mcdonald's, 34
McDonald's Canada, 14
McDonald's International, 12–13, 139, 140, 141, 185, 201–2n4; and antiglobalization, 186–90

McDonald's Moscow, 14
McDonny, 34
McDuck's, 34
MacFastFood, 34
McHuevo, 24
McJoy (magazine), 173
McKim, 140
McKiver's, 34
McLaks, 24
McLean Deluxe, 24, 236n38
McLibel trial, 187–88
McNuggets, vegetable, 23
McPloughman, 24
McSpagetti, 24
McSpotlight.org, 188
Maharaja Mac, 23
Mai-Dang-Lao, 120
Mai-Dang-Nu, 120
Mak Dong Lou Suk-Suk, 103
Malaysia, 23, 121
Management, 12–13, 87
Manners: Japanese, 175–80
Martial arts, 11
Meals: vs. snacks, 45–47, 84–85, 143f, 164, 166–69; as events, 77–78; concept of, 155–56; obesity issues and, 192–94
Meat, 144, 167, 229n21. *See also* Hamburgers
Meiji period, 166
Men, 55, 146–47
Menus: modification of, 23–25
Mid-Autumn Festival, 59
Middle class, 16–18, 33–34, 120f
Miller, Daniel, 75, 180
Ministry of Agriculture, Forestry, and Fishing, 137
Mintz, Sidney, 73
Mitsukoshi department store, 172

Modernization, modernity, 41–42, 44, 65–66
Modornol, 34
Monster Thickburger, 192
Morito Masahiko, 173
Morris, Dave, 187–88
Mos Burger, 165–66, 174, 229n27
Moscow, 27–28, 29, 209nn79, 80
Muslims, 188
Mutton, 23

NACF. *See* National Agricultural Cooperative Federation
Nagai Kafu: *Amerika Monogatari*, 178
Nancy's Express, 34
Napkin Wars, 96
National Agricultural Cooperative Federation (NACF), 136f, 155
National Day (China), 40–41
Nationalism, 116, 136–37
National Restaurant Association, 192
Neighborhood committees, 54
Netherlands, 24, 29
Newlyweds, 15
Newman's Own, 193
New Territories, vf
New York: obesity lawsuit in, 190–91
New Zealand, 121
Ng, Daniel, 13f, 82f, 86f, 88f, 204n30
Nihonshoki, 178
Nike Corporation, 11
Nonghyop, *see* National Agricultural Cooperative Federation
Noodles, 165
Noodle shops, 170

Norway, 24
Nutrition, 44–45, 175, 219n13

Oak Brook (Ill.), 12
Oaxaca, 187
Obesity politics, 190–94, 197, 235nn34, 35, 236n38
Offshoring, 185–86
Ohnuki-Tierney, Emiko, 138
Olympic Games (1996), 23, 208n61
Operations and Training Manual, 21
Osaka, 162, 165, 170, 172
Outsourcing, 185–86
Owner-operators, 13, 21

Paraguay, 190
Perry, Commodore, 167
Personal Responsibility in Food Consumption Act, 191–92
Philippines, 24, 121
Pizza, 165, 221n30
Pizza Hut, 4, 47ff, 73, 133, 152, 221n30
Politics, 2, 58, 97–98; and Taiwanese culture, 111–13, 119; and betel-nut chewing, 117–18; bombings and, 122–23; of food, 138–39, 140–41; obesity, 190–94, 235nn34, 35, 236n38
Predictability, 34
Production: dispersed, 11–12; standardized, 20–23, 44–45
Profits, 13
Protests, 98–99
Public relations, 60
Public space, 130

QSC & V, 44
Quanjude Roast Duck Restaurant, 75

Queuing, 29–30; in Moscow, 27–28; in Hong Kong, 93–94, 221n28

Rachmadi, Bambang, 188
Rāmen, 165, 174
Receptionists, 59, 60–61
Republic of China, 113. *See also* Taiwan
Residence patterns, 15
Restaurants, 3, 42, 81, 147; service in, 29–31; family, 59–60; theme, 63–64; in Beijing, 70–71; in Taiwan, 111–12
Restrooms, 150, 220–21n23
Rice, 175; symbolism of, 137f, 154–56; in food system, 167–68
Rio de Janeiro, 30
Rituals, 57, 58, 62
Ritzer, George: *The McDonaldization of Society*, 35
Ronald McDonald, vi, 19, 64, 103–4, 224n47
Ronald McDonald House for Sick Children, 99, 223n39
Ronald McDonald Scholarships, 55
Ronald Room, 103
Ronghua Chicken, 74
Roppongi, 170
Rose, Bill, 121, 133
Russia, 31f

Sanitation, 89–90, 134, 151, 210n91
Santa Cruz (Calif.), 34
San Tin village, 77
School lunches, 131–33
Schools, 54–55
Self-provisioning, 95f
Seoul, 7, 9f, 12, 18, 33f, 136, 139–40, 153
Service: education about, 27–28; variations in, 29–31; expectations about, 31–32, 89–90, 91–92; in Beijing, 50–51
Shanghai, 34, 184
Sheldon, Allen, 30
Shenzhen Special Economic Zone, 87–88, 89
ShinMc, 140
Shopping: in China, 67–70
Singapore, 23
Single-child-family policy, 16
Sint'oburi, 154–55
Slow food movement, 189
Smiling, 210nn85, 88; service, 28, 31–32, 90–91
Snacks: vs. meals, 45–47, 84–85, 143f, 164, 166–69, 181–82
Soba, 165
Social behavior: changes in, 20, 52–53; importance of, 176–80
Social mobility, 66
Sourcing, 13, 66–67, 153
South Korea. *See* Korea
Space: as commodity, 147–48, 149, 160
Spam, 35f, 157
Standardization: of production, 20–23, 41–42, 44–45
Standards of living, 184
Status, 9, 53–54, 117f
"Stealth fries," 25
Steel, Helen, 187–88
Steel, Ronald, 5
Stephenson, Peter, 29
Street stalls, 6, 71, 74
Students, 7, 212–13n14; protests by, 98–99; in Hong Kong, 105–7
Sumptuary laws, 186–87
Sun, David, 121
Suppliers, supply, 13, 66–67, 153

Sushi, 26
Suzumo Machinery Company, 26
Sweet, Robert, 190–91
Symbolism: cultural, 45, 128–29; food, 137, 138–40, 141, 154–55, 158–60, 166–69

Tachigui, 178f
Tachisoba shop, 170
Taipei, 7, 10, 19, 30, 33, 113, 114–15, 119–20, 128–29, 225n14; customers in, 125–28, 129–30; children in, 130–31; school lunches in, 131–33; localization in, 133–35
Taipei Municipal Bureau of Education, 132
Taiwan, x, 2, 6, 15, 32, 45, 52, 140, 183, 190, 207n60, 219–20n15; children in, 16, 20; consumerism in, 17–18; menu variation in, 24; cuisine in, 110–11, 114–15; Kuomintang on, 112–14; betelnut chewing in, 115–19; and United States, 120–21; bombings in, 122–23; youth culture in, 123–25
Takashimaya department store, 172
Taste: biological, 22, 207n59; cultural, 9, 203n19
Teachers' Day (China), 55, 63
Teahouses, 6
Teenagers, 17, 19, 29, 124–25
Teikyo period, 165
Thailand, 121
"Theater of equality," 30
Tianjin, 63
Tillotson, James, 192
Toilets, *see* Restrooms; Sanitation
Tokyo, vi, 16–17, 27, 166, 170, 174, 220n19, 229n20

Tourism, 39, 48
Transnationalism, 7, 10–11
Trinidad, 190
Tsimshatsui, 93
Turkey, 24

Udon, 165
Umeda, 162
Uncle Joe's Hamburger, 143
Uncle McDonald, 10, 61. *See also* Ronald McDonald
Uncle McDonald's Adventures, 63–64
Uncle Sam's, 70
United Kingdom. *See* Great Britain
United States, 113, 120–21, 180–81, 234n21, 236n36, 237nn47, 49; and globalization, 185–86; obesity issues in, 191–92
U.S. Food and Drug Administration, 191
U.S. House of Representatives: obesity legislation, 191–92
Urban legends, 174–75
Uruguay, 24

Values, 144–45, 210n85
Vegetable McNuggets, 23
Vegetarianism, 190
Victoria (Hong Kong), 93
Vie de France, 70
Vietnam, 108

Web sites, 188
Wendy's, 133, 193
Winner's Burger, 34
Women, 9, 90; in Beijing, 46–47, 55, 56; as customers, 126–28, 146; in Korea, 141–42
Working-class, 10, 62–63

World Anti-McDonald's Day, 188
World Trade Center attack, 185

Xi'an, 34
Xiangfei Roast Chicken, 74

Yokohama, 167–68, 174, 230n41

Youth, 16ff, 42; and cleanliness, 33, 90; in Beijing, 49–51, 55; in Hong Kong, 86, 96–97, 102, 105–7; in Taiwan, 123–25, 135; in Korea, 148, 160; in Japan, 171–72; anti-globalization and, 185–86
Yuen Long, v–vi, 93, 221n29
Yuppies, 2, 9, 49–50